US Foreign Policy in the Post–Cold War Era

US Foreign Policy in the Post–Cold War Era

Restraint versus Assertiveness From George H. W. Bush To Barack Obama

Tudor A. Onea

palgrave
macmillan

US FOREIGN POLICY IN THE POST–COLD WAR ERA
Copyright © Tudor A. Onea, 2013.

All rights reserved.

First published in 2013 by
PALGRAVE MACMILLAN®
in the United States—a division of St. Martin's Press LLC,
175 Fifth Avenue, New York, NY 10010.

Where this book is distributed in the UK, Europe and the rest of the world,
this is by Palgrave Macmillan, a division of Macmillan Publishers Limited,
registered in England, company number 785998, of Houndmills,
Basingstoke, Hampshire RG21 6XS.

Palgrave Macmillan is the global academic imprint of the above companies
and has companies and representatives throughout the world.

Palgrave® and Macmillan® are registered trademarks in the United States,
the United Kingdom, Europe and other countries.

ISBN: 978–1–137–36463–0

Library of Congress Cataloging-in-Publication Data

Onea, Tudor A., 1975–
    US foreign policy in the post-cold war era : restraint versus
assertiveness from George H.W. Bush to Barack Obama. /
by Tudor A. Onea.
        pages cm
    Includes bibliographical references and index.
    ISBN 978–1–137–36463–0 (hardback)
        1. United States—Foreign relations—1989– I. Title.

E840.O54 2013
327.730090′49—dc23   2013016344

A catalogue record of the book is available from the British Library.

Design by Newgen Knowledge Works (P) Ltd., Chennai, India.

First edition: October 2013

10 9 8 7 6 5 4 3 2 1

CONTENTS

ACKNOWLEDGMENTS

This book would have been impossible to write without the immense help of Richard Ned Lebow, who has read through several drafts of the manuscript, and has provided invaluable suggestions on the psychology of prestige, and of William Wohlforth, who has also been a vital source of inspiration and of critical feedback. These amazing scholars rightfully deserve the highest praise as embodying the pinnacle of erudite achievement, but to me deserve even more accolades for their generosity as friends and mentors. I would also like to extend my warmest recognition to the outstanding Benjamin Valentino, who has found insightful ways to reexamine key chapters and has provided stalwart support throughout my time at Dartmouth. Furthermore, I would like to convey my deepest appreciation to Stephen Brooks, Darryl Press, Jennifer Lind, Bridget Coggins, Brian Greenhill, and to the other participants in the International Relations and Foreign Policy seminars organized by the Dickey Center for International Understanding at Dartmouth College for providing countless ideas and alternate viewpoints that have helped sharpen my argument. I also want to thank the anonymous reviewers for their considerably helpful comments on my manuscript.

I want to thank in particular the Social Sciences and Humanities Research Council of Canada, which has provided the funding to undertake a two-year postdoctoral stage at Dartmouth.

I would like to express my sincerest gratitude to my doctoral supervisor David Haglund, whose door has always been open and who has shown remarkable patience in dealing with my frequent (sometimes daily) queries, and to Charles Pentland for providing me with consistent support and advice. For some extraordinary help in separating the wheat from the chaff, as well as for his constant encouragement, I would also like to thank my external examiner, Norrin Ripsman. Special recognition should also be due to my very first supervisor Harald

Kleinschmidt, who more than a decade ago taught me the virtues of dedication, honesty, and commitment in the academic profession.

My sincerest thanks and gratitude to Brian O'Connor, my excellent editor, who has been extraordinarily patient and helpful in seeing this project brought to fruition.

I also want to thank an old and dearest departed friend, Aaron Iarovici, who was like a father to me. He was one of the very few people I have known who, having both the gifts of genuine wisdom and intelligence, has never given in to the sin of arrogance.

Last, but certainly not least, I would like to thank my amazing mother for so many things that I must end up thanking her for everything. This book is in many respects as much my work as hers, except that of course all the remaining faults are mine. Tennyson may have said it best: "Happy is he with such a mother!...trust in all things high comes easy to him, and tho' he trip and fall, he shall not blind his soul with clay."

1

INTRODUCTION

"We are going to do a terrible thing to you—we are going to deprive you of an enemy."[1] This 1988 statement by Georgi Arbatov, a top Soviet foreign policy adviser, showcases the considerable strategic difficulties met by the United States once it was left without a superpower rival to compete against. Deploring the demise of an enemy irreducibly committed to the obliteration of your way of life may impress observers as making little sense. Nonetheless, the presence of an enemy equips a state with a grand strategy connecting means to objectives in its international undertakings.[2] Despite its many facets and critics, containment had provided for more than four decades a straightforward purpose in the more predictable, even if more dangerous, world of the Cold War. But once the Soviet Union conceded defeat, soon to be followed by its disintegration, the United States was left without a successor strategy, and, consequently, with no clear road map to follow.

Hence, the post–Cold War US foreign policy is frequently described as a fruitless quest for a grand strategy to replace containment.[3] For many analysts, US foreign policy during George H. W. Bush's and Bill Clinton's time in office constitutes an incoherent and often ungainly attempt to implement at once various mutually contradictory strategic options.[4] Following September 11, this seeming embarrassment of choice was understood to have been replaced by clarity of purpose in the so-called "Bush revolution," defined by the preservation of US military supremacy, unilateralism, and preventive war. But the Bush revolution ended abruptly as well, even before the political exit of its originator, plagued by a worsening economy and insurgency in Iraq, leaving the United States once again without a strategic rudder in the murky waters of world politics. This apparent uncertainty continues under the Obama administration.[5]

Yet, despite this lack of a clear strategy, the United States has shown a steady propensity in the last 20 years for strategies favoring assertiveness over restraint, even though restraint seemed not only feasible, but also more advantageous. Therefore, the question under investigation consists in why the United States chose assertiveness over restraint as the cornerstone of its foreign policy. Restraint refers to the infrequent and slight use of the military capabilities at one's disposal, the scaling down of political commitments abroad, and the reluctance to impose one's preferences unilaterally over one's allies and partners. Restraint does not impose a choice between doing all and not doing anything, or action and passivity, but rather confronts decision-makers with a choice between more and less international involvement. Hence, if restraint pleads for reduced implication overseas, assertiveness advocates sustained activism abroad. As such, assertiveness covers a policy array encompassing conquest, the constitution of protectorates and spheres of influence, the acquisition of military bases, activist diplomacy, interventionism, and increased unilateral decision-making.[6] In the end, the US choice of a grand strategy is reducible to a decision between assertiveness and restraint, or on whether to begin the defense of the United States on the American side of the water or on the other side. This question represents the oldest and most fundamental issue of US foreign policy.[7]

THE PUZZLE

Why is US post–Cold War assertiveness puzzling? Before the onset of the ongoing economic crisis in the fall of 2008, there were few reasons to fear that the United States risked being supplanted as the dominant power. Dominant power refers to a state that surpasses others in economic and military capabilities as well as their successful use, and thus possesses broad-spectrum capabilities exercised across the global system. Nevertheless, a dominant power is not strong enough to lay down the law to other states, which would represent a condition of hegemony. Basically, the dominant state is the strongest state in the system at any given time without necessarily being omnipotent. Unipolarity is simply a subcategory of dominance, as it designates a power configuration in which one state both "excels in all the component elements of state capability" and has significantly more capabilities than other great powers. In other words, a greater gap separates the dominant state from its nearest competitor in unipolarity than under other configurations of power.[8]

The US lead over other great powers has never been so pronounced as in the post–Cold War. In the words of Kennedy: "Nothing has ever existed like this disparity of power; nothing. I have returned to all of the comparative defense spending and military personnel statistics over the past 500 years that I compiled in *The Rise and Fall of the Great Powers*, and no other nation comes close."[9] Since no other state can realistically compete against it, the United States has been enjoying since the end of the Cold War a period of uncommon security- and status-plenty. Therefore, the United States should have been able to afford the benefits of leadership exercised with fewer expenses, which suggests that conditions were particularly ripe for putting into practice a policy of restraint. As Jervis put it, "The United States should be then a very conservative state in its foreign relations; with its power and dominance thus assured, it should be the quintessential status quo power. It makes a puzzle of Washington's current behavior, which is anything but conservative."[10] Restraint should have been all the more recommendable because it is also arguably the smartest course of action for a dominant power to reassure the world it is not going to abuse its power. No wonder then that the majority of post–Cold War foreign policy studies have recommended restraint as the guiding principle of US grand strategy.[11] Furthermore, while in over two decades of post–Cold War, assertiveness has produced undeniable costs in treasury and lives, it is yet to provide tangible benefits in security and power for the United States.

Nonetheless, by the time US troops rolled into Baghdad, few would have disagreed with the assessment that restraint had failed, being supplanted by an unambiguous policy of assertiveness. This new orientation, inaugurated in the last stages of the Bosnia War, included the bombing of Iraq and Yugoslavia in 1998 and 1999 without a UN Security Council sanction, the rejection of treaties such as the International Criminal Court (ICC) and the Anti-Ballistic Missile (ABM) Treaty between 1998 and 2001, and the 2003 invasion of Iraq. Hence, there is a legitimate reason to inquire into what brought about this paradoxical course of action.

THE ARGUMENT

The answer I suggest is based on three hypotheses. The first hypothesis is that US assertiveness in the post–Cold War was caused foremost by a growing concern among US leaders with maintaining the state's prestige in the eyes of the world. Prestige designates the deference that the United States demands from the other states in the system on account of being recognized as the dominant state. The second hypothesis is that even though the United States was not threatened by any competition, its prestige was vulnerable to symbolic challenges. By symbolic challenges I mean the failure of lower-ranked actors to award the proper level of deference to a superordinate state. While such challenges do not affect the actual status of the state, they cast a doubt as to its competence and effectiveness in holding a higher rank. The third hypothesis is that these symbolic challenges led the United States to favor an assertive course of action that would have allowed it to reassert its prestige, as well as to exact retribution on the challengers.

The higher the status or hierarchical rank of a social actor, the more pronounced its prestige in that respective group. If this demand for prestige is not recognized in a way that satisfies its expectations of appropriate deferential treatment, the actor is likely to take measures to assert its credentials through demonstrations of achievements and through the castigation of those who would challenge its superiority through real or imagined offenses. A dominant power, and, even more so, a unipole requires more prestige than ordinary polities on account of being in possession of formidable military and economic capabilities, as well as of its perceived ability to use them successfully. If prestige is not granted to the degree it requires, this is seen as an offense, since it calls into question its right of being worthy of a superior rank. These challenges have to be answered, both to demonstrate the state has "what it takes" to preserve its dominant status and to take revenge on those who offend it. As a result, the United States has to resort to assertive measures, such as using military force or/ and treading on the sensibilities of other states, in order to support its claim to world leadership. Thus, the requirements of prestige and those of restraint cannot help but clash.

In the aftermath of the fall of the Berlin Wall, the United States thought it would be automatically granted prestige by other states. Accordingly, from the Gulf War to the conclusion of the ethnic warfare in Bosnia, the United States predicated its foreign policy on the assumption that restraint would prove the most effective strategy in providing a more peaceful and cooperative world with governance and at the same time safeguarding American values and interests. That is certainly not to say that foreign policy under George H. W. Bush and Clinton represented the most restrained policy imaginable, but rather that it constituted a relatively moderate strategic choice. But as the decade progressed, the world frustrated American expectations that it was about turn into a more peaceful place, through turmoil in Somalia, Bosnia, North Korea, Haiti, Rwanda, Kosovo, and Iraq. Furthermore, the United States found out that it could not rely on the full-hearted support of other states for its political initiatives. As a result, by the late 1990s, despite its superiority in capabilities, the United States faced a context where it was flouted by much weaker international actors, such as Belgrade and Baghdad; and its allies and partners refused to allow it special dispensation in its initiatives on international crimes, missile defense, or dealing with challengers. Therefore, US decision-makers arrived at the conclusion that the experiment with restraint was too costly in terms of prestige. The result of this mounting dissatisfaction with restraint was the launching of an assertive strategy aimed at recouping prestige and punishing challengers. The United States conducted large-scale military operations against Baghdad and Belgrade without the seal of approval of the UN Security Council and claimed special treatment in the contexts of the negotiations over the ICC and missile defense. When its demands for peculiar privileges and exemptions were rejected by the other sides involved, the United States abandoned participation in the respective institutional frameworks. Finally, in the aftermath of the September 11 attacks, the United States needed to demonstrate to the world its steadfastness. Iraq provided the most suitable ground for mounting such a convincing demonstration of strength.

The field of International Relations has recently witnessed a heightened interest in status and prestige.[12] This new-found popularity has to do with the need to explain better instances of conflict that would be perplexing if considered from the points of view of material gains and of physical security. These instances are much more frequent than previously thought: a recent study found that out of the 94 interstate wars fought between 1648 and 2008, 62 (or 58 percent) were motivated by standing, and a further 11 (or 10 percent) by revenge, as compared to traditionally accepted causes such as security or material interest (18 and 7 percent, respectively.)[13] Moreover, accounts based on status and prestige appear increasingly persuasive in an interval in which the traditionally accepted material incentives for conflict are muted, due to factors such as the declining benefits of conquest, the spread of democratic peace, and the influence of nuclear weapons.[14] Yet, the vast majority of the status and prestige studies are devoted to the role these factors play in the foreign policy of rising states, who claim more prestige as they rise. Therefore, the effect of prestige for the dominant power has so far been neglected.[15]

This inquiry helps fill this gap. Furthermore, this endeavor is also policy relevant by shedding light on whether assertiveness represents a correctible anomaly, or whether it is a harbinger of things to come in US foreign policy. One testimony of how hard it is to practice restraint is the continually increasing number of analyses over the last two decades urging it. Hence, if US decision-makers had really been able to heed this advice, there would have been little reason to repeat it so often. Consequently, this investigation highlights the limitations restraint is likely to encounter and suggests a reexamination of the policy recommendations regarding US grand strategy.

Alternative Theories and Evidence

This inquiry compares and contrasts the hypotheses of a prestige-motivated assertive foreign policy against the main three alternative accounts as well as against the historical record. These alternative theories are structuralism, exceptionalism, and revisionism:

- For structuralism, the United States cannot help but seek additional power—this strategy being compulsive for any state that has reached an unrivalled level of power capabilities vis-à-vis the other great powers. States that have the power to conduct an assertive foreign policy, and nevertheless refuse to do so, are eventually forced into it by the international system by means of multiplying security threats.
- For exceptionalism, the United States follows an assertive policy in order to spread to other shores its cherished political values—democracy and freedom.
- For revisionism, the question to be asked is really "cui bono?" or "who stands to profit" from assertiveness? The culprits are then found in the ranks of US socioeconomic interest groups.

What sort of evidence would confirm/falsify the relevance of the prestige hypothesis relative to the accounts provided by structuralism, exceptionalism, and revisionism?

In order to attest the salience of prestige, an analyst should expect to encounter two possible kinds of evidence. First, when faced with symbolic challenges, decision-makers should exhibit in official documents as well as in their public and private statements preoccupation for the maintenance of the image of the United States as an effective international leader through public displays of prowess. A related clue to concerns over prestige may be the decision-makers' insistence on the United States being granted privileges on account of its status as an international leader. Second, the presence of prestige may be ascertained if the statements convey a sense of humiliation at the challenge by a lower-ranked actor, as well as an angry impulse to castigate the challenger.

The case for prestige will also be strengthened if the contending three schools of thought are unable to fully explain the US post–Cold War record. For structuralism to be disconfirmed, the absence of worries over US physical security or that of US allies when addressing challenges should be in evidence. Meanwhile, exceptionalism would be refuted by a weak impact in decision-making of convictions regarding the international promotion of democracy and human rights. Finally, revisionism would be falsified by evidence showing that considerations of private benefits or losses by domestic groups did not affect foreign policy decisions. To be sure, owing to ambiguous evidence, the incentives of decision-makers to misrepresent their position, and the possibility that decisions are influenced by unconscious factors, a question mark is always left hanging on the "real intentions" behind policy. Nonetheless, some interpretations may be shown as less persuasive through the use of process-tracing and of counterfactuals.

Process-tracing involves tracking the intermediate steps between a possible cause and its likely effect so as to understand the precise sequence of events that have led to the eventual conclusion scrutinized. For a theory to be valid, "all the intervening steps in a case must be as predicted by a hypothesis...or else that hypothesis must be amended—perhaps trivially or perhaps fundamentally—to explain the case." In this case, process-tracing considers the evolution of US foreign policy throughout the post–Cold War. For a theory to be valid, it would have to account not only for each case examined, but also for the whole development of US orientation in this time period. Counterfactuals are alternative scenarios based on the actions a rational actor would have to perform in order to meet a given goal and on the differences existing between such hypothetical behavior and the policy record. This reasoning follows the form, "If A were present, one could expect B." However, if B cannot be found, or if we find evidence of C, then chances are that A did not cause the event under scrutiny and that a different factor may be responsible.[16]

Restraint, being a matter of degree, is hardly ever absolute. The choice between America's assertive and restrained strategic options may be illustrated alongside a spectrum running from the ideal types of perfect restraint or complete political and economic isolation to that of perfect assertiveness or coercive hegemony. As such, these extremes may never exist in practice, but, nevertheless, represent a useful assumption as they indicate the orientation of a particular strategy according to the distance that separates the strategy from the respective ends of the spectrum (figure 1.1).

In this spectrum, isolationism stands for the most restrained strategic option: avoiding foreign political entanglements, while allowing for economic and diplomatic relations. Offshore balancing is a slightly more assertive strategy, in which the United States stays clear of

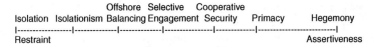

Figure 1.1   Spectrum of US grand strategy options.

permanent foreign alliances and commitments, but reserves the right to create such arrangements and intervene if another state threatens to become dominant by overcoming the resistance of regional actors. Selective engagement is even more assertive, allowing for long-term alliances, foreign military bases, and commitments, as well as intervention under a larger number of possible scenarios. Yet, selective engagement is at the same time more restrained than other strategies because it restricts US involvement to areas deemed critical from the point of view of their value as geopolitical real estate, or/and as locations of economic resources. Hence, this is a strategy of prioritization, in which the United States devotes less attention to other less-significant areas of the world. Cooperative security is more assertive than selective engagement in that it encourages alliances and foreign undertakings regardless of geopolitical or economic importance, provided the United States receives the support of other states in the system, preferably with the blessings of international institutions such as the UN. Lastly, primacy is the most assertive strategy as it recommends that the United States preserves its dominance in perpetuity, by further increasing its military capabilities, by containing would-be rivals, and by disciplining misbehaviors all over the world without relying on outside approval or support.[17] If the George H. W. Bush and first Clinton administrations flirted with implementing a cooperative security approach, the second Clinton and George W. Bush administrations were unmistakably relying on primacy. Initially, Obama has attempted to push the clock back toward cooperative security, before producing a foreign policy hybrid owing more to primacy. It is in this sense that the early post–Cold War can be qualified as relatively restrained, and the latter timeframe since 1998 onward as relatively assertive.[18]

PLAN OF THE BOOK

The volume is organized into eight chapters. Chapter two defines prestige and explains why human beings and state pursue it. The chapter also outlines a theory of how the prestige of a dominant power such as the United States may be challenged in world politics, insisting on the relevance of symbolic challenges in an era of unipolarity. It also surveys the main assumptions of structuralist, exceptionalist, and revisionist models as well as discusses how US foreign policy in the post–Cold War may confirm/refute these assumptions. Chapter three describes the background of America's assertive strategy: the years between the fall of the Berlin Wall and the end of the war in Bosnia, which witnessed the unsuccessful experiment with restraint. Chapters four through six explore the causes and the course of America's assertiveness. Chapter four investigates the intervention over Kosovo in 1999. Chapter five examines the rejection of the ICC and of the ABM Treaty, as well as the decisions to use force without Security Council authorization from 1998 to 2003. Chapter six examines the causes behind the 2003 invasion of Iraq. These are hard cases for the prestige hypothesis because there is already a large amount of established literature that ties these instances to alternative theories. For instance, the intervention over Kosovo is explained by reference to the protection of human rights in the face of abuse; unilateralism is accounted for by the discrepancy of power on the US side and by its historical penchant for eschewing foreign entanglements; and the invasion of Iraq is explained either by reference to the perception of Iraq developing weapons of mass destruction (WMD) or by the desire to promote democracy in the Middle East. Therefore, the prestige model would have to prove superior to explanations based on power and security, values, and domestic interests, respectively. Chapter seven is concerned with the likely future of restraint and assertiveness in US foreign policy by examining the record of the Obama presidency. Chapter eight presents the conclusion in terms of the confirmation or refutation of the prestige hypothesis.

2

US PRESTIGE AND ITS CHALLENGERS

Prestige refers to extraordinary deference and corresponding privileges bestowed by any social group upon a member, whether an individual or a group, on account of the rank or status it occupies.[1] Prestige has a close affinity with respect, recognition, or consideration.[2] But while every group member, irrespective of social position, wealth, or background, has the right to a minimal degree of respect, which entitles it to a basic deferential treatment by other members, prestige, by contrast, implies the bestowal of an excessive amount of respect based on the qualities, the achievements, or the office the member holds. Therefore, prestige entitles the recipient to preferential acknowledgement compared to other members. As such, the distinction between respect and prestige is the one between raising the hat to one's peer on the street and bowing deep enough to an upper-ranked actor. Consequently, striving for prestige is an endeavor that aims for more than the achievement of equality with other social actors. Prestige requires that others recognize one's right to a superior position, and behave accordingly.

Prestige has two defining features: social character and hierarchy. On the one hand, a social actor cannot confer upon itself prestige solely on account of how worthy of deference it regards its own conduct, achievements, and capabilities. This aspect of prestige places the opinion of society above one's own opinion of oneself, which may warrant the appellation of external honor or honor conferred by outsiders.[3] Accordingly, "Prestige is a social-psychological category; an individual or social group cannot enjoy it unless their prestige claims are recognized by others willing to give them deference."[4] This is so because deference is indicated by behavior that explicitly signals priority or precedence or/and prescribes or proscribes a certain behavior in social interactions: for instance, allowing another actor to speak, sit, enter, exit, or pass first; using honorific formulas when greeting, inviting, or complementing the actor in speech or writing; granting the actor restricted access to a specific way of life in terms of housing, dress, food, transportation, entertainment, and education; conferring it particular rights and responsibilities (such as the right to bear weapons, hold office, or vote on certain issues); or excluding it from common obligations or punishments.[5] This is to say that one cannot enjoy prestige in social isolation: other actors have to be willing to acknowledge it for it to be present. Robinson Crusoe on his island has no prestige whatsoever before the arrival of Friday. Accordingly, the crux of prestige-related politics consists in obtaining, conserving, or recuperating the recognition by others of one's claims to superior deference.[6]

Furthermore, prestige is the product of status, which means that prestige is really a response from other actors to an actor's position in the social hierarchy. Prestige constitutes perhaps the quintessential positional good—a concept designating goods and benefits that are both scarce and in high demand. Because everyone lays a claim to them, positional goods create the problem of social crowding—the more people seek to enjoy them, the less satisfaction is being derived from them. As a result, positional goods cannot be enjoyed unless some claimants are excluded from their full enjoyment.[7] Hence, not everyone in a given society can claim prestige in the same amount—for some members to enjoy more respect and admiration, other members must enjoy less. Thus, prestige is distributed unevenly on a hierarchical basis, with the social actors occupying the superior rungs claiming amounts in excess of the lower ranks.[8]

Why Do Actors Care about Prestige?

By contrast to political philosophers and evolutionary biologists, who trace the drive for prestige to individual psychology or to a hard-wired evolutionary instinct that contributes to better chances of survival for the species, respectively, I propose a social psychology explanation.[9] Basically, prestige is a requisite for a social actor achieving self-esteem. According to theories of social identity and social categorization, there is no such a thing as an individual identity preexisting or divorced from appurtenance to diverse social groups. A person is who he or she is by reason of belonging to certain gender, age, family, professional, religious, national, etc., groups. These overlapping identities come in turn loaded with roles and expectations as to the requisite behavior vis-à-vis fellow group members and other groups, and, as such, both localize the individual's position in larger social networks and provide him or her with schemas for social orientation.

One is expected to act in a certain prescribed way as a father, teacher, Christian, US citizen, etc. It is therefore impossible to understand who one is without taking into account one's respective social affiliations. In this sense, if individuals make up groups, group inclusion also shapes decisively who the individual is and how he or she is likely to behave.[10] By implication, the only plausible sense in which an individual is able to secure self-esteem or a good opinion of one's merit is to secure recognition from other group members.

Self-esteem represents a fundamental human need, which provides a sense of stability and meaning to a person's existence. This psychological need for constant self-esteem is just as critical as physical survival.[11] To function effectively, the psyche relies on routines emphasizing self-worth, whether images, rituals, or narratives designed to both create an orderly environment for the psyche and assert one's intrinsic significance in the universe. Psychological evidence abounds as to human dependence on such routines, as to the traumatic effect resented when they are placed in jeopardy, and as to the strong resistance to any changes of routines. Human beings exhibit cognitive dissonance—they suppress, ignore, or adapt information that contravenes their image of the world. According to terror management theory, when reminded of their mortality, and as such of the potential eradication of their personal identity, people show increased support for the group's routines and decreased attention to those groups who disagree or contest them. Children experience trauma due as a result of the disequilibration between their image of the world, which provides them with a predictable and secure environment and hence routines, and the contradicting external reality. Therefore, human beings have a basic psychological stake in feeling significant and in maintaining continuously a high level of self-esteem.[12]

To this extent, prestige is a necessary means toward achieving self-esteem, and, as such, is valued primarily for the psychological satisfaction it provides rather than for tangible benefits. As Rosen has suggested, prestige and social rank may be desirable "not because of what we get after we win, but because we enjoy *the process* of beating people," thus proving by comparison our own superiority.[13] Therefore the above-mentioned privileges associated with prestige are not significant solely or principally in terms of satisfying physical needs, but are also important for an actor's psychological needs, as indicators of one's social importance, and, by implication of one's excellence relative to other human beings.

Evidence of such behavior is found in everyday life, for instance, in the ubiquitous consumption of pricey luxury items, from cars to hi-tech gadgets, mansions, and fashion, which do not add to one's material happiness, but rather have the added value of making the consumer feel privileged compared to the nonconsumer. Or consider the competitiveness of games, sports, and professional contests, where the very stakes are prevailing over an opponent, "the desire to excel others, to be first and to be honored for that."[14] On a more scientific level, one notices a verified tendency of human beings to favor options that give them modest increases of material benefits relative to a competitor over larger increases that are universally spread. Tests involving functional magnetic resonance imaging of brain activity have shown that human beings prefer to perform better than others even in contexts where they receive as a result a smaller quantity of material rewards.[15] Moreover, a person would prefer to gain an additional 10 percent more than another person, rather than for both incomes to go up 50 percent.[16] In support of this view, a recent foreign policy poll found out that 50 percent Americans would prefer a future in which the US economy increases by only 10 percent, but stays ahead of China, compared to 20 percent of respondents who chose a future in which the average American's income doubles, but China overtakes the United States in economic productivity.[17] Social identity theory experiments have also shown that individuals prefer outcomes that maximize the difference of resources division between their group and a competitor group over outcomes that provide larger rewards, but which are jointly shared by groups. Prestige, not cost-benefit calculus, is at work here, since actors place extra value on social rank rather than on absolute profit, which attests to the enduring need to secure a positive comparison vis-à-vis other actors.[18]

This does not mean that prestige-seeking should be construed as altruistic. The actor who seeks prestige seeks primarily his or her own psychological satisfaction at the expense of others. But neither can this behavior be construed as egoism of the same kind as material cost-benefit calculation, since its payoff is not palpable and may raise the prospect of trade-offs with physical well-being. Hence, prestige-seeking constitutes an intermediate behavior between material egoism and altruism.[19]

PRESTIGE IN WORLD POLITICS

At this point, it may be objected that it is one thing for individuals to desire prestige, and quite another for states to do so. States are often referred to as if they were "like individuals," endowed with a similar range of emotions and psychological requirements. To exemplify, there is constant reference to what the United States did, wanted, thought, feared, etc. But, in the end, states are not people.[20] States exist only because individuals exist, and, therefore, it may be problematic to extend conclusions valid for individuals to abstract collectivities such as states. Nonetheless, this is not an insurmountable challenge.

For social identity and social categorization theories, the boundary where the individual ends and the group begins is obscure, since one shapes the other. For these theories, individuals have a fundamental stake not only in how they perform relative to other individuals, but also in how well their groups fare relative to other groups. One of the most important experimental findings of social identity theory consists in the pronounced and constant discrimination individuals implement on behalf of their groups, in terms of both allocating resources and assessing qualities. In other words, groups to which one belongs are by necessity seen as better and worthier of rewards than other groups. To quote Tajfel and Turner, "the mere perception of belonging to two distinct groups—that is, social categorization per se—is sufficient to trigger intergroup discrimination in favor of the in-group."[21] This finding remains consistent even if the "glue" holding the group together is extremely weak: if groups are selected on the basis of random characteristics, if they have no prior history of interaction, or if they lack any face-to-face communications.

The explanation of this behavior consists in that "individuals evaluate themselves in terms of their group memberships. They seek to establish positively valued differences between their own and other groups to maintain and enhance their self-esteem as group members. In other words, there is a tendency to define one's own group positively in order to evaluate oneself favorably."[22] Individuals bask therefore in the reflected achievements of their groups and, correspondingly, resent their groups' setbacks as personal defeats. Furthermore, individuals will seek whenever possible feasible association with higher-ranking groups, such as sports teams, precisely because of the satisfaction derived out of membership even if they did not contribute directly to the success of the group; while fewer would pledge loyalty to a group constantly ranking low, and thus reflecting poorly on its members.[23]

The same principle holds irrespective of group size, as seen from the strong identification between individual and nation. Individuals often resort to sacrificing their material well-being, and their very existence, to the advancement of the nation, an abstract group, the majority of whose members the individual will never know or meet. Moreover, studies have shown how individuals are ready to support the superiority of their nation through aggressive means even though they may not be aggressive themselves in their personal lives.[24] Hence, the support for one's nation is not solely instrumental, in terms of the nation providing members with security and material support most of the time, but also psychological, in terms of vicariously providing them with feelings of pride, that is, with reflected status and prestige. In a comparative study of the emergence of nationalism in France, Britain, Germany, Russia, and the United States, Greenfeld argues that in all societies nationalism was related to the need to protect or to enhance group status vis-à-vis other groups. Even in the case of the United States, the violent reaction to taxation without representation was caused more by unsatisfied prestige claims ("don't tread on me") than by genuine economic grievances. As she concludes: "Nationality elevated every member of the community which it made sovereign. It guaranteed status. *National identity is, fundamentally, a matter of dignity.* It gives people reasons to be proud."[25]

By implication, individuals will care considerably how their state, which represents the political manifestation of their nation, ranks relative to other states, and, as a consequence, about the amount of deference the state will be extended internationally. On the one hand, political leaders act both as members of the national group and as its chief representatives, so their own prestige is intimately tied to the performance of their state.[26] To this extent it does not matter that the state itself has no emotions since, to paraphrase Wendt, decision-makers "experience state emotions on its behalf."[27] On the other hand, because their domestic audiences regard it as an essential matter of national pride, decision-makers are compelled to cater to the public's demand for achieving or/and maintaining high national prestige or risk being driven out of office.[28]

INSULTS AND INJURIES TO PRESTIGE

Challenges to an actor's prestige, be it an individual or a state, will be interpreted as personal injuries and trigger angry responses, possibly resulting in violence. Violence often begins by the exchange of insults, and hence by another actor failing, whether accidentally or on purpose, to recognize the actor's right to prestige.

This is so because an assault on an actor's upper rank represents an attack directed against its self-esteem. Admitting another actor's superiority or/and being forced to acknowledge one's inferiority in a valued dimension conferring prestige is traumatic in an emotional sense, since it involves a feeling of humiliation, a public exposition of the absence of self-worth. As a word, "humiliation" itself is derived from the Latin word "humus" or "earth" and has the meaning of bringing one down, abasing, belittling, or lowering one's sense of deference. Humiliation stands for unmasking, puncturing, or deflating the claims of an actor to superior status, hence questioning his or her right to receive deference from other actors.[29] Thus, the offender questions the justification of the offended party's social position and the hierarchy that confers it status.[30]

According to Aristotle, there are three types of humiliating offenses, slights, or insults. First are the offenses that show contempt and convey the message that the victim is unimportant. As such, contempt is present chiefly in relations when an actor is denied recognition of its status aspirations by would-be peers or by higher-ranked actors. Second are the offenses that convey spite, or the desire to thwart the target's wishes, even though the challenger does not extract profit from frustrating the victim's desires. Third are those offenses that show insolence, by which the challenger arrogates unjustified superiority over the target by "robbing people of the honor due to them."[31] This last category designates injuries in which lower-ranked actors fail to extend appropriate deference to higher-ranked actors or/and attempt to demean their status. In other words, insolence marks conduct toward superordinate actors deemed inappropriate for the offender's lower status and prestige. As will be seen later on, it is this last type of injury that emerges as the most important for US foreign policy in the post–Cold War.[32]

The offense to a superior actor's status may be deliberate or unintentional, since what matters most is the target's perception of being humiliated. Furthermore, the offense may be expressed by deeds or words, and may consist in the failure to extend appropriate deference or/and in the active effort to demean it. Both variants produce the same result: asserting the inferiority of the offended party by comparison to the offender. As Neu writes, "To insult is to assert or to assume dominance, either intentionally claiming superiority or unintentionally revealing lack of regard. To be insulted is to suffer a shock, a disruption of one's sense of self and one's place in the world. To accept an insult is to submit, in certain words to be dishonored."[33] The offense may also take the form of provocation or daring to a public competition, testing whether the challenged person really possesses a quality on which its status is based. Failure of such a test or failure to participate is seen as humiliating by revealing the challenged party as lacking the disputed quality.[34]

Suffering humiliation encourages the victim to respond violently for two interrelated reasons.[35] First, the target of humiliation wants to reassert its superiority, in the process recuperating its lost or questioned self-esteem. Prestige represents a fluctuating amount of deference that can be reduced or added to—it is not lost in one go or won definitively. Hence, if humiliation decreases an actor's share of deference, and, as a result, impacts emotionally its self-esteem, reassertion restores it to the point where it is in accordance with its expectations so that the ordering routines on which its self-esteem is based are reaffirmed. Reassertion occurs in the form of taking up a test challenge so as to prove one's continued right to prestige; or may involve showcasing the disputed quality through a demonstrative achievement.[36] In either scenario, the offended actor feels that it has to demonstrate publicly, to *show* others its effectiveness so as to recover prestige.

Second, the target of a prestige offense resents anger at the wrong suffered, and experiences the desire for retribution, in the form of a similar infliction of abasement, and hence of suffering, upon the responsible party. Thus, revenge produced by anger is not rational in a material sense, since the injury is a sunk cost, and the suffering of the party having caused the injury does not better the material condition of the revenger. Nor is revenge the equivalent of sadism or pure pleasure in causing suffering, because it is understood as a response to a prior offense. Revenge fulfills, however, the psychological need of restoring to order one's injured sense of self-esteem and could be seen as a negative form of reciprocity. The thirst for revenge will be stronger the more the injured party experiences a sense of injustice and the more the offender acknowledges its action as intentional and gloats (expresses pleasure) at the harm caused.[37]

It could be objected that such emotions vitiate an otherwise rational conduct of foreign policy and that, therefore, they should be guarded against in all contexts. But this statement should be qualified. It is true that public demonstrations and anger-fueled vengeance may lead decision-makers astray by prompting them to lash out against perceived offenders without carefully weighing the likely material consequences of their actions. To this extent, mounting public demonstrations of strength and punishing challengers may prove in the end strategically counterproductive. However, a state does not only have to protect material interests, but also must cater to equally significant psychological needs. Thus, suboptimal strategic conduct may be necessary for the purpose of satisfying the state's demands for self-esteem. Accordingly, a genuinely realistic foreign policy has to balance both material and psychological requirements. Ignoring the first leads to policies that are prohibitively costly or that produce no benefits. Yet, ignoring the latter leads to policies that are not sustainable because they take an unbearable toll on the self-esteem of decision-makers or/and the public.[38]

PRESTIGE AND US FOREIGN POLICY UNDER UNIPOLARITY

It is now time to explore how these findings "scale up" when applied to the United States in an era of unipolarity. When analyzing the implications of unipolarity, a rarely seen structure prior to 1989, we are proceeding into an intellectual terra incognita since the experience of unipolarity is by far restricted to the current configuration of world politics. In order to find comparable instances of domination by a single power, scholars may have to go all the way back to Imperial Rome or China.[39] Accordingly, innovative theories have to be devised to deal with the new subject matter. One such theory, put forward by Wohlforth, argues that status and prestige play an important role in accounting for a peaceful unipolarity.

For Wohlforth, the steeper or more stratified the international pecking order of states, the less conflict-prone it is likely to be. This is so because there are no incentives to fight over status and prestige, if the proper ranking of states is beyond doubt. Under unipolarity, since there is little ambiguity over who holds claims to the higher rank, lower-ranking polities will realize the futility of challenging the status of the dominant power and, as a result, will resign themselves to its privileged position as a given. Hence, unipolarity will dampen status-generated conflict. To quote Wohlforth, "Dissatisfaction arises not from dominance itself but from a dominance that appears to rest on ambiguous foundations." As such, "status competition is unlikely in cases of clear hierarchies" dominated unambiguously by one actor. Unipolarity contrasts with both multipolar (several great powers) and bipolar (two great powers) environments, which represent instances of comparatively flatter hierarchies, and, as a result, are more open to disputes over the allocation of proper rank and prestige. Therefore, the US position seems secure from challenges to its prestige for as long as unipolarity endures.[40]

However, this argument does not necessarily cover all instances of conflict that may arise over prestige under unipolarity.[41] Challenges to a state's prestige may be of two kinds, which are labeled for the purpose of this discussion as *positional* and *symbolic* challenges. The two types of challenges differ according to the stakes involved, the social position of the challenger, and the form the challenge assumes.[42] A leading state faces a positional challenge whenever a competitor state threatens (or more appropriately is perceived to threaten) *to overtake it* in one or several of the key dimensions conferring prestige internationally, especially in economic capabilities, military force, and the successful use of these military and economic capabilities. Thus, fear of losing its high status on the world stage in favor of an upcoming rival triggers anxiety of a commensurate decline in the level of deference the state receives internationally and encourages conflict. This is to say that positional challenges involve matters of succession and of rank maintenance, that is, determining which state is number one. Such positional challenges necessarily come from states that represent next-in-line rivals, which are therefore high-ranked themselves, and whose growing capabilities encourage them to seek even further advancement in the international pecking order. Emblematic examples of positional conflict are rivalries pitting great powers against each other in a competition-like format in a given dimension susceptible of ranking. Hence, the goal of these contests is to get one better than the other player whether one is competing in terms of economic productivity, trade tariffs, arms races, the acquisition of colonies, military exercises, interventions, or even status indicators of dimensions such as space races, palace building, Nobel prizes, or Olympic medals.[43] A possible such future positional conflict may emerge once again between a declining United States and a continually rising China.

Wohlforth's argument as to the absence of incentives for status conflict is valid in this sense, since the United States faced no positional competitor in the post–Cold War.[44] A cursory overview of statistics for the 1990s and early 2000s confirms a pronounced US lead in military and economic capabilities. If in 1989 the United States and the Soviet Union were neck-to-neck militarily, with budgets approximating $280 billion, a decade later the United States' slightly lower military budget of $267.2 billion was larger than the combined defense expenses of the ten next-in-line powers. By 2006, the US enlarged defense expenditure represented 46 percent of the world's total and 65.6 percent of the defense expenditures of other great powers. Washington was spending ten times as much as second-place China. The United States remained from the collapse of the Berlin Wall onward the only state able to project its power globally, thanks to its unmatched sea power and airpower, even entertaining the possibility of simultaneous deployment in battle theatres situated on different continents. In economic terms, if in the late 1980s the United States was in decline relative to the growing GDPs of Germany and

Japan, by contrast, in 2000 the US GDP of $9.25 trillion put it in first place before China, Japan, and Germany ($4.8 trillion, $2.95 trillion, and $1.3 trillion, respectively). By 2006, the US share of the world GDP, 27.5 percent, was larger than the combined percentages of the four next-in-line powers: Japan, China, Germany, and Britain. Furthermore, the United States also maintained a lead in high-technology manufacturing, and its 1997 budget devoted to Research and Development was close to the combined total of the other six G-7 countries. Finally, throughout the post–Cold War there was a clear understanding, and a signaling that the United States was the only power able to provide a resolution to pressing issues, whether in former Yugoslavia or Iraq, or in terms of promotion of international regimes. As such, there was never an expectation that another state could prevail where the United States had not, or that it could have done a better job in its stead.[45]

But a dominant power's rank and prestige may also be challenged in a very different sense. Such challenges are *symbolic* when they do not threaten the actual position of the upper-ranked state, but rather raise a question mark as to its will or ability to hold its status. The intention behind these challenges is not to actively usurp the target's rank in the international hierarchy, but to force it to demonstrate that it continues to possess the qualities requisite by its high rank. In case the upper-ranked state fails this symbolic test, it does not automatically suffer demotion, and its victorious rival is not elevated in its stead, but its prestige is nevertheless weakened.

Thus, symbolic challenges are not actual attacks on the relative rank of the state. Instead, they represent a virtual test of *its right to a superior rank*. In this sense, symbolic challenges are akin to the above-mentioned failures to extend proper deference and insults, whose consequence is to humiliate the target by reducing its self-esteem. And, as is the case with individuals, or domestic groups discussed above, humiliating offenses to one state's rank constitute serious emotional injuries to the state's self-esteem, triggering the desire for reasserting prestige as well as the thirst for retribution.

Prestige is conferred in international politics not solely on the basis of economic or military capabilities, but also on the perceived skill of a state in successfully using these capabilities. As Levy writes, "Symbolic interests of national honor and prestige are also given high priority by the Great Powers, for these are perceived as being essential components of national power and necessary for Great Power Status."[46] Accordingly, being perceived as a great power is a de facto condition of being a great power. Throughout history, a great power's credentials were revealed not through its amassing of capabilities, but by surviving the public test of war against an already acknowledged great power. By extension, prestige is enhanced also by success off the battlefield—in diplomatic confrontations in which a state manages to promote an initiative, prevent other states from following policies harmful to its interests, or compel dissenters to bow to its wishes.[47] Ergo, a great power and more to the point a dominant power's perceived victories will increase its prestige, while perceived setbacks will lower it correspondingly. By implication, symbolic challenges, while not disputing the dominant power's primacy in capabilities, nevertheless raise the prospect of exposing it as an incompetent or/and pusillanimous leader by showing that it can be defeated/defied/crossed on a given issue by a lower-ranking state.

In order to be perceived as victorious, a dominant power seeks, on the one hand, to perform better than other states, but, on the other hand, it also has to meet or exceed its and others' expectations of success. As Jervis has argued, success and failure are measured not just according to how far the outcome matches one's preferences, but also according to preexisting expectations—low expectations can mean that even a modest performance may count as a success, but, conversely, high expectations may make even a victory appear as a setback.[48]

From this perspective, a dominant power faces the highest expectations and, consequently, has to meet a constant requirement of delivering public success, or at any rate the impression of public success. In this, dominant powers follow the logic of Napoleon: "My power depends on my glory and my glories on the victories I have won. My power will fail if I do not feed it on new glories and new victories."[49] Consequently, the condition of dominant power has a demonstrative publicity dimension, that is, the dominant power has to mount public displays of effectiveness so as to be seen as worthy of maintaining its top ranking. The dominant power will also go to great lengths to avoid or minimize the impression of defeat, or, if defeated, to insure a compensating success elsewhere so as to recoup its prestige loss.

This is not to say that dominant powers will never admit defeat publicly. As Morgenthau writes: "The prestige of a nation is very much like the credit of a bank. A bank with large, proven resources and a record of successes can afford . . . to make a mistake or suffer a setback."[50] An isolated military defeat or diplomatic setback, while lowering a state's prestige, will not obliterate it, since the state is still seen as overall successful. But since both victories and defeats cumulate over time, not even a dominant power can afford to be perceived as suffering an uninterrupted string of failures, without seeing its prestige seriously affected. A dominant power that perceives itself on the retreat must compensate eventually for losses through a public display of success that would be proof of its continued entitlement to high prestige.

A dominant power's response to a symbolic challenge is also motivated by the anger-fueled desire for revenge. As an emotion, anger is not associated with the social underdogs, who are mistreated by the upper ranks, because, as long as these underdogs have no expectations of better treatment, they would not object to receiving a reduced share of respect. Rather, anger comes from those members of the higher status group who are not extended a level of deference corresponding to their expectations. As Lebow contends, following Aristotle: "In terms of at least foreign policy, it is powerful states not weak ones who feel the most humiliation...[Anger] is a response to... a slight, lessening or belittlement. Such a slight can issue from an equal but provokes even more anger when it comes from an actor who lacks the standing to challenge or insult us." Consequently, "anger is a luxury that can only be felt by those in a position to seek revenge." Therefore, anger may be provoked in instances when a rising power is not extended appropriate recognition of its status pretensions by established great powers, such as Imperial Germany's anger at being denied its right to a "place in the sun." In Aristotelian terms, such parvenu states resent the contempt of established powers, which treat them as if they are polities of little importance.[51]

However, anger will be also, and perhaps even more so, characteristic of scenarios in which a dominant power experiences a sense of lèse majesté in relation to lower-ranked polities, which are expected to behave with special deference and, nevertheless, fail to do so. This is not just a matter of disregarding proper etiquette toward a superior, but also one of refusing to submit to a superior's preferences and therefore should be equated with the Aristotelian notion of insolence.

The United States has itself a long history of reacting to such "insolent" challenges. One may recall here the dispatch of naval forces against the Barbary pirates of Algiers, Tripoli, and Tunis in the 1800s and 1810; the 1891 Chile crisis; the war against Spain over Cuba in 1898; the 1900s and 1910s interventions in the Caribbean and in Mexico; and the more recent military involvement in Korea, the Taiwan Straits, Cuba, Vietnam, Libya, Nicaragua, and Panama. To elaborate, the United States did not become a second-ranked state once it admitted defeat by withdrawing from South Vietnam in 1975, but the eventuality of withdrawal and its actual execution were never-theless construed by US decision-makers as severe humiliations, owing to the disparity in status of the opposing forces and to the expecta-tions of success on the American side. To quote Richard Nixon in his 1970 message to the nation announcing intervention in Cambodia: "We will not be humiliated. We will not be defeated...if when the chips are down, the world's most powerful nation, the United States of America, acts like a pitiful, helpless giant, the forces of totalitarian-ism and anarchy will threaten free nations and institutions through the world. It is not our power but our will and character that is being tested tonight...If we fail to meet this challenge all other nations will be on notice that despite its overwhelming power the United States, when a real crisis comes, will be found wanting."[52] This was not just fiery rhetoric, as shown by Assistant Secretary of Defense John McNaughton's 1965 memo, which argued that America's goals in South Vietnam were "70% to avoid a humiliating US defeat."[53] Indeed, in the Cold War, the United States was not only maintain-ing its prestige as dominant power in a positional sense vis-à-vis the Kremlin, but also obsessed with its credentials vis-à-vis the symbolic challenges of lesser states. As Gaddis wrote, throughout the Cold War, the United States manifested a continual fear "of embarrassment, of humiliation, of appearing to be weak."[54]

The United States may not have met with any positional challenges in the post–Cold War, but, at the same time, it faced a multitude of symbolic challenges coming from lower-ranked actors. Accordingly, the United States was challenged continuously by much weaker offenders: the governments of Iraq, North Korea, and Yugoslavia, the militias in Somalia, the Bosnian Serbs, al Qaeda, and the Taliban. Furthermore, the United States faced steep international resistance to seeing its preferences enacted in the case of the ICC, the revision of the ABM Treaty, or the sanction by the Security Council of the use of force against Baghdad and Belgrade.

None of these challenges succeeding would have hurt the United States sufficiently for it to cease to be a superpower, let alone pose a threat to its survival. The very point of these challenges did not con-cern the particular issue at stake, but rather involved the point that a lower-ranked political actor dared to challenge the dominant power. Hence, for the United States, the stakes of symbolic challenges did not consist in negligible strategic or economic losses. None of these contexts endangered directly the three key material national inter-ests of the United States, which may be summed up as ensuring its physical security against an existential threat; the absence of a peer great-power contender in Europe, East Asia, and the Middle East; and the continued flow of oil exports especially in the Gulf region.[55] Rather, the stakes of symbolic challenges consisted in their repercussions in terms of US prestige. As a consequence, despite its comfortable lead in capabilities, which might otherwise have translated into restraint, the leitmotif of the US foreign policy in the post–Cold War was its recurring worry of failing to live up to its full unipolar potential. For a state nominally so powerful to meekly endure symbolic challenges without answering them was interpreted as humiliating. Therefore, mounting a response to symbolic challenges became imperative. First, the United States needed to demonstrate publicly that it could pass the test proposed by the challenger—that it actually *did* have the requisite qualities of a world leader. Second, the US decision-makers, having experienced anger, wanted to punish the challengers by exacting retribution.

Symbolic Challenges and Challengers

Symbolic challenges come either from recalcitrant actors, whether states or groups, or from free-riding states.[56] Recalcitrant actors are foes who contest the order the dominant power is striving to implement.[57] Conversely, free-riding states are allies and partners, who, while deriving benefits from the preservation of *Pax Americana*, benefit even more by withholding or conditioning their logistical, financial, or/and diplomatic support to the preservation of this order. Neither recalcitrant nor free-riding challengers wish to supplant the dominant power, but seek to maximize their own gains at its expense.

Dominant powers are entitled not only to certain rights, but also act as custodians of the international system concerning the promotion, maintenance, and administration of rules. Thus, dominant powers impose order—a pattern of prohibitive and requisite behavior—on the other states in the system. Obviously, in so doing, these other states benefit from the ability to conduct political, economic, and cultural exchanges in the peaceful context provided by the dominant power; but at the same time the international order is also a self-interested enterprise, conferring the dominant power special privileges for its managerial role.[58] Consequently, other political actors may find it on occasion advantageous to contest or get a free ride against the dominant power's efforts to induce and preserve order in the system. Insofar as the challengers cross the dominant power, they cannot help but challenge its prestige, because if they prevail, their prestige will accrue and that of the dominant power will diminish. As Pitt-Rivers argues, "The victor in any competition for honor finds his reputation enhanced by the humiliation of the vanquished."[59] However, it is problematic whether recalcitrant and free-riding actors really mean to inflict humiliation on the dominant state, as it is more probable that humiliation is only a by-product of their policy to enhance their influence, wealth, and security. It is for this reason that symbolic challenges (barring exceptions such as al Qaeda) fall in the category of injuries caused by insolence, that is, the lack of appropriate respect to a higher-ranked state, rather than of injuries caused by spite, or the desire to demean the United States on purpose.

Typically, the dominant state is more likely to lash out against symbolic challengers when (a) the challenge is particularly brazen, (b) the challenge is repeated by the same actor so that the effect is cumulative, and (c) when the state has suffered reverses in other contexts and wants to put an end to a course of drift.brazen challenges describes those challenges that contest the most important principles for US identity and self-esteem, or those in which the challengers gloat over or express an open satisfaction at the humiliation and the discomfiture of the United States at their hands.[60] The more brazen the challenge, the stronger the prestige response of the United States is likely to be, because an open offense, which is not accompanied by excuses, guilt, or remorse, cannot be seen as an accident but conveys an intention to inflict harm. Brazen challenges are more likely to come from recalcitrant actors because, while free-riding states are able to disguise their challenges as legitimate actions, such as voting against US initiatives in the Security Council, recalcitrant challenges represent open acts of defiance and hence lack the cover provided by institutional legitimacy. Hence, the United States would lash out more often against recalcitrant adversaries than against free-riding ones, and would seek to punish them more harshly, including by force.

Second, the United States is more likely to lash out against challengers in order to put an end to a perceived streak of prestige losses, whether they are caused by repeated challenges of the same actor over time or by various actors issuing separate challenges. A dominant state refraining from doing so risks seeing its prestige slowly eaten away by consecutive setbacks, leaving it in the position of a weak, ineffective international leader.

As Kissinger argued in advocating force to liberate the US merchant ship *The Mayaguez*, which had been seized by the Khmer Rouge in 1975, after South Vietnam had collapsed two weeks before, it was precisely due to that setback that "the United States must carry out some act somewhere in the world which shows its determination to continue to be a world power."[61] This consideration is also detectable in President Kennedy's concern for keeping South Vietnam out of Communist hands, not because of its intrinsic value but in order to put an end to a sequence of setbacks: "There are limits to the amount of defeats I can accept within a twelve-month period. I've had the Bay of Pigs, and pulling out of Laos, I cannot accept a third."[62]

Accordingly, taking the above into consideration, one can conclude that unipolarity does not absolutely eliminate the incentives of conflict over prestige involving the dominant power. If unipolarity minimizes positional challenges, it may at the same time be prone to generate symbolic challenges. First, unipolarity raises the expectations bar for the United States. A unipolar dominant power is more vulnerable to symbolic challenges than other states simply because it is held up to a higher standard of success than any other polity based on its superior capabilities and record of using them. Second, in unipolarity every other state ranks lower than the unipole, since the gap that separates the dominant power from its nearest rival is too great to overcome. Hence, the unipole demands deference from a much larger group of lower-ranking states, comprising not only small and middle powers, but also the group of former great powers, now fallen to a devalued secondary rank. Ergo, there is more opportunity for instances of controversy regarding the proper level of deference vis-à-vis the unipole (especially concerning the second-tier great powers) than is the case in either bipolarity or multipolarity. Third, another reason for the proliferation of symbolic challenges in unipolarity derives from the multiplication of responsibilities the unipole assumes, simply because it is the only state able to address these issues. As the sole superpower left, the United States is burdened with the Herculean tasks of creating and enforcing world order, which it previously could either shirk on account of larger Cold War concerns or share with its Soviet rival. Rejecting this responsibility is not acceptable, as it exposes Washington to accusations of being an ineffective international leader, and hence risks damaging its prestige. Thus, any unaddressed disturbance in the international order becomes a blemish for the US claim to world leadership.

Prestige and Reputation

An important objection is that prestige may not be the actual drive behind US assertiveness, which is rather prompted by reputation, that is, "a judgment of someone's character or disposition," typically involving considerations of resolve in the face of threats and loyalty to one's commitments.[63] Traditional wisdom holds that analysts should differentiate between prestige, which is valued for its own sake, and reputation, which is seen as contributing to a state's deterrent ability. To quote the economics Nobel prizewinner Thomas Schelling: "It is often argued that 'face' is a frivolous asset to preserve [...] But there is also the more serious kind of 'face,' the kind that in modern jargon is known as a country's 'image,' consisting of other countries' beliefs (their leaders' beliefs, that is) about how the country can be expected to behave. It relates not to a country's 'worth' or 'status' or even 'honor,' but to its reputation for action." Reputation is an assumed prized asset because it is thought to function as a protective shield: if a state has a reputation for standing firm to challenges and for respecting its commitments, other states will likely refrain from challenging it. [64]

Nonetheless, operationalizing such a distinction, hence deciding which kind of "face" or "prestige" is frivolous to preserve, and which is cardinal to the security of state, is an exercise in futility. An inevitable overlap exists between prestige and reputation as both are aimed to impress other actors, both require establishing the possession of leadership qualities such as resolve and effectiveness, and both dictate the avoidance of conduct that conveys the impression of weakness and defeat. The only difference seems to consist in the assumption that reputation may have instrumental material results, while prestige does not.[65] Yet, even this distinction is blurred by studies that ascertain the absence of an actual link between reputation and deterrence. States do not acquire a reputation for weakness by giving in to their challengers, and, similarly, do not gain a reputation for resolve by standing firm, which means that past instances of firmness or of weakness do not affect the opponents' decision-making in future crises, compared to the stakes of the particular issue at hand.[66] Initial studies found only a single instance out of 16 crises where reputation had an effect on the challenger's future policy. This involved Germany's decision to invade Poland, apparently as a result of the weakness demonstrated by Britain and France at Munich. But later studies cast doubts on this case as well, as Hitler wavered in his assessment of the British commitment to Poland according not to the past British reputation for weakness but rather to situational specifics (the drop in support from Italy), and relied on power assessment more than on reputation to forecast the likely British course of action (lack of funds would prevent Britain from intervening, and Britain would find it logistically difficult to assist Poland).[67]

However, if reputation has no proven material consequences, any distinction with prestige cannot help but be impossibly fuzzy. Hence, it is not surprising that scholars use the two concepts interchangeably. For instance, Gilpin writes that prestige represents "the reputation for power and military power in particular," and that "prestige involves the credibility of a state's power and its willingness to deter or compel other states in order to achieve its objectives." Meanwhile, O'Neill states that "in the ambiguities of ordinary language, prestige overlaps reputation" and that, while reputation is the belief that an actor possesses a certain quality, prestige refers to a second-level belief about such a reputation, prestige being "the reputation of reputation."[68]

Why Bringing in Prestige Matters

Therefore, this overlap leaves one in a conundrum when interpreting the often ambiguous statements of decision-makers attributing their decisions to prestige or reputation.[69] Such statements could indicate either concern for prestige as a goal in itself or for reputation as an instrument to further the state's security. So, in other words, why opt for a psychological interpretation over an instrumentalist one, with the evidence plausibly pointing either way? The pragmatic answer is that the prestige interpretation emerges as the better fit, that is, the more useful choice in terms of added explanatory power. This does not mean that the prestige interpretation is necessarily true or false, only that, other things being equal, it is preferable for the purposes of theory-building.[70]

Reputation is supposed to produce larger material benefits than costs, which is to say that reputation accounts for regular strategic behavior by states. But reputation cannot account well for policies that are wasteful or strategically suboptimal. By this it is meant policies that entail significant material costs, do not add in a verifiable way to the material well-being of the state, and whose ends are out of proportion with the threat faced.[71] Why, therefore, should a state invest materially in defending its reputation, and, moreover, continue to do so, if reputation is not worth the candle?[72] Hence, in contexts where the state engages in suboptimal strategic behavior, prestige may be seen as the better explanation. The reason prestige is better equipped than reputation to account for such scenarios is precisely because it delivers psychological gratification rather than material utility.

The case of the US foreign policy of assertiveness may be described as strategically suboptimal because of two considerations. First, as suggested above, none of the challenges the United States responded to involved a crucial, pressing threat to key material interests. Second, while assertiveness has produced undeniable costs, particularly as chapters seven and eight show in the war in Iraq, it is very hard to prove with any certainty what exactly the policy has contributed in over two decades of post–Cold War to producing a sensibly more secure or powerful United States than it would have been otherwise.[73]

By the time the United States initiated military action against actors that were challenging it, deterrence had arguably already failed in the respective instance at stake, so seeking to establish a reputation no longer served a practical purpose. Effectively, throughout the period, the United States was unable to prevent its opponents from taking actions contrary to its preferences, whether this concerned Milošević's repeated attacks on the Kosovars or Saddam's restriction of access of UNSCOM weapon inspectors.[74] Of course, one could object that the United States was seeking to establish a reputation not for the present, but in view of averting future challenges. However, in support of the above-mentioned studies of reputation, this investigation has found no evidence that the United States demonstrating firmness in one context has resulted in the prevention of ulterior challenges. Standing up to the Bosnian Serbs and to the defiance of Saddam did not curb the propensity of Milošević to issue repeated challenges in Kosovo; acting in Kosovo did not prevent al Qaeda from attacking the United States; and not even the invasion and occupation of Iraq avoided subsequent offenses by the Taliban or by North Korea.

This argument holds even assuming that the US actions represented instances of using its image of effectiveness so as to elicit compellence (seeking to determine a change in the target's behavior or seeking to determine it to reverse a step already taken) rather than deterrence (seeking to prevent it from initiating an action in the first place).[75] A study of compellence in the post–Cold War found that out of eight cases only in two did the United States succeed in persuading the target to bow to its wishes without initiating major hostilities: Haiti and Bosnia. Even those cases are borderline, because in neither did the United States rely solely on its image. In Haiti, the United States was on the point of initiating a major invasion, and the Bosnian Serbs were convinced to cooperate not only by the bombing, but also by the simultaneous Croatian-Muslim offensive. By comparison, compellence failed in the five cases of Iraq (1991–1998), Somalia, North Korea, Kosovo, and the war against terrorism.[76] Thus, standing firm in one instance did not impact upon the future compelling ability of the United States.

Accordingly, from the point of view of advancing its instrumental reputation, US assertiveness in the post–Cold War constitutes a paradox. But this is no longer a paradox if the US policies are understood in terms of psychology rather than instrumentality, because the United States still has a prestige stake in its number one position, and in behaving assertively so as to maintain it even if doing so does not pay off materially.

The second advantage of choosing a prestige lens over a reputation lens is that doing so allows scholars to include into the theory emotional variables that are lacking in instrumentalist accounts. Accounts stressing reputation are predicated on the notion that decision-making is or should be a cool-headed calculation of material costs and benefits. However, emotion is an inevitable component of *any* instance of decision-making. Neurological studies have shown how individuals whose emotional capacity had been impaired, even though their cognitive functions were not, were unable to make up their minds about the simplest decisions, such as fixing a meeting time, in an endless calculation of the pros and cons of each option.[77] Moreover, emotions allow human beings to adjust to changes in the environment that may require urgent shifts between the pursuit of multiple goals.[78] Thus, the enabling role of emotions has to be factored in foreign policy analysis simply because nonemotional decision-making is impossible. This does not mean that emotions lead always to strategic optimal decisions, but rather that the denial of emotions is unfeasible for decision-makers. Even if the leaders would be able to resist their own emotions they still would have to contend with political pressure from an emotional public.[79]

Prestige is a better-suited explanation than reputation when dealing with emotions since, as seen in the above, defending one's prestige from challenges supposes reacting emotionally to a perceived humiliation through public demonstrations of effectiveness and the angry castigation of the offender. As later chapters will argue, US foreign policy in the post–Cold War was prone to such impulses: the US decision-makers felt compelled to show the world the United States effectively had what it took to be a leader, and angry at challenges, sought retribution against the offenders.

Accordingly, since bringing prestige into the analysis offers gains for scholars in theoretical explanatory power, it should be seen as preferable to reputation for the purpose of analyzing US foreign policy in the post–Cold War.

ALTERNATIVE THEORIES

Prestige is not the only theory accounting for the US foreign policy of assertiveness in the post–Cold War. Alternative, but not necessarily mutually exclusive, explanations are provided by structuralism, exceptionalism, and revisionism. These schools of thought are derived from the literature on US foreign policy. They are not the equivalent of International Relations theories, and hence are not fully identifiable with realism, liberalism, constructivism, or Marxism. Basically, structuralism emphasizes the role of the imbalance of power capabilities between the United States and other great powers, hence of structure; exceptionalism that of the peculiar US political culture, hence of values; finally, revisionism that of the pursuit of global economic openness, hence of socioeconomic US domestic interests. Each school represents an ideal type that covers an array of related, but often widely competing theories, which, nonetheless, proceed from the same assumptions.[80]

Structuralism

For structuralism, unlike in the popular *Spiderman* movies, with great power may not come great responsibility, but rather the appetite to acquire yet more power.[81] Structuralists see assertiveness as the outgrowth of power imbalance, in which one state is left, however temporarily, with substantially more capabilities than the others, and decides to make the most of its advantage. That is to say for structuralism, assertiveness is the product of the window of opportunity created by the international distribution of power. It is just as if at a standing-room-only horse race, a seat suddenly became open in the front row.[82] Just like spectators scrambling to reach the front-row seat, a state will take advantage of the favorable occasion that happens to come its way. Thus, systemic shifts automatically push the fortunate great power to further expand its international influence. Dominant powers at their apex, such as the United States, become more assertive as they become cushioned against security threats by other states, meaning that they gain a free hand in pursuing their objectives aggressively, with little concern of adverse repercussions from other parties.

As Waltz argues, "Where gross imbalances of power exist…the more capable naturally exert a considerable influence over those less able to produce surpluses."[83] Waltz writes at length about this so-called "imperialism of great powers," meaning that "it would be odd for states affecting others more than they are affected by them not to engage in outwardly imperialist activity" and that, this being the case, "the absence of imperialism in the face of imbalanced power would sorely require explanation."[84] This is why US assertiveness 30 years down the road constitutes no mystery. "The winner of the Cold War and the sole remaining great power has behaved," writes Waltz, "as unchecked powers have always done."[85]

For structuralism, the United States does not have a choice between restraint and assertiveness, because, try as it might, structural pressures would push it over time in the direction of assertiveness. A state that refuses to follow a line of assertiveness when presented with the opportunity to do so is punished by the system with the multiplication of threats to its security, as its rivals expand their influence in its stead and grow therefore more powerful and more menacing and as unrest spills out across borders. Hence, since "the greater the military advantage one state has over others, the more secure it is," states should never flinch from consolidating their power further so as to preserve their security.[86] To this extent, while the one-sidedness of power provides the opportunity, security concerns provide the chief motive for assertiveness. Moreover, the security of a dominant state may require substantial assertiveness, not restraint, as the interests that it needs to protect multiply, especially in terms of involvement in additional geographic areas (such as the Balkans or the Gulf) and of increased attention to previous minor threats (such as rogue states).[87]

A good deal of dissent exists among structuralists as to the exact mechanism through which systemic pressures and incentives are translated into actual assertiveness, with some analyses suggesting the additional relevance of ideology or/and domestic politics factors. Furthermore, defensive-minded structuralists, who are the chief proponents of the strategy of offshore balancing, point out that assertiveness will lead over the long run to counterbalancing by other great powers, and thus will prove self-defeating. Yet, structuralists of all hues tend to view power imbalances as too tantalizing for a dominant power to resist.[88] Hence, to wager that decision-makers can fight off the lure of expansion offered by unbridled power is likely to prove a losing bet.[89]

In regard to the post–Cold War, structuralism would be confirmed if, on the one hand, power imbalances favoring the United States translated into the temptation to use/abuse them, and, on the other hand, if assertiveness was the result of US decision-makers' concerns regarding physical security in the face of growing threats.

Exceptionalism

For exceptionalism, assertiveness is driven by an enduring US faith in having been entrusted a mission on behalf of global liberal-democracy.[90]

Accordingly, for exceptionalism, US decision-makers believe that the United States both holds a special place among other nations as defenders or champions of democracy and was chosen, "whether by God, 'Destiny,' or 'History'" to embody "the greatest, most successful, oldest, and most developed form of democracy."[91] US liberal-democracy is understood to rest on a creed, that is, a set of political principles—liberty, equality, individualism, and free markets—that is pervasive throughout US institutions and practices. From here derives both a strict adherence of the United States to "a fixed, dogmatic...liberal way of life" and a definition of American-ness as commitment to the creed. As Lipset puts it, "Being an American is an ideological commitment. It is not a matter of birth. Those who reject American values are un-American." This is why, for exceptionalism, US foreign policy cannot escape a liberal pattern that suffuses all political life.

These beliefs suppose a foreign policy of assertiveness in several ways. First, since John Winthrop's sermon a self-described city upon a hill, set high above all other nations, the United States cannot be burdened with the obligations and restrictions that apply to ordinary states. This belief accounts for the US soft spot for unilateral foreign policies, since the United States prefers to act with few or no partners so as to suffer no hindrances in the way it carries out its mission and no adulterations of the values it champions. Furthermore, because of this assumption, any manifestation of opposition to US initiatives is seen as illegitimate since it challenges what is held to be an evidently valid American mandate on behalf of global democracy.[92]

Second, the United States is persuaded of a symbiotic relation between its own interests and the best interests of the world.[93] As a result, the more states are cajoled or pressured to adopt the US liberal-democratic model, the better off the whole of humankind will be. Besides, this outcome will also be highly beneficial for the United States itself, because the progress of democracy in the world will contribute to US security and prosperity.[94]

Third, to be chosen involves a particular moral imperative in propagating liberal democratic values worldwide. Woodrow Wilson best exposed this crusader agenda: "The world must be made safe for democracy. Its peace must be planted upon the tested foundations of political liberty. We have no selfish ends to serve. We desire no conquest, no dominion...We are but the champions of the rights of mankind."[95] This fondness for crusades may be somewhat moderated by the influence of the opposite covenanted conviction that the US mission on behalf of liberal democracy may be carried out better by concentrating on liberty at home, thus providing the world with an example to follow, rather than, in John Quincy Adams' words "going abroad in search of monsters to destroy."[96] However, the promotion of liberal democracy has incontrovertibly emerged as the more influential approach for US foreign policy in the aftermath of World War Two, which has been pronouncedly internationalist.[97]

In the case studies, exceptionalist arguments would be confirmed if the record shows that a "crusader" effort on behalf of democratic principles and human rights determined assertiveness. Exceptionalist arguments would be valid whether the aim of the US policy was to promote or, alternatively, to protect from abuse democracy and human rights, both being consistent interpretations with the Wilsonian call of "making the world safe for democracy."[98] Conversely, exceptionalism would be falsified if ideology did not affect policy decisively.

Revisionism

For revisionism, US assertiveness can be traced to the interests of particular domestic groups set to achieve or consolidate political and economic gains. Approached from a revisionist perspective, US foreign policy is striking mainly by its obsession with assertiveness or as revisionists would put it, informal empire, since at least the 1890s. For revisionism, the United States spurns the complications of a formal political dominium: a simple economic connection suffices to secure a position of privilege for US elites without presenting them with the burden of actually administrating a subject territory. In this sense, US dominance does not rely excessively on coercion, at least as long the validity of the principle of unimpeded access to world markets and capital outlets is not in question.[99]

For revisionists, the gains social elites derive from assertiveness do not consist in brute economic profit, but in the preservation of these groups' dominance over US society. In effect, even though assertiveness does not actually deliver the economic bounty it promises, US decision-makers are socialized in the conviction that the prosperity and survival of the United States depend on the continual export of goods, services, and capital.[100] Thus, the guiding principle of US foreign policy came to be defined in terms of ensuring the unimpeded access of American products and capital to foreign economic outlets, a principle embodied by the Open Door notes of Secretary of State John Hay in 1899 and 1900 on maintaining a free market in China. Accordingly, revisionism argues that the United States has ever since pursued a foreign policy aimed at spreading and maintaining the Open Door abroad.[101]

Current revisionism updates the original accounts for the post–Cold War context.[102] Accordingly, revisionists argue that the Open Door has gone global in the 1990s, thanks to the boom in means of communication, transfer of information, financial transactions, and trade exchanges that link together the various parts of the world into a single global economy, with the US at its helm. As a result, the main preoccupation of US decision-makers in the post–Cold War, irrespective of administration, is to ensure the definitive triumph of globalization through dismantling the last remaining obstacles to US trade and capital.[103]

However, a key difference between the original revisionists and the present practitioners lies in the degree of importance the latter attach to the use of military force by the United States in order to safeguard openness. For Williams, the use of force was episodic and a last-resort instrument. Not so for new revisionists, for whom the United States has become much more trigger-happy.[104] Furthermore, the more openness the United States promotes, the more threats to the unimpeded functioning of the Open Door System are identified. In order to address them, the United States has turned assertive, with substantial authority devolved to the Pentagon and to regional military commanders in chief (CINCs) who act as a modern counterpart of the Roman Empire proconsuls. A particular class, constituted of a motley group of professional soldiers, multinational corporation bureaucrats, petroleum industrialists, hedge funds speculators, intellectuals supporting globalization, and businessmen catering to US bases around the world, stands out to profit from assertiveness. Hence, the point of assertiveness is not to benefit the United States, but instead to preserve the privileges of this oligarchic group.[105]

Two kinds of evidence may confirm/falsify revisionism in the case studies. First, the expectation of gains and the avoidance of losses related to the application of the Open Door constitute key clues for revisionism. Second, revisionism also implies the presence of a causal link between the alleged influence of domestic groups and the conduct of foreign policy, which can be tested against the policy record.

CHAPTER CONCLUSION

Prestige represents an inordinate amount of respect. As such, it is valued by any social actor because it provides a sense of self-esteem, which is a fundamental psychological requirement. In world politics, prestige can be obtained through the possession of formidable military and economic capabilities as well as through the achievement of success. A state would fear for its prestige if faced with either positional challenges from a competing state, or with the symbolic challenges of recalcitrant and free-riding actors that contest its right to superior rank and respect. Such symbolic challenges are regarded as serious offenses and have to be answered with assertiveness, both so as to regain one's lost prestige and so as to take revenge on the challenger. As the dominant power in an interval of unipolarity, the United States became the target of challenges, which it ultimately had to respond to.

However, this is not a plea for monocausality, since in foreign policy analysis a "mosaic" model is superior to the one resulting from the consideration of a single overriding factor. This is to say that an account of US foreign policy in the post–Cold War has to combine elements of the prestige model and of the other three schools of thought: the international distribution of power capabilities from structuralism, the liberal- democratic political culture from exceptionalism, and US domestic politics from revisionism. Nonetheless, necessary as they undoubtedly are for understanding US fondness for assertiveness, capabilities, ideology, and domestic interests are also not sufficient. The United States would not have resorted to an assertive foreign policy, but for the additional, yet crucial factor of prestige.

3

THE US FAILED EXPERIMENT WITH
RESTRAINT

Following the Gulf War of 1991, when asked whether he envisioned the post–Cold War as a new era of using US military power, and, hence, of assertiveness, President George H. W. Bush was unequivocal. "Because of what's happened we won't have to use US forces around the world. I think when we say something... people are going to listen. Because I think out of all this will be a new-found—let's put it this way: a reestablished credibility for the United States of America."[1] That was to say that with US power and prestige at an all-time high, the post–Cold War seemed to usher in a golden age of restraint. Yet the roots of assertiveness are to be found precisely in this interval headed for uneventful tranquility. When the United States chose assertiveness in the late 1990s, it did so chiefly because the alternative option of restraint was seen as having been tried and having backfired.

One may object to the designation of an interval that witnessed high defense spending and the extension of defense commitments to the Middle East and to Eastern Europe, as well as a war in the Gulf and several military interventions, as restrained. However, US efforts to implement a strategy of cooperative security show that this period, while not an epitome of restraint, witnessed, nevertheless, a more moderate US foreign policy compared to the unbridled assertiveness of later years, particularly in the areas of multilateralism and the propensity to employ limited force. Therefore, the early post–Cold War should be seen as the years of a US experiment with restraint, which eventually ended in failure.

The perception of failure was caused by the proliferation of symbolic challenges both from recalcitrant actors and from free-riding states. Symbolic challenges were humiliating, given the disparity of forces in the balance in the post–Cold War, yet, owing to the constraints imposed by restraint, the United States was hampered in taking action by the requirements of avoiding or minimizing the use of force, and of securing the consent of other states for its preferred policy. As a result, a striking contrast was created between America's superior capabilities and its mediocre achievements. As the then-editor of *Foreign Affairs* put it: "American credibility and influence have declined at a time when this country's power is unmatched."[2] By 1995, the United States had become increasingly disenchanted with this state of affairs, and began resorting to assertiveness.

THE THREE ILLUSIONS

Relative restraint was the product of three illusions that gathered popularity among academics and decision-makers alike: order, cooperation, and peace.[3] First, there was the illusion that the end of the Cold War had resulted in a much more manageable international environment; second, that other states would wholeheartedly assist the United States in its managerial burden; and, finally, that in an age of globalization, matters of war and peace had been superseded by economic issues.

The three illusions were predicated on the belief in a post–Cold War revolutionary transformation in the conduct of international affairs. As Nye wrote, "The world has changed more rapidly in the past two years than at any time since 1945."[4] The transformation was at the same time structural, ideological, economic, and technological—and worked to the great advantage of the United States. It is uncontestable that a far-reaching change had taken place as the result of the collapse of communism, but, with the benefit of hindsight, contemporary observatories were exaggerating the consequences of these events to the point of assuming the advent of a lasting orderly, cooperative, and peaceful environment.

A typical illustration of these views came from the theory of the end of history. For Fukuyama, liberal-democratic states had moved "beyond history," meaning that they had reached a point where war had become an unthinkable prospect, except in those limited contexts where the opponent (by necessity a nondemocracy) was still "stuck in history."[5] In practical terms, since Fukuyama argued that democracy and wealth went hand in hand, "the post-historical" states tended to be clustered in the developed North, while "the historical" states occupied most of the South. Moreover, the Soviet Union and China were gravitating increasingly toward the post-historical camp. This imagery essentially divided the planet into a zone of prosperity and peace where the leading world states shared the same interests, and a zone of poverty and disorder still mired in history, but that was going to be moving inexorably on its own toward liberal democracy.[6] This conviction was in turn reinforced by the democratic peace theory, whose main conclusion was that democracies do not go to war against other democracies. Hence, taking into account that the world had become increasingly democratic since 1974 and decisively more so since 1989, the United States could count on a markedly more peaceful environment.[7]

If in this respect, the George H. W. Bush cabinet was reluctant to accelerate the drive toward democracy of post–Tiananmen China, the Middle East autocracies, and the Gorbachev-led Soviet Union, the first Clinton administration was outspoken in its belief in democratic peace. As National Security Advisor Anthony Lake argued, "The successor to a doctrine of containment must be a strategy of enlargement—enlargement of the world's free community of market democracies." Lake contended that as a key component of "enlargement," the United States "should help foster and consolidate new democracies and market economies, where possible, especially in states of special significance and opportunity…our strategy must be to help democracy and markets expand and survive in other places where we have the strongest security concerns and where we can make the greatest difference."[8] In the same vein, Undersecretary of State Strobe Talbott wrote that "the larger and more close-knit the community of nations that chose democratic form of government, the safer and more prosperous the Americans will be, since democracies are demonstrably more likely to maintain their international commitments…and less likely to make war on each other." By Talbott's own account, this bright future was already in the making, since 61 percent of the world population in the 1990s was already living in democratic states.[9] This faith in the advent of democracy was even enshrined by the Clinton administration in the official National Security Strategy of the United States: "We believe that our goals of enhancing our security, bolstering our economic prosperity, and promoting democracy are mutually supportive…democratic states are less likely to threaten our interests and more likely to cooperate with the US."[10] Accordingly, with most of the world already democratic, and with Russia and China set to follow suit, there was no reason to worry about the prospects of international order and peace—they were assumed to have become self-maintaining.

This was more so since a consensus reigned in the early 1990s among analysts that the United States could rely on an eager and wide international following. For conservatives, cooperation was going to be the automatic effect of America's unrivalled power, since other states would have sought to ingratiate themselves with the unipole. As Krauthammer put it: "The true geopolitical structure of the post–Cold War world...consists of the United States at the apex of the industrial West. Perhaps it is more accurate to say the United States and behind it the rest, because where the United States does not tread, the alliance does not follow...The unipolar moment means that... an ideologically pacified North seeks security and order by aligning its foreign policy behind that of the United States."[11] Meanwhile, liberals shared a similar faith in international cooperation, only they attributed it to the constraints of globalization. Globalization created new challenges that could be addressed efficiently only in a multilateral format. Thus, Nye, who had become undersecretary of defense in the Clinton administration, argued that the magnitude of transnational problems, such as nuclear proliferation, AIDS, and global warming, meant that the best approach to an interdependent world was some form of coalition headed by the United States and blessed by international institutions. Both the United States and the institutional components were necessary, but neither was sufficient on its own: "The way to steer a middle path is...to renew American commitment to multilateral institutions...The use of multilateral institutions, while sometimes constraining, also helps share the burden that the American people do not want to bear alone."[12]

The consequence of these views was the elevation of cooperation to the level of guiding principle for the post–Cold War policy, on par with enlargement or democracy promotion. No wonder therefore that the most coherent foreign policy document put forward by the first Clinton administration was entitled "A National Security Strategy of Engagement and Enlargement." Engagement was a concept developed by a group of the Brookings Institution scholars, comprising the future numbers one and two at the Pentagon, Secretary of Defense William Perry, and his assistant Ashton Carter. By engagement they meant "a strategic principle that seeks to accomplish its purposes through institutionalized consent rather than through threats of material or physical coercion. It presupposes fundamentally compatible security objectives and seeks to establish collaborative rather than confrontational relationships among national military establishments." Such cooperation implied the conclusion of arms limitation and arms reduction agreements, greater security transparency, and a commitment to "an internationally supported concept of effective and legitimate intervention which is always multilateral and elected only as a last resort."[13]

Hence, in this line of thought, when the "National Security Strategy" spoke of engagement, it referred to the imperative of multilateral cooperation. The document made the explicit point that "no matter how powerful we are as a nation, we cannot secure these basics goals unilaterally...the threats and challenges we face demand cooperative, multinational solutions. Therefore, the only responsible US strategy is one that seeks to ensure US influence over and participation in collective decision-making in a wide and growing range of circumstances...Accordingly, a central thrust of our strategy of engagement is to sustain and adapt the security relationships we have with key nations around the world." Thus, the United States was not going to just consult with other states and institutions—it also was going to take their objections and concerns to heart, and, in case no consensus was achievable, it should have forgone action instead of pressing ahead on its own. But this scenario was not judged likely, since as long as the United States intended to act in concert with other states and institutions, the expectation was that the concert would not run afoul of US wishes. While the United States reaffirmed its right to act alone if "its vital or survival interests are at stake," this was a last-resort solution. On most matters at most times, cooperation was the preferred instrument: "As much as possible, we will seek the help of our allies and friends or of relevant international institutions...working together increases the effectiveness of each nation's actions."[14]

A third illusion propped those of order and cooperation: that of the decline in relevance of large-scale military force. This alleged obsolescence was caused by the *deus ex machina* of globalization, which rewarded certain states for showing openness to foreign products, services, capital, and ideas, while punishing those resisting them. Once a state had been engulfed by the transnational forces of economy, technology, and information, it was less likely to use violence against another similarly developed polity. War would have disrupted commercial and financial ties; states would have advanced their objectives by much cheaper means through embracing globalization than through conquest; and markets would have abhorred the instability inherent in a military conflict. So if a state was foolish enough to resort to fighting, investment would have immediately left its shores in quest for more peaceful havens, wrecking the warmonger's economy.[15] Hence, for the purpose of prevailing in the realm of global economic competition, the use of force by a developed nation was pictured as an "act of desperation."[16] The only practical use of force was dealing with challenges in the Third World, for which a minimum amount of troops and hi-tech weaponry would have been sufficient.

As a result, the early 1990s marked a low point of military matters and the simultaneous peaking of interest in the economy. Between 1990 and 1998, the United States cut back its military spending from the Cold War levels of 5.7 percent to 3.4 percent, reducing both its active manpower by more than 700,000 troops and its total force structure (numbers of army and marine divisions, warplanes, bombers, aircraft carriers, and battleships) by almost 25 percent.[17] At the same time, Clinton created in 1993 a counterpart to the National Security Council in the form of the National Economic Council, in charge of coordinating domestic and foreign economic policy, thus placing economy and security on formal parity. Special Trade Representative Mickey Kantor summed up this trend by stating: "Past administrations have often neglected US economic and trading interests because of foreign policy and defense concerns. The days when we could afford to do so are long past. In the post–Cold War world, our national security depends on our economic strength."[18]

Hence, while economic issues gained prominence in US foreign policy, the Clinton administration was perceived as inhibited when it came to employing large-scale force.[19] This much maligned trait cannot be attributed just to the fear of domestic backlash due to casualties or the influence of the Pentagon, which through the 1990s swore by the Powell Doctrine.[20] After all, both these factors should have still been at work in Clinton's second term, but, nevertheless, did not derail the decision to intervene massively against Yugoslavia. Hence, a supplementary factor needs to be considered: the conviction of the Clinton administration that force itself had become a blunt tool, ill-suited for use in the globalized post–Cold War world and relegated to the role of an instrument of last resort.

Considered together, the three illusions of order, cooperation, and peace, amounted to a minimalist, and hence restrained, US exercise of international leadership. However, as US decision-makers found out to their dismay, the United States' uncontested dominance did not result in order, or cooperation, or not even in peace.

THE EXPERIMENT BEGINS: THE GULF CONFLICT

The issue that helped the three illusions and hence restraint to take hold of US foreign policy was the Gulf conflict.[21] Insofar as it represented the first major crisis to arise in the aftermath of the fall of the Berlin Wall, this was more than a question of who controlled the oil-rich emirate of Kuwait. Instead, it was interpreted by US decision-makers as setting the pattern of international relations in the post–Cold War era. In the words of Bush's National Security Advisor Brent Scowcroft: "In the first days of the crisis we had started self-consciously to view our actions as setting a precedent for the approaching post–Cold War world. Soviet cooperation in condemning the attack [by Saddam Hussein on Kuwait] provided the initial impetus for this line of thinking, inasmuch as it opened the way for the Security Council to operate as its founders envisioned. That in turn had led to our August [1990] discussions of a 'new world order.'"[22] Scowcroft emphasized this precedent-setting point further: "One of the underlying premises of the Gulf War...for the president and me, probably for Baker, was to conduct this whole thing in a way that would set a useful pattern for the way to deal with crises in an area of cooperation."[23]

What exactly was the pattern that US decision-makers wanted to set? Again this is explained by Scowcroft: "Our foundation was the premise that the United States henceforth would be obliged to lead the world community to an unprecedented degree, as demonstrated by the Iraqi crisis, and that we should attempt to pursue our national interests, wherever possible, within the framework of concert with our friends and the international community."[24] As a result, the top US decision-makers derived from the Gulf conflict the lessons that first, the United States could exercise international leadership to a degree it had never experienced before and second, that the support of other states was crucial to its success.

The Gulf conflict proved conclusively that the United States was a force to be reckoned with. According to Pentagon estimates, Iraq fielded at the time the world's fourth largest army in terms of troops and had proved in its eight-year war with Iran that it could withstand conflict against a numerically superior foe. By some forecasts, the losses likely to be suffered by the coalition in an attempt to liberate Kuwait were estimated to be as high as 20,000, with 7,000 dead. Astonishingly, the United States freed the emirate, with only 458 casualties, including 148 dead, while inflicting casualties in tens of thousands on Iraq.[25] Given these impressive results, it is no wonder that US decision-makers did not seriously contemplate the prospect of challenges to US leadership. Even a self-defined realist such as Secretary of State James Baker subscribed to the buoyant mood: "The entire world suddenly wanted to get closer to the United States...The principles and values of the American experience—democracy and free markets—were being embraced around the globe as never before. It seemed as though everyone wanted to be America's best friend."[26]

Furthermore, the Gulf conflict was also a path-opener because, had Saddam proceeded to invade Kuwait just a decade earlier, he could have counted on backers that would have prevented both sanctions and intervention by a coalition under the UN flag. Instead, in the post–Cold War, the Iraqi attempt at conquest was met with unambiguous unity, which, moreover, survived Saddam's wedge-driving efforts. The United States succeeded in all its major diplomatic initiatives: the deployment of 250,000 troops to Saudi Arabia in Operation Desert Shield, the worldwide imposition of a blockade on Iraqi products, and, finally, the authorization through UN Security Council resolution 678 of the use of "all necessary means" in order to free Kuwait.[27] It was therefore clear to US decision-makers that Saddam could not have been isolated and defeated without the support of a large number of states, whether their contribution came in the form of financial burden-sharing, of granting the use of territory for armed operations, of enforcing sanctions, of contributing troops, or simply of not sabotaging US initiatives.

Cooperation involved a self-conscious quid pro quo policy. In return for logistic, diplomatic, financial, and legitimacy assistance from other nations, the United States committed itself to a course of restraint, manifested by consultations as well as by concessions in terms of policy timing, wording, style, and even content. In effect, the United States went to unprecedented lengths to secure international support in the Gulf crisis. For instance, on the occasion of the vote on resolution 678, Baker engaged in a diplomatic marathon ranging from the USSR and China to Columbia and Yemen, meeting with representatives of all the other 14 countries occupying a seat in the UN Security Council. This included even the usually shunned Cuban foreign minister, whom Baker met in New York.[28] Perhaps the single most significant instance in which international cooperation affected US foreign policy content was the decision to stop the terrestrial advance into Iraq before Saddam could have been unseated. This decision was in great part due to the conviction of Bush decision-makers that toppling Saddam would have exceeded the mandate of the UN Security Council and thus would have been disavowed by Soviet and Arab partners. As Scowcroft argued, there was no single rationale for the United States to stop its offensive into Iraq, "but one of the factors was we had a UN mandate to take whatever measures necessary to get the Iraqi troops out of Kuwait. And that was all."[29] Thus, in the aftermath of the Gulf War, the cooperation of other states had become a requirement of US foreign policy-making.

Restraint and the New World Order

This pattern of restraint for cooperation became the foundation of Bush's doctrine of the new world order. The first time the concept was hinted at was in a conversation between President Bush and Scowcroft on August 23, 1990, which concluded that "the United States and the Soviet Union could, in most cases, stand together against unprovoked interstate aggression."[30] Accordingly, the United States could employ the formula of broad cooperation under UN auspices inaugurated in the context of the Gulf conflict so as to exercise leadership in the post–Cold War. The new world order buzzword then appeared repeatedly in Bush's speeches.[31] As he put it to Congress: "The crisis in the Persian Gulf...also offers a rare opportunity to move toward an historic period of cooperation. Out of these troubled times...a new world order...can emerge: a new era—free from the threat of terror, stronger in the pursuit of justice, and more secure in the quest for peace. An era in which the nations of the world, East and West, North and South, can prosper and live in harmony."[32] For all the extravagant rhetoric, the new world order was not meant as the advent of a golden age. To quote Scowcroft: "We certainly had no expectation that we were entering a period of peace and tranquility." Instead, "the phrase, as we thought of it, applied only to a narrow aspect of conflict—aggression between states," and more to the point, on how to handle world governance problems in a cooperative framework.[33]

In this sense, the new world order was a conservative rather than a reformist enterprise: it implied making concessions to US partners and allies as well as refraining from actions that risked provoking their concerns or bruising their sensibilities in return for their support. It is for this reason that the UN briefly became the instrument of choice for exercising US leadership, first because of its all-inclusive character, and second because it provided guarantees of nonaggressive US behavior since as long as it was committed to Security Council authorization, the United States could not have acted without the other permanent members' express consent.[34]

Yet, the major weakness of the new world order was that it ignored the features that had set apart the Gulf conflict, "the perfect war with the perfect enemy," as a unique development.[35] Iraq's occupation of Kuwait had represented a challenge to the interests of all the great powers and oil-dependent developed economies, while Saddam's violation of the taboo on conquest in place since World War Two alienated the support he might have gathered regionally and in the Third World. Furthermore, the United States relied on the presence in power in the Kremlin of the most accommodating Soviet leadership ever. It was therefore highly debatable whether this amount of international support was going to be equally forthcoming for US endeavors in different contexts, and, as such, basing future policy on such exceptional circumstances constituted a risky gamble. Unfortunately, the genie was out of the bottle, since Bush, Scowcroft, and Baker clearly understood the post–Cold War in terms of a world order that was to be brought and maintained by a restrained US leadership, with the automatic (and presumably wholehearted) help of other states.[36]

The commitment of the Bush administration to a course of relative restraint was particularly detectable in its negative reaction to the Pentagon's 1992 Defense Planning Guidance (DPG). The document advocated that the United States' top priority should have been preventing the reemergence of any power capable of mounting a challenge to US supremacy as formidable as the one posed by the Soviet Union. This meant opposing the effort of *any* power to gain regional dominance of Europe, East Asia, or the Middle East. As Khalilzad, the DPG's chief author, later clarified, the United States should not have concerned only by potential challenges from China and Russia. Instead, America had stakes in preventing the reemergence of a multipolar environment, which implied blocking even efforts by US allies to catch up militarily or economically.[37] This prevention effect was to be achieved by retaining an unrivalled lead in military capabilities over any would-be challenger. In the words of the DPG, "We must maintain the mechanisms for deterring potential competitors from even aspiring to a larger regional or global role."[38]

As such, the DPG was seen as counterproductive, since by throwing its weight around, the United States risked alienating states whose contributions were deemed crucial to the maintenance of the new world order. The motives to resist the DPG therefore ran deeper than just the concern to avoid domestic public outcry following the leaking of excerpts of the document in March 1992.[39] Even though both the DPG and the new world order were predicated on the assumption that the United States should remain dominant, they were at loggerheads on the best means to achieve it: whether by assertiveness or by restraint. In this respect, the key Bush foreign policy-makers, with the exception of Secretary of Defense Dick Cheney, unambiguously repudiated assertiveness. To quote Scowcroft: "It [the DPG] didn't go anywhere further. It was never formally reviewed."[40]

RESTRAINT AND ENGAGEMENT

The pattern of relative restraint inaugurated by Bush did not vanish with the advent of the Clinton team. This is shown by the State Department's transition memo written by Secretary of State Lawrence Eagleburger to his successor Warren Christopher. According to the memo recommendations, the United States should be "a provider of reassurance and architect of new security arrangements; an aggressive proponent of economic openness; an exemplar and advocate of democratic values; a builder and leader of coalitions to deal with problems."[41]

Clinton came into office with little personal interest in shepherding foreign affairs except in matters concerning globalization. One disaffected former aide refers to him as a president "less interested in international affairs than at any time in the previous six decades combined." In the first months following his election, he even turned the entire responsibility of foreign policy decision-making to his officials, with the advice to keep him informed, but not to take too much of his time.[42] This was by no means a plunge into isolationism. Rather, Clinton acted on the new world order premise that the system had become much more manageable than it had been throughout the Cold War, and that the United States could rely on its partners to help it ensure order.

Much as the accusation of lacking an overarching grand foreign policy strategy became a litany among critics and spurred an obsession to come up with a catchy bumper-sticker phrase within the administration itself, Clinton's foreign policy amounted to exercising relative restraint in return for cooperation. The only addition from the days of George H. W. Bush was that the United States meant to promote, besides objectives such as peace and stability, values such as democracy and respect for human rights.[43] This was not, however, a revolutionary call for the indiscriminate overthrow of dictatorships and for punishing human rights violators. Despite the rhetoric of his main foreign policy advisors (Lake, Talbott, and the UN ambassador Madeleine Albright), which Bush ironically referred to in the 1992 presidential campaign as "the vision thing," Clinton was not a genuine visionary. The promotion of US values was a desirable goal, but one that could only be achievable in contexts where international consensus on the matter existed and where there was no risk of using force on a large scale.

However, the net effect of these measures was a foreign policy widely interpreted as adrift.[44] Although they appeared compatible, the illusions of order, cooperation, and peace could and actually did clash. For instance, the spread of democracy contravened the requirements of cooperation and of economic globalization in relations with China; or the desire to avoid using massive military force in Bosnia led to strained cooperation with the European allies who argued that the United States was not sharing the same risks they faced. In such instances, the victory of one principle meant the concomitant defeat of the others, which meant that the administration had to time and again suffer the embarrassment of backing down from its initial position. Furthermore, the United States had no back-up plan in the plausible scenario it could not secure international support or compliance. Finally, although it obsessively styled itself as the world's leader—for instance, in one speech, Clinton's Secretary of State Warren Christopher mentioned leadership no less than 23 times—the United States was reluctant to lead, particularly when large-scale use of force was actually needed to prevail.[45] Consequently, in the early 1990s, the United States preferred to muddle through. These compromises, while successful in preserving consensus and in avoiding the use of significant force, could only do so at the cost of tolerating human rights abuses, war, WMD proliferation, ethnic cleansing, and genocide. Unlike in the imagined grand bargain of US restraint versus allies and partners' compliance and deference, relative restraint came at a cost. Whenever it could not persuade its partners, especially the other permanent members of the UN Security Council to embrace its viewpoint, the United States had to consent to deadlock. Whenever a challenge solicited a sustained military commitment, the United States preferred to leave the issue unaddressed. This resulted in a corresponding decline in prestige, since the United States was perceived and perceived itself as having failed as international leader.

Restraint and Free-riding: Russia and China

In the early 1990s, Moscow and Beijing were markedly inferior to the United States in capabilities: Russia was caught in an economic and political free fall, while China was still struggling to recapture the goodwill of the world in the aftermath of its repression of the Tiananmen protests. To this extent, both states needed US benevolence more than the United States needed theirs. However, and even though neither was an ally, the United States exhibited forbearance in relations to Russia and China because of its overall policy of restraint. The United States put up in both cases with domestic policies that flouted democratic values, and showed leniency to foreign policies that undermined or blocked US initiatives. This is not to say that Russian and Chinese actions were necessarily illegitimate, as they were meant to cater to their own interests and values; only that, from US perspective they represented an embarrassment and hindrances to the orderly management of the international scene.

The future of Russia's pro-Western orientation and of its fledgling democracy was seen as hinging on the survival in power of President Boris Yeltsin. "Helping the Russian people to build a free society and a market economy" was regarded by US officials as "the greatest strategic challenge of our time," comparable in magnitude with the two World Wars.[46] To this end, the United States allowed the Kremlin considerable leeway, both to strengthen the domestic hand of Russia's pro-Western camp and to preserve its cooperation, which had been so important during the Gulf conflict. The United States turned therefore a blind eye to Yeltsin's heavy-handedness, such as the shelling of the Russian Duma in the fall of 1993 and the 1994–1995 war against the breakaway republic of Chechnya. On the front of Russian foreign policy, the United States put on ice the planned eastward expansion of NATO, which was diluted in 1993 into the imprecise formula of a Partnership for Peace. Furthermore, the United States did not object to displays of Russian coercion outside its borders in Georgia, Moldova, and Tajikistan; accepted the modification of the Conventional Forces in Europe treaty to allow a Russian deployment in the Caucasus; did not insist on Russia giving up its sales of missile and nuclear technology to India and Iran; and bowed to Russian concerns about NATO military intervention in Bosnia.[47]

In respect to China, the United States exhibited similar restraint. China had been a tacit US partner since the time in office of Nixon, but this did not imply Chinese malleability in favor of US policies. Thus, the Bush administration's moves to repel the US diplomatic and financial punitive measures for the Tiananmen crackdown and to veto in 1992 a Democrat-sponsored bill that linked the renewal of China's Most Favored Nation (MFN) status to progress on human rights and on missile proliferation to Iran and Iraq generated only modest Chinese reciprocation. Attempts to pressure China into offering wider concessions in return backfired. To give a typical example, when the Bush team sought to signal US displeasure at the Chinese abstaining instead of fully endorsing resolution 678 by refusing access to the president to the visiting Chinese foreign minister Qian Qichen, China threatened to cancel the visit, forcing the US officials to backtrack and grant after all a meeting with Bush, the first since June 1989.[48]

Chinese intransigence also pushed Clinton into a humiliating volte-face. Throughout the 1992 presidential campaign, the Clinton team had lambasted Bush for "coddling dictators from Beijing to Baghdad." Accordingly, once in office Clinton decided to press China in the direction of democracy by signing in May 1993 an executive order that conditioned renewal of MFN status on Beijing's progress on human rights.[49] However, by that time, as the world's fastest growing economy, China attracted alternative trade partners such as Germany, France, and Canada, which risked jeopardizing the competing chances of US businesses. A last-ditch effort in early May 1994 by Christopher to journey to Beijing turned into a diplomatic fiasco. Even before the secretary of state had reached China, the government had cracked down on known dissidents, a repression that continued through the visit. Christopher's reception by the Chinese leaders was in his own words "rough, somber, sometimes bordering on insolent."[50] In subsequent meetings with China's leaders, Christopher was informed that "China will never accept the United States' concept of human rights" and that Beijing was confident it would be awarded the MFN regardless of its internal policies. Faced with the prospect of a trade conflict with an inflexible Beijing, and mindful of the virtues of Chinese assistance in the context of a confrontation with North Korea, the Clinton cabinet retreated. The same month, it announced not only that China's MFN status was going to be renewed, but also that in the future the administration would no longer tie the renewal to human rights.[51]

While both the Bush and Clinton teams brushed off these Russian and Chinese rebukes as of little importance, the requirements of restraint had trumped America's effectiveness as international leader.

THE ILLUSIONS DISPELLED: THE BOSNIAN MORASS

The context that contributed the most toward ending the illusions was the conflict in Bosnia. As far as the Bush administration was concerned, the United States "didn't have a dog" in the fight taking place in the former Yugoslavia.[52] Admittedly, officials of the Bush administration had qualms about the wisdom of allowing a free hand to the strongest party in the conflict, the Serbs. However, they also agreed that any involvement in Yugoslavia could reach alarming proportions, necessitating a long-term commitment and the deployment of tens if not hundreds of thousands of US troops—one estimate put the figure of forces for policing a cease-fire in Bosnia at 400,000.[53] Hence, the responsibility of order maintenance was going to be transferred to the Europeans who seemed eager for the job.

However, as much as the chairman of the European Commission Jacques Poos of Luxembourg may have claimed that "the age of Europe has dawned," it soon became clear that the major European players, Germany, France, and Britain, had little appetite for peace-maintaining. In fact, any European military option for the former Yugoslavia had been ruled out both by the European Community and by the Western European Union since the summer of 1991.[54]

This inaugurated the pattern for the post–Cold War, which proved far more tenable than the alternative Gulf quid pro quo of restraint versus cooperation: whenever major challenges to international order arose, only the United States had the capabilities to effectively handle them, even though it might not have wanted to act. As chapter two has argued, unipolarity might mean that the dominant state is more susceptible to symbolic challenges. In crises such as Bosnia, the United States could not pass the buck to anyone else—hence the blame for the lack of results in any crisis of international order was going to be laid squarely on its shoulders. Doing nothing would therefore have affected US prestige as the dominant power. This concern thus led to the initial extension of a US commitment to solve the crisis, which, if challenged, had to be defended at the risk of losing even more prestige, ultimately pushing the United States into a course of assertiveness.

In Bosnia, instead of direct intervention, the European states encouraged a multitrack approach consisting of the deployment of UN peacekeepers under UNPROFOR (United Nations Protection Force), the pursuit of negotiations, and the imposition of an embargo on all warring parties through UN resolution 713. This new approach was, however, disowned by the United States, where Clinton had come into office in January 1993. In the opinion of Clinton's advisors, the European-proposed Vance-Owen peace plan, named after the UN and EU negotiators, was both unworkable and rewarding Serb ethnic cleansing of Bosnian Muslims. As a result, the United States decided to undermine it, by making clear it would only "endorse," "wel-come," or "support" an agreement that was acceptable to all conflict-ing parties. The United States favored instead the so-called "lift and strike" solution: lifting the arms embargo imposed on the Croats and Muslims, while at the same conducting limited air strikes on the Bosnian Serb positions near the Bosnian capital Sarajevo.[55] But this option was in turn unacceptable to the Europeans, since their forces ensuring peacekeeping were the ones exposed to Serb retaliation in the form of potential hostage-taking. The European powers main-tained that the United States could not employ airpower as long as it did not have troops of its own in harm's way.[56]

At this point, the United States became trapped by its shibboleths. The commitment of US boots on the ground represented a major use of force, and as such was seen by the Clinton administration as counterproductive. The deployment risked degenerating into a quagmire and resulting in heavy economic and political costs. It is telling in this respect that in the very same speech in which he stressed the need for US leadership, Christopher referred to Bosnia as a "problem from hell," "a morass," and "a quagmire." For his part, Clinton refused to send troops in the Bosnian "shooting gallery."[57] Peace and its global economic rewards could not therefore be jeopardized for the sake of promoting order in Bosnia through ground intervention. Yet, on the other hand, pressing ahead with "lift and strike" without the approval of the Europeans was equally unpalatable, since it violated the principle of using force only under multilateral auspices. As Clinton repeatedly argued: "Europe must be willing to act with us. We must go forward together."[58] The problem was, however, that if Europe was not willing to act, neither could the United States.

The US predicament became evident on the occasion of the European visit by Christopher in the beginning of May 1993, a diplomatic disaster from which the secretary of state returned, as one commentator put it, "with bullet holes all over him." Having left in order to sell "lift and strike" to London, Paris, and Moscow, Christopher was met with a frosty reception by European leaders. British Prime Minister John Major flatly rejected it, arguing his own government could fall if there was escalation in Bosnia. The Serb-leaning French President François Mitterrand unconditionally rejected lifting the arms embargo and French Foreign Minister Alain Juppé even threatened to withdraw France from UNPROFOR should such an event occur. By the time Christopher was heading to Moscow, where Yeltsin refused even to talk about the use of force in Bosnia, he found out from Secretary of Defense Les Aspin that the White House had lost the heart to pursue "lift and strike"—in Aspin's words: "The President has gone south on us."[59] Christopher himself put his finger on the very problem when reporting to Clinton that "we have to tell [the Europeans] that we have firmly decided to go ahead with our preferred option and that we expect them to support us."[60]

However, instead of the United States imposing its policy of choice on its allies, it was the Europeans' view of creating and defending UN safe areas within Bosnia that prevailed. Thus, in May 1993, the United States committed itself to the defense of the six safe havens, a pledge repeated by NATO in August of the same year. Yet even this modest commitment was heavily qualified by the so-called dual key mechanism: In order for a strike against the Bosnian Serbs to proceed, the United States had to formally go through the process of securing prior permission from *both* NATO and the UN Secretary General or the Secretary General's representative, who were not forthcoming.[61] Hence, relative restraint resulted in a policy of forced passivity. While the United States pressed for massive air strikes to defend the safe haven Bihac in the fall of 1994, Britain and France objected out of concern for their peacekeepers under threat of Serb retaliation and cautioned that such a course would result in their pullout from Bosnia. As a result of unproductive negotiations throughout late November, Lake argued in a memo to Clinton that the allies' opposition to strikes meant that "the stick of military pressure is no longer viable." In the words of a senior official: "The principals agreed that NATO is more important than Bosnia."[62] Accordingly, the United States ended up by stating it would not insist on "strategic strikes." The conclusion was unavoidable: the United States preferred inertia to acting without its allies and partners. So, as will be shown, was the consequence to follow: Bosnia had turned, as Lake put it, into "a cancer" for US foreign policy by harming US prestige as an effective leader.[63]

RESTRAINT AND RECALCITRANCE: SOMALIA

While the majority of the recalcitrant challengers had no particular interest in humiliating the United States, this was, nonetheless, the unavoidable effect, since the challengers' goals and tactics contravened US preferences and values, and as such questioned the US-ensured international order. Accordingly, the United States had to respond to such challenges so as to demonstrate its qualifications as the dominant state. But how could it punish these various provocateurs if it denied itself the ability to employ its full military might and if it required the prior blessing of other states? US inaction allowed challenges to metastasize as in Bosnia, creating a vicious circle of embarrassment and frustration.

Somalia was since 1991 in the throes of interclan warfare that wreaked havoc on its fragile economy. Faced with the threat of mass starvation, the UN, which already had a peacekeeping presence in the country under UNOSOM I (United Nations Operation in Somalia), appealed to the United States for help in the fall of 1992. The US decision to deploy 25,000 troops to help the UN deliver food to the famished Somalis—the UNITAF (Unified Task Force) mission—was determined by the need to back the rhetoric of a new world order with some semblance of action.[64] In the opinion of US decision-makers, Somalia represented, by contrast to Bosnia, a context where intervention both would have made a sizable difference in saving lives and could have been undertaken on the cheap, with no risks of escalation attached. Thus, Somalia was a demonstration of goodwill: according to Scowcroft, the United States had to show that "it was not that we were afraid to intervene abroad; it was just that the circumstances weren't right in Bosnia." By contrast, Somalia had all the markings of a new world order showcase: "It was a Southern Hemisphere state; it was black; it was non-Christian; it was everything that epitomized the Third World." Consequently, as he put it: "We did not want to portray the administration as wholly flint-hearted realpolitik, and an airlift in Somalia was a lot cheaper to demonstrate that we had a heart."[65] Moreover, success in Somalia would have represented a model of future peacekeeping operations conducted under UN mandate.[66] The incoming Clinton administration shared this view, as shown by its support of the Presidential Review Directive 13, a project that supported increased US support for UN peacekeeping and peace maintaining.[67]

However, the outcome of Somalia was a political debacle. While the United States and the UN were shackled to each other in their first joint peacemaking operation since the Gulf War, they pursued nevertheless different agendas. For the UN, the mission was transformational: to stabilize Somalia by disarming the warlords and conducting nation-building. Conversely, for the United States, the mission was strictly humanitarian: US troops were deployed solely to ensure food reached those in need of it, and they would have departed once this was accomplished. A tug-of-war ensued between UN Secretary General Boutros Boutros-Ghali and the United States throughout the winter of 1992–1993, which resulted in the worst of both worlds.

In the interest of US-UN cooperation, the Clinton administration agreed to maintain a reduced military presence in Somalia, consisting foremost of the Quick Reaction Force (QRF) to continue to assist the UN mission.[68] Moreover, in line with enlargement, the Clinton administration agreed to the March 1993 Security Council Resolution 814, which gave US troops a wider mandate to rehabilitate Somali political institutions and economy and to promote a countrywide political settlement by confiscating weapons and raiding the warlords' arms caches. This was hailed by Albright as an "historical undertaking," the administration was ready to "support vigorously." Yet at the same time, the US troops of the QRF were denied at the Pentagon's insistence, consistent with the reluctance to employ massive force, the heavy weapons to carry out the job so to avoid being dragged into a protracted intervention. Hence, to illustrate this contrast between means and ends, the United States expected its 1,500 light-armed troops and a contingent of 400 commandos to accomplish an objective that the previous US force of 25,000 had had qualms pursuing.[69] As it turned out, even more was asked of the QRF, as the mission objective went from just disarming warlords to apprehending those who resisted.

In June 1993, following an arms inspection, the Pakistani contingent of the UNOSOM II came under fire by soldiers under the command of warlord Mohamed Farah Aideed. A series of attacks culminated in August in the death of four American troops. Albright summed up the prevalent view in the administration: "The decision we must make is whether to pull up stakes and allow Somalia to fall back into the abyss or stay the course and help lift the country and its people from the category of a failed state into that of an emerging democracy."[70] Hence, so as to preserve world order, Aideed had to be made an example as a warning to other "perpetrators of crimes against the United Nations."[71] Nevertheless, to implement this agenda the administration did not send heavy armament, choosing instead a moderate escalation: sending in the elite formations of the Army Rangers and of the Delta Force. On October 3, the Rangers botched an attempt to capture Aideed to put him on trial, as Boutros-Ghali had requested. In the ensuing battle, 18 US troops were killed, 74 were wounded, three Black Hawk helicopters were downed, and the body of a US pilot was filmed being dragged through the streets of the Somali capital Mogadishu. An immediate decision was made on October 5 to withdraw all US troops from Somalia.[72]

Somalia represented a heavy blow to US prestige, coming on the heels of Bosnia. In both contexts, the United States tried to put a brave face on the setbacks by presenting them as irrelevant. In regard to Bosnia, Christopher argued that the Bosnian war did not concern NATO, even though the organization had taken charge of coming to the defense of UN troops protecting the safe havens.[73] In Somalia, so as to avoid the impression that the United States was running away, Clinton decided to send over as a symbolic gesture the requested tanks just before the US troops were withdrawn.[74] Yet Clinton himself was far from convinced that the United States had managed to avoid the appearance of humiliation. During the pullout from Somalia, the president complained bitterly that the United States was being pushed around by "two-bit pricks" and worried that US "leadership in global affairs would be undermined at the very time when people are looking to America to help promote peace and freedom in the Post Cold War."[75] There was good reason for such concern, as US prestige soon came under fire in a multitude of other contexts.

RESTRAINT AND RECALCITRANCE: HAITI, RWANDA, NORTH KOREA, AND IRAQ

In Haiti, the United States was committed to restoring to power the elected government of President Jean-Bertrand Aristide, overthrown in 1991 by a military junta led by General Raoul Cedras in a coup that produced a massive Haitian refugee flow toward Florida. While Cedras had agreed to the restoration of Aristide, in practice the junta sabotaged the transition of power. The most egregious such episode was the orchestration of a demonstration in October 1993 that prevented US police advisers under the banner of the UN, who were going to monitor the transition, from landing on the island. Faced with mobs chanting "Somalia!" the ship carrying the peacekeepers, *The Harlan County*, left Haitian waters. After this incident, Clinton was so enraged that his officials had allowed him to be ridiculed by Third World strongmen that he told them he wished he had better people working for him, like Reagan did: at least if the United States suffered a setback in Lebanon, it compensated for the loss of credibility by invading Grenada.[76] Eventually, by September 1994, after having threatened Cedras with intervention, and having issued an ultimatum, the Clinton administration authorized an invasion.[77] Yet this uncommonly muscular response did not go through either, as the United States attempted a last-minute effort at negotiations with the junta. Thus, invasion plans were cancelled with the troops already in the air as the United States negotiated past its own deadline. While the United States managed to restore Aristide, which was undeniably a plus, it did so in a less-than-impressive fashion, not by punishing, but by agreeing to a deal with the challengers.[78]

Force was not even an option for the United States in the context of the "most pure and unambiguous genocide since World War Two" committed in Rwanda in the spring of 1994 by the Hutu army and militias against the Tutsi minority and those Hutu seen as having ties to the Tutsi. Following the debacle in Somalia, the United States had become reluctant to participate in peacekeeping operations that could lead to an escalation in violence and, hence, to deeper US commitment. In the words of a Department of State official: "Bosnia was already almost dead in terms of United States participation in peacekeeping, but Mogadishu put the last nail in the coffin."[79]

Thus, the administration put forward the Presidential Decision Directive (PDD 25), which not only superseded the vision intended by the earlier PRD 13, but which also conditioned participation in UN peacekeeping on whether the United States considered the goals clear and feasible, on whether the intervention represented the best means to advance US interests, and on whether other nations contributed their share to the common effort.[80] Since action in Rwanda did not satisfy the requirements of PDD 25, the United States did not only abstain from intervening, but also did its best to make sure that no intervention was contemplated. Therefore, the response to genocide went beyond inaction: the United States actively worked to prevent intervention. Initially, the United States lobbied for the withdrawal of the entire UN mission from Rwanda, then voted to substantially reduce UN presence, and then prevented references to events in Rwanda as genocide, an admission that might have required military involvement.[81] Nonetheless, the dimensions of the killing taking place in Rwanda, where 800,000 Tutsi were killed in a matter of weeks, were such as to represent a blemish on the US pretensions of being the custodian of world order. Clinton later referred to the failure to intervene as one of the greatest regrets of his presidency.[82]

Meanwhile, the hermit state of North Korea was able to conduct a successful nuclear blackmail of the United States. North Korea's actions were not solely a security threat to South Korea and to US troops in the peninsula, but also a blatant issue of defiance of non-proliferation, and by implication, of US leadership. The regime in Pyongyang developed a highly effective cat-and-mouse pattern of bargaining with the United States, by restricting the access of the International Atomic Energy Agency (IAEA) monitors to its nuclear facilities, by conditioning its endorsement of the Non-Proliferation Treaty (NPT), and ultimately by announcing its withdrawal from the NPT altogether. Then, North Korea offered concessions, such as suspending its withdrawal from the NPT or authorizing limited monitoring, only to issue a renewed challenge. In so doing, Pyongyang counted on two US weaknesses associated with restraint: first, the United States was unable to either impose sanctions or gain Security Council approval for strikes without the assent of China. Beijing might have been unhappy with the North Korean brinkmanship, but it was also wary that if the North Korean regime was pushed with its back to a wall, it could have unleashed war on the South or sent massive waves of refugees into China. As such, it refused to endorse US calls for tougher measures to punish North Korea.[83]

A second important consideration for the United States, which was hesitant to use massive force anyway, was that military conflict with North Korea, even if pursued to victory, would have come at an especially galling cost—Pentagon analyses gave estimates of hundreds of thousands of casualties. In March 1994, Pyongyang was not averse to threaten to transform Seoul into "a sea of fire." As new Secretary of Defense William Perry and Chairman of the Joint Chiefs of Staff John Shalikashvili summed the options to Clinton in June 1994, the United States had a choice "between a disastrous option—allowing North Korea to get a nuclear arsenal, which we might have to face someday—and an unpalatable option, blocking this development, but thereby risking a destructive non-nuclear war."[84]

Nonetheless, even though the Clinton administration contemplated the "unpalatable" prospect of a conventional military conflict and though most Americans (51 percent in June 1994) favored a preemptive attack on the Yongbyon nuclear site, its preference was to reach an accommodation with Pyongyang. Thus, the agreement, reached through the ad hoc office of former President Jimmy Carter, exchanged the North Korean freezing—but not the elimination—of its nuclear program and allowing inspections by the IAEA, in return for the United States putting an end to the Team Spirit yearly joint military exercises with South Korea, agreeing to continuing bilateral negotiations, and providing economic and assistance for a civil nuclear energy program to the communist state.[85]

The United States also proved unable to dislodge Saddam Hussein from power in Iraq, or, for that matter, to curb his propensity for issuing periodic challenges: undermining sanctions, repressing Shiite opponents, intervening into the Kurdish safe haven areas, massing troops on the Kuwaiti border, cracking on the US-sponsored Iraqi National Congress, and allegedly attempting to assassinate former President Bush on a visit to Kuwait City. As chapter six will elaborate, following the conclusion of the Gulf War, the United States had made the toppling of Saddam its explicit goal, deciding to keep Iraq bottled up by means of sanctions until that desiderate was seen through, which in the US understanding was not going to take long.[86] Saddam, however, remained in power, creating therefore a constant irritant, as well as a conundrum on how to maintain sanctions against Iraq. By 1995, Russia, France, and China, all permanent members in the Security Council, were interested in rehabilitating rather than in sanctioning Iraq so as to resume oil trading, which meant that the United States was increasingly isolated when it came to mustering diplomatic and military coalitions to punish Saddam for his transgressions.[87] Accordingly, the message of "don't tread on me" that the United States wanted to send out to Saddam and presumably to other recalcitrant challengers never got through.[88] These incidents do not suggest that taken in each separate context US foreign policy was necessarily mistaken—it managed after all to avoid a potentially catastrophic conflict with North Korea, to contain Iraq, and to find a settlement allowing the restoration of democracy in Haiti. But considered together, and in conjunction with the similar context of Bosnia, these instances exhibited a pattern of US inability to punish recalcitrant actors for their transgressions. Restraint, therefore, proved an impediment in managing world order. Increasingly, US decision-makers became convinced that the pursuit of this line was taking a toll on America's prestige in the eyes of the world. Consequently, instead of complaining of the disproportionate US power under unipolarity, other states had begun to complain about the lack of results of US foreign policy. Matters eventually came to a head in Bosnia.

THE "WORLD'S PUNCHING BAG" NO LONGER

Throughout 1994, NATO was called to the rescue several times when the Bosnian Serb forces endangered the safe havens. The threat of bombing and the conduct of what the media referred to as pinprick strikes in April and November 1994 were sufficient to make the Serbs back down. But in the spring and summer of 1995, this pattern changed as the Bosnian Serbs sought to consolidate their territorial hold by eliminating the remaining Muslim enclaves. Not only were the safe havens repeatedly attacked, but the threat of NATO airpower proved increasingly unworkable, as 400 French, Canadian, and Dutch peacekeepers were used in May as human shields against strikes. Worse was to come. In June, the Serb forces occupied Srebrenica, one of the Muslim safe havens, and ethnically cleansed it, killing in the process an estimated number of 8,000 men. Srebrenica constituted the worst mass atrocity to occur in Europe since the end of World War Two as well as a major act of defiance against the United States, since it had guaranteed the security of safe havens. After the fall of Srebrenica, the Serbs went on to conquer another safe haven, Zepa, and predicted conquering by the fall the remaining safe havens, including Sarajevo.[89]

The US position was further worsened by the incensed response of its partners, especially France. A change of administration had taken place in Paris, and the new president Jacques Chirac was far more belligerent than his predecessor François Mitterrand in regard to Bosnia, going so far as to propose retaking Srebrenica and deploying troops around Goražde so as to deter a Serb attack. Chirac felt humiliated by the French troops being taken hostages without a shot being fired and pressed for an immediate military response. But faced with US equivocation, he went so far as to accuse the United States of having abdicated the role of world leader by tolerating Serb abuses. "The position of leader of the free world," said Chirac, "is now vacant," adding that France stood alone in wanting to act on Bosnia, and, if it was not humored, it was ready to abandon its participation in UNPROFOR. This opened the possibility of a nightmare scenario in which the UN would have pulled out of Bosnia. If this occurred, the United States and NATO were committed to intervention including the deployment of 20,000 US troops to extract the peacekeepers. Hence, Clinton would have faced the choice between agreeing to an all-out domestically unpopular intervention on the ground, with a presidential election looming, and abdicating the US commitment to NATO intervention, with further damage to US prestige. In this predicament, it was the concern for prestige rather than domestic considerations that forced the United States into action. If reelection had been the dominant factor, it would have been even safer to continue not doing anything about Bosnia owing to Republican opposition to any involvement past lifting the arms embargo.[90]

This interpretation is strengthened by the administration's private statements concerning Bosnia, which was increasingly perceived as the latest and the most serious of the series of setbacks suffered by the United States. Restraint was seen as having tied the US hands in dealing with challenges falling into the Aristotelian category of "insolent" offenses. US decision-makers exhibited therefore not only humiliation at the Serb outrage, but also anger at being unable to respond. Mounting international and domestic criticism of Bosnia enraged Clinton to such a degree that it provoked the president on July 14 into a half-hour angry rant complete with expletives directed at his National Security officials. "I am the President of the United States," complained Clinton. "I am checkmated on the most important issue I face by people who should not be able to checkmate our policy. This can't continue." Furthermore, as Clinton confided to Lake in the aftermath of Chirac's outburst, Bosnia was "killing the US position of strength in the world" and "doing enormous damage to the United States and our standing in the world." "We look weak," concluded a beleaguered Clinton. Lake agreed: "This is larger than Bosnia. Bosnia is the symbol of US foreign policy." In his view, "The issue was US credibility as a world leader, its credibility in NATO, the United Nations, and at home." This opinion was also endorsed by Albright, who saw Bosnia as eating away at US prestige: "Reluctance to lead an effort to resolve a military crisis in the heart of Europe has placed at risk our leadership of the post–Cold War world," she argued in a memo to the president. Clinton accepted Lake's and Albright's conclusions. As he put it, the United States could not be the world's punching bag any longer. And tellingly for prestige reassertion, in the same breath he conceded the "need for robust airpower."[91]

Therefore, the United States would no longer let recalcitrant actors get away with their insolence, even if it had to distance itself from restraint. When the United States decided to punish the Bosnian Serbs, it no longer kept its response confined to isolated strikes, but launched a full-scale bombing campaign, and no longer asked the prior permission of the Europeans and of Russia. In contrast to the former "ask, don't tell" approach, allies and partners were simply politely informed of the action the United States was going to take and then told that while they were welcome to join it, Washington will proceed alone if necessary.[92] After a (presumed) Bosnian Serb mortar attack on Sarajevo, the United States conducted a thorough eight-day bombing of the Serb artillery and communication centers. In conjunction with an offensive of the Croat army supplied with US weapons in the Krajna Serb republic in Croatia, and with incentives offered to Milošević, the strikes compelled all sides to commit to negotiations. The seemingly intractable conflict in Bosnia was settled in less than a month of talks conducted at the US Air Force Base in Dayton, Ohio, in October-November 1995.[93]

The chief lesson that the United States extracted from this experience was that cooperation and the nonuse of force if taken as sine qua non conditions could turn into major liabilities. As long as the United States had been committed to get West European and Russian assent and had hesitated to employ its military might on a large scale, Bosnia had been trapped in limbo. But once the United States opted for a more assertive policy, based on an explicit "don't ask, tell" approach and the large-scale use of force, success materialized quickly, and, what is more, the US partners rallied behind its position. Hence, US decision-makers concluded that the post–Cold War context required a similarly more determined exercise of leadership. The United States would no longer be bound "by concerns over niceties or allied consensus," and would favor a course of action driven by "the desire to get things done."[94] The US role was to charter the course to follow and then to pursue it resolutely, by force if necessary, instead of attempting fruitlessly to hammer out consensus. Consequently, this moment proved, as Christopher put it, a watershed for Clinton's foreign policy: the United States experienced "a palpable feeling of relief that impotence had been replaced by determination... the success at Dayton reaffirmed the imperative of American leadership. Some Europeans grumbled about how we had dominated the Dayton process... but... they really knew that without us the settlement would not have happened."[95] The same impression was relayed by Holbrooke, the main architect of Dayton: after Bosnia, US foreign policy had become more assertive, a clear sign that "America was back."[96]

In the aftermath of Bosnia, the foreign policy of indulgence toward China and Russia was replaced by a more confrontational approach, in which the United States moved to expand NATO in 1997 by allowing in Hungary, Poland, and the Czech Republic over the Kremlin's objections, and stood up to Beijing by dispatching two air carrier battle groups to the vicinity of the Taiwan Straits (even if not in the Straits as such) in response to Chinese military exercises in the spring of 1996.[97] Moreover, the United States became more assertive in responding to the challenges of recalcitrant states, in particular those coming from Iraq and Yugoslavia.

CHAPTER CONCLUSION

The Bosnian endgame had represented the initial impulse in the direction of policy change, but, despite its newly found propensity for assertiveness, the United States was still reluctant to contemplate the deployment of ground forces, and still clung to solutions reached and implemented multilaterally. To paraphrase Krauthammer, the United States was still worshipping at the altar of cooperation and of peace, though the ardor of its faith in these principles had been reduced by repeated setbacks.[98] Thus, in the cases of both Iraq and the former Yugoslavia, the reflex was to handle the challenges through the usual Security Council mechanism. Obviously, the United States expected, as in Bosnia, that the other permanent members as well as the relevant regional states would fall into line once the United States made clear its preference for a given course of action and threatened resorting to unilateral measures. But as events were about to show, this expectation was about to be proven mistaken, as US attempts to assemble coalitions to punish these two serial misbehaviors came to nil due to the dogged opposition of its partners. Increasingly, with its prestige on the line, the United States found itself in a context where it had to throw restraint completely overboard.

4

PRESTIGE AND ASSERTIVENESS
IN KOSOVO

During the years of illusions, the United States had downplayed the seriousness of any challenge to its prestige as the dominant power. Even the cautious Colin Powell was won over by this optimism: "I would be very surprised if another Iraq occurred. I'm running out of demons. I'm down to Castro and Kim Il Sung."[1] But the unfolding decade proved Powell wrong, as the United States wandered from crisis to crisis, each instance further reducing its prestige. Recognizing this problem, the Clinton administration sought to address it with a renewed resoluteness, as in Bosnia.

In this respect, Operation Allied Force—the three-month-long bombing campaign in response to Belgrade's actions in Kosovo—represents the decisive moment of change toward a more assertive foreign policy. True enough, the operation was still clothed in appropriately humanitarian and multilateral rhetoric, and there continued to be considerable US reticence to authorize ground deployment in Kosovo. Nonetheless, the intervention stands out from the established post–Cold War practice. First, instead of delegating responsibility to the UN and the EU on the model of Bosnia, and intervening at the last possible moment, the United States took the lead in putting pressure on Belgrade from the beginning of the crisis. Second, the United States moved away from multilateralism by giving up on the previously obligatory seal of approval of the UN Security Council and by claiming legitimacy from NATO.[2] Third, the bombing of Yugoslavia constituted the single largest military operation undertaken by the United States in the aftermath of the Gulf War. NATO carried out nearly three months of uninterrupted pounding of Yugoslavia, conducting more than 40,000 sorties, and employing in the process 1,000 allied warplanes, of which more than two-thirds belonged to the United States.[3]

This chapter argues that US decision-makers felt the need to act in Kosovo in response to what they saw as repeated transgressions by Milošević, which called into question US prestige as the world leader.[4] In so doing, the Clinton administration expected the intervention would be confined to a limited period of bombing, as had been the case in Bosnia.[5] But since Milošević did not prove pliable, and responded to bombing by emptying Kosovo of its Albanian population, the United States had no choice but to up the ante to the point of contemplating sending ground troops into a nonpacified Kosovo. Before proceeding, it may be useful, as some statements may be compatible with interpretations in terms of either reputation or prestige, to recall the difficulty of operationalizing a distinction between the two, and that prestige seems preferable, given its ability to account for strategic suboptimal behavior and for emotions.

KOSOVO'S PRESTIGE STAKES

Perhaps the most striking aspect of the intervention is the discrepancy between the two sides: the US-led NATO alliance against the rump Yugoslav federation. In military statistics, NATO's 1999 defense spending totaled $475 billion (of which the United States represented 59 percent), as compared to that of Yugoslavia, which barely amounted to $1.5 billion; while NATO had four million military personnel on active duty, Yugoslavia fielded only 110,000. In economic terms, the combined NATO GDP stood at a towering $16.5 trillion compared to Yugoslavia's $19 billion. Figures speak for themselves: the economic ratio was 870 to 1 in favor of NATO, 67 to 1 in terms of population, 35 to 1 in terms of military manpower, and 300 to 1 in military budgets.[6] Moreover, the United States was aware of the disproportionate advantage it enjoyed over Yugoslavia. In the words of the new National Security Advisor Sandy Berger: "We had a thousand-to-one advantage over Milošević from the air once we took out his air defenses."[7] Thus, despite this obvious disproportion of power, the United States found out that it could not sway the policy of repression of Belgrade toward Kosovo's ethnic Albanians. Confronted with an armed rebellion by the Kosovo Liberation Army (KLA), the Yugoslav authorities responded by cracking down on civilians, which resulted in the exodus of hundreds of thousands of Kosovars. This policy represented a symbolic challenge to US prestige for two main reasons: the cumulative effect of Yugoslav defiance, and the fact that the perpetrator was seen as having escaped retribution over Bosnia only to renew his challenge in Kosovo.

On the one hand, Yugoslavia could not aspire to the status of a great power—clearly not an actor in the same league as the United States. While Yugoslavia was in no position to endanger the United States, its behavior was nevertheless very much contravening its preferences, since, to invoke the Aristotelian categories of insults, it showed insolence toward a higher-ranked actor. What made Belgrade's transgressions in Kosovo alarming to Washington was not the extent of the Serb infractions per se. Worse human rights violations in terms of proportions were simultaneously occurring in Afghanistan, Angola, Sierra Leone, Liberia, Sudan, the Democratic Republic of Congo, Burundi, Somalia, Eritrea, Iraq, Sri Lanka, and Colombia. In terms of worldwide refugee figures at the end of 1998, Yugoslavia placed at number 20, while in numbers of internally displaced persons, it appeared only at number 19.[8] Clinton responded to this implication of double standards by asserting that "we cannot, indeed, we should not do everything and be everywhere. But where our values and our interests are at stake, and where we can make a difference, we must be prepared to do so."[9] However, the geopolitical interests that Clinton was alluding to remained, as will be shown later on, ambiguous.

Furthermore, the United States was not even opposed to a Yugoslav response against the KLA, as indicated by the US chief envoy to the region Robert Gelbard in a direct conversation with Milošević: "You can deal with this terrorist group in a way that is consistent with dealing with terrorism, but don't go after the population—find a way to resolve the Kosovo problem politically."[10] For more than a year before the bombing started, the Milošević regime managed to elude US demands. From February to December 1998, Milošević's forces conducted no less than four major offensives in Kosovo. The first offensive provoked only mild economic and diplomatic sanctions. In a meeting of the principal US decision-makers, Berger vehemently rejected the suggestion to employ force: "You can't just talk about bombing in the middle of Europe…What would you do the day after?" Secretary of Defense William Cohen equally rejected the possibility of the US acting as "the KLA air force."[11] Similarly, the second Serb offensive in June 1998 caused solely an air exercise in which NATO warplanes flew over Albania and the Former Yugoslav Republic of Macedonia (FYROM). The third offensive in the summer and fall of the same year produced a more serious response, with threats of strikes on Yugoslavia, and a complex set of negotiations involving Holbrooke and Milošević. Not even the fourth Serb offensive in Kosovo starting in December 1998, which ended with the massacre of 45 Albanians in the village of Račak, determined the United States to bomb Yugoslavia on the spot. Instead, the United States preferred talks at the Rambouillet chateau near Paris. It was only after these talked failed to produce an accord signed by both Serbs and Kosovars that the United States decided to intervene militarily, and even then, after granting a last chance to Belgrade by dispatching Holbrooke to meet Miloševíc.[12] Clearly, to quote Berger, "Force was the last option, not the first option."[13]

Hence, this equivocal US response suggests that the Serb actions in Kosovo were not so significant in themselves as to justify an immediate military response. Rather, the challenge posed by Yugoslavia was significant to the United States compared to other contexts because it was cumulative—consisting of recurring challenges that ate away at US prestige. With each US threat that was not carried out in the face of Serb noncompliance, the prestige of the United States and of NATO was reduced a little further, in the same pattern that had characterized for four years the war in Bosnia. Just as in Bosnia, and at least in part because of that experience, the United States could not turn a perpetual blind eye to the situation in Kosovo, which, if left unaddressed, would have generated anew doubts as to its credentials as the dominant power.

As Albright argued, Kosovo "was emerging as a key test of American leadership and of the relevance and effectiveness of NATO. The Alliance was due to celebrate its fiftieth anniversary in April...that event would coincide with the spectacle of another humanitarian disaster in the Balkans. And we would look like fools for proclaiming the Alliance's readiness for the twenty-first century when we were unable to cope with a conflict that began in the fourteenth."[14] The indispensable nation doctrine only reinforced the discrepancy between the capabilities and the leadership pretensions of the United States and its mediocre achievements over Kosovo. Consequently, the magnitude of each US failure over Kosovo paled by comparison with the general pattern of failure that was emerging in Washington's relations with Miloševíc. That is to say, it was Miloševíc's refusal to mend his ways despite repeated US warnings that made his symbolic challenge in Kosovo particularly humiliating.

On the other hand, the other factor that could have driven US decision-makers to respond to the challenge over Kosovo was the identity of the perpetrator: Miloševíc. Because of the technicality that the war in Bosnia had not actually been fought by Belgrade, but by the Bosnian Serbs of the nominally independent Republika Srpska (in great proportion consisting of the former Yugoslav federal troops in the province), Milošević had avoided being indicted as a war criminal, the fate that met the Pale leaders Radovan Karadzíc and General Ratko Mladíc. Actually, Milošević had emerged out of the Dayton negotiations not as the villain, but rather as the savior of the agreement because of his last-minute intervention to provide the Muslims with an additional 1 percent of territory, which the Croat side had refused to surrender.[15] Yet US decision-makers could not exculpate him of responsibility in the outbreak and the continuation of hostilities in Bosnia, which had gone on with his logistical support. This was particularly the view of Albright, who thought that if unaddressed, "Bosnia's past would become Kosovo's future."

As she put it, "Kosovo is not Bosnia because we have learned the lessons of Bosnia—and we are determined to apply them here and now. We know—and we are seeing again—that the only reward for tolerating atrocities is more of the same." James Rubin, the Department of State spokesman reaffirmed this view in December 1998: "Milošević has been at the center of every crisis in the former Yugoslavia over the last decade. He is not simply part of the problem; Milošević *is* the problem." Ivo Daalder, formerly the director for European Affairs on the National Security Council and the coauthor of the most comprehensive account to date of US involvement in Kosovo, also agrees with this assessment: "The administration's experience in Bosnia was the single most defining element in how it approached the impending crisis in Kosovo...you had to act in a way that was consistent and forceful against the main perpetrator of the conflict, which was believed to be Mr. Milošević."[16] Milošević was therefore perceived by US decision-makers as a brazen serial offender, who, having managed to get away with his first crime, was preparing to now add the insult of Kosovo to the many previous injuries of Bosnia. As Clinton put in his war message: "We learned that in the Balkans inaction in the face of brutality simply invites more brutality, but firmness can stop armies and save lives. We must apply that lesson in Kosovo, before what happened in Bosnia happens there too."[17] Hence, another reason for intervening was to exact long-awaited retribution against Milošević for his repeated offenses.

This motivation, moreover, augmented by the events of the spring of 1999, may also account for US policy in the aftermath of the Milošević-Ahtisaari accord that ended hostilities in Kosovo. As William Montgomery, the person in charge of the Office of Yugoslav affairs in Budapest, the office in charge of fomenting regime change in Belgrade, and the future ambassador to Belgrade reminisced: "Milošević was personal for Madeleine Albright, a very high priority...

She wanted him gone . . . Seldom has so much fire, energy, enthusiasm, money—everything—gone into anything as into Serbia in the months before Miloševíc went." Consequently, the United States did not rehabilitate the Yugoslav strongman, even though it had negotiated with him, via mediators, a settlement of the Kosovo conflict. Instead, Albright stated repeatedly that the United States "wanted Miloševíc out of power, out of Serbia, and in the custody of the war crimes tribunal."[18] After the cease-fire, the United States not only maintained in place economic and diplomatic sanctions against Belgrade, but also sought Miloševíc's political departure by extending millions of dollars' worth of aid as well as providing training to the Serb opposition. Sanctions were lifted only after Miloševíc was brought down by popular protests following his attempt to rig presidential elections in October 2000. Moreover, the United States conditioned reconstruction aid to the successor regime of Vojislav Koštunica on its cooperation with the Hague Tribunal, which demanded and eventually secured Miloševíc's extradition on war crimes charges.[19]

Prestige considerations were also significant in determining the United States to stay the course and even to accept the risks of escalation. Only three months before the Kosovo crisis, the United States had attempted to coerce Iraq to provide unlimited access to UN weapon inspections, and had been forced to abandon course after just four days of bombing.[20] A similar walkout was not an option in the case of Kosovo because, in response to the bombing, Miloševíc refused to capitulate and expelled hundreds of thousands of Kosovars from the province.

Thus, the prestige that the United States and NATO stood to lose was significantly larger, because the offender had issued an even more outrageous challenge. Accordingly, the perspective of failure in Kosovo was, to quote a Senior US official, "too awful to think about."[21] Democratic Senator Joseph Biden, chairman of the Senate Foreign Relations Committee, argued that "if we do not achieve our goals in Kosovo, NATO is finished as an alliance."[22] A similar line of reasoning caused Henry Kissinger, otherwise a wholesale critic of the intervention, to throw his support behind the campaign because "the future of NATO, the credibility of the alliance, and the commitments of the United States require we achieve success."[23] Daalder also gives credence to this interpretation by stating that the decision-makers believed that "politically we can't lose the war, militarily we can't lose the war, strategically we can't lose the war. If we lose this war, NATO is ended, and the credibility of American foreign policy is at an end."[24]

"MADELEINE'S WAR"

Evidence to the relevance of prestige considerations comes from two indicators: the evolution of the US position regarding the use of force against Belgrade in the months preceding the bombing, and the change in the ban on a ground invasion.

At first, the only serious partisan of employing force against Belgrade had been Albright, who fought a three-pronged battle to sell intervention to a skeptical cabinet, the European allies, and the US public opinion.[25] Convinced that recalcitrant misbehaviors such as Milošević understood only the language of force, Albright wanted to head off Kosovo as early as possible, before there was a repetition of the massacres and ethnic cleansing on the pattern of Bosnia. As she put it, "We knew better now, that we shouldn't allow these kinds of things to happen." Hence, she argued that "there still was time to do something about this, and that we should not wait as long as we did on Bosnia to have dreadful things happen; that we could get it ahead of the curve."[26] But Albright found herself isolated in the cabinet, which was concerned with gaining the assent of the European allies and of Russia for a Security Council's resolution authorizing action. Moreover, the other principal decision-makers were sharing the optimistic view advocated by Holbrooke that a deal could have been struck with Milošević.

The factor that contributed the most to undermining this view and, conversely, strengthening Albright's was the unrepentant policy of Belgrade, which after announcing a deal, was renewing its onslaught against the Kosovars. Consequently, Albright's case was essentially that US prestige was suffering proportionally with each new Serb infraction and that only assertiveness would break this pattern of repeated offenses.[27] As she argued in February 1999: "We know that the longer we delay in exercising our leadership, the dearer it will eventually be—in dollars lost, in lost credibility and in human lives. Simply put, we learned in Bosnia that we can pay early, or we can pay much more later."[28] In this respect, the four offensives carried out by the Serb forces in Kosovo provided the best excuse to advocate escalating the response from weapon rattling to ultimatum, and then to intervention.

The first Serb campaign began in February 1998, with police attacks on prominent KLA members, and reached its apex on March 5, with the killing of 58 members including 28 women and children of the Jasheri clan, the founding fathers of the KLA, in the village of Denji Prekaz.[29] These dramatic events were followed on March 9 by a meeting of the foreign ministers of the Contact Group on Yugoslavia in London, where Albright delivered a plea for a stern response, reminding her audience that "in 1991, the international community did not react with sufficient vigor and force . . . this time we must act with unity and resolve" and concluding on a dramatic note: "History is watching us. In this very room our predecessors delayed as Bosnia burned, and history will not be kind to us if we do the same . . . we have an opportunity to make up for the mistakes that had been made four or five years ago."[30] Albright obtained a firm but not forceful response, as the United States along with the Contact Group sponsored UN Security Council resolution 1160, which demanded under the threat of sanctions that Miloševíc stop targeting civilians, that the Serb special police forces be withdrawn, and that a dialogue be initiated between Belgrade and Kosovars. By May, diplomatic and economic sanctions as well as an arms embargo were put into place, since no sustained talks had materialized despite the Serb strongman's promises to Holbrooke.

By June 1998, however, the Serb forces launched a second round of attacks on Kosovo in response to a guerilla campaign begun in May by the KLA. This time around, NATO responded through the conduct of a military exercise known as Determined Falcon, in which 80 warplanes flew over Albania and FYROM. However, at the same time, the other US decision-makers worried about strengthening the KLA too much—as a background briefing put it, "The KLA need to know and NATO has made clear, the US government has made this clear, that the cavalry is not coming."[31] The fighting in June and July actually ended with the KLA in the advantage—at one point in July the guerillas controlled about 40 percent of the territory of Kosovo. To reclaim the lost territory, Miloševíc began in July a third offensive that drove almost 200,00 Kosovars away from their homes. The United States answered on September 23 by passing Security Council resolution 1199, repeating the demands of resolution 1160, and then delivering an ultimatum to Belgrade.

Albright was instrumental in this process by organizing a key meeting on October 8 with the foreign ministers of Britain, France, Germany, and Russia in London. The conclusions of the meeting were on the one hand, that the United States could press ahead with international support and threaten Miloševíc; and on the other hand, that Albright had managed to get the United States committed to using force if Miloševíc did not comply. As Albright emphasized, "Time and again, Miloševíc has promised us to do things he had no intention of doing . . . But he has to understand that the minimum is not good enough. The only thing that is good enough is full compliance… one of the key[s] to diplomacy is knowing when diplomacy has reached its limits. And we are rapidly reaching that point now."[32] To press the seriousness of the situation, in the aftermath of the meeting, Holbrooke and US General Michael Short, the person in charge of NATO's air force, were dispatched to Belgrade and laid open their cards to Milošević. "I've B52s in one hand and U2 surveillance spy planes in the other," Short warned. "It's up to you which I'm going to use."[33] On October 12, Holbrooke announced an agreement, whose main points comprised a reduction of Serb forces in the province and the conduct of serious negotiations with the Kosovars. Nevertheless, while the Holbrooke accord appeared to have diffused the crisis, it made it much harder for the United States to ignore further Serb infractions in Kosovo.

Predictably, the United States found itself with its back against the wall in January 1999, when violence flared again in Kosovo. Responding to a series of KLA attacks in late December 1998, Belgrade launched its fourth offensive, which culminated with the killing of 30 Kosovar civilians on January 15 in the village of Račak. Račak was the catalyst of intervention because it confirmed Albright's previous warnings about the risks of not standing firm against Milošević. Just as the massacre was taking place, US decision-makers had come together to discuss Kosovo. During the meeting, Albright summed up three possible avenues of action: "Stepping back, muddling through or taking decisive steps." Even though she was again overruled in the meeting by Cohen and Berger, who favored a "Status Quo Plus" solution, which reaffirmed the Holbrooke accord with the only addition of restoring the autonomy of Kosovo, Albright's position eventually carried the day thanks to the developments on the ground.[34]

After the offense of Račak, even the skeptics in the Clinton cabinet came to accept Albright's viewpoint that the use of force constituted the only viable policy left. To do anything else would have meant, as an enraged Albright put it in the January 15 meeting, to be reduced to the condition of "gerbils running on a wheel," forever trapped by the reluctance to take decisive steps in order to achieve effective results.[35] A second meeting of principals on January 19, supported Albright's conclusion this time around that a credible threat of force was necessary. As Cohen later argued, US credibility was "at the heart" of the intervention over Kosovo, "to the extent NATO was telling Milošević he could not do what he was doing." Berger agrees with this assessment: "In international affairs you never threaten things you are not prepared to do."[36] Consequently, as Cohen summed up the attitude of the cabinet, "The Račak massacre served as a galvanizing and rallying point for the NATO allies, saying we've had enough of Milošević lying and misrepresenting himself to NATO and to the world—that this could not stand."[37] Albright's argument had at long last won the day in the administration.

PICKING UP A FIGHT IN THE BALKANS

Since US decision-makers did not believe that Belgrade would comply with the United States' demands without the infliction of some punishment, they agreed in a January 19 meeting on a formula that would provide an appropriate justification for NATO intervention by laying the responsibility for the conflict on Milošević.[38] Thus, the purpose of the negotiations conducted from February 6 to 23 between Serbs and Kosovars at the French chateau of Rambouillet and mediated by the states of the Contact Group, by the EU, and by the OSCE, was less to hammer an accord between Serbs and Kosovars, than to get the latter to endorse an agreement, and then, once Milošević rejected the deal, to blame him for scuttling diplomacy. In the words of Daalder, the US strategy was to "get the Kosovars to sign on, get the Serbs to renege, bomb the Serbs, get the Serbs to sign on, deal—that's the strategy."[39]

There was little expectation in the ranks of US decision-makers for a genuine breakthrough at Rambouillet. As the president put it to his team as the talks were about to proceed: "I hope we don't have to bomb, but we may need to."[40] This manner of proceeding had the further advantage of extracting before the talks the commitment of the more reluctant NATO allies to bombing if Milošević did not comply fully. This was achieved by a joint communiqué on January 30 stating that "NATO is ready to take whatever measures are necessary... by compelling compliance with the demands of the international community and the achievement of a political settlement. The Council has therefore agreed today that the NATO Secretary General may authorize air strikes against targets on FRY territory."[41] In so doing, the Europeans had, presumably unwittingly, signed on what was for all intents and purposes a military campaign against Belgrade.[42] As Berger argued, if Milošević "was playing a game with us at Rambouillet by building up his forces while pretending to negotiate seriously, so were we. We needed to demonstrate a real commitment to get a peaceful resolution in order to get the allies to go along with the use of significant force."[43]

Accordingly, the terms of the Rambouillet agreement were presented as nonnegotiable and included the provision, aimed to rattle Miloševíc, of a NATO-led force that would deploy in Kosovo to oversee the agreement's implementation. Moreover, the United States exerted strong pressure on the ragtag Albanian delegation, composed of mortal rivals, to sign the agreement in order to give it a free hand against Belgrade. The United States correctly gambled that the Serb delegation was both not interested in negotiating (unlike Dayton, Miloševíc had not bothered to come to Rambouillet) and under the belief that the differences between the Albanians will preclude the signing of an accord that required inter alia that the KLA should disband.[44] Therefore, at Rambouillet Yugoslavia was going through the motions of the talks, without the expectation of any concrete result. The United States turned this insouciance to its advantage, by presenting the Albanian side with an offer it could not refuse: either the Kosovars signed, and bombing could proceed, or Yugoslavia will be allowed a free hand in Kosovo. This offer was explicitly spelled out in a press release on February 21 by Rubin: "We believe it is extremely important to put pressure on the Serbs. We cannot put the full amount of pressure if we don't get an agreement from the Kosovar Albanians...in order to move towards military action, it has to be clear that the Serbs were responsible."[45] A day later, Albright, desperate to get the Kosovars to sign, extended them a written pledge for a referendum on the statute of the province three years after the agreement.[46]

To the US allies' surprise, at the Paris signature ceremony on March 15, while the Yugoslav delegation predictably refused to do so, the Albanians unanimously signed on, stressing their right to conduct a referendum after three years. The NATO members thus found themselves committed overnight to a bombing campaign against Yugoslavia. Simultaneously, the United States ensured that Miloševíc could not back out yet again at the last minute by agreeing to token concessions. This time around, in order to escape bombing, he would have had to be subjected to humiliation himself by accepting harsh terms such as the unimpeded access of NATO (instead of the UN or the OSCE) to the entire Yugoslav territory, withdrawal of Serb forces from Kosovo except for police, autonomy for the province, and the referendum, which while not written in the accords was still heavily implied.[47] The essential meaning of Rambouillet was that the United States was so headset to castigate Miloševíc for his offenses that it was willing to go many an extra mile to guarantee that a fight was going to take place.

"WE WILL WIN. PERIOD. FULL STOP. THERE IS NO ALTERNATIVE."

Prestige explains not only why intervention was chosen to begin with, but also why it was not abandoned once it became clear that the expected folding on Milošević's part was not going to occur. Facing higher prestige stakes, the United States escalated the intervention by dispatching more warplanes to the front, by increasing the number of targets in Yugoslavia, and, ultimately, by breaking the taboo on ground operations in Kosovo. Clinton had been particularly emphatic on this point in his war message: "I do not intend to put our troops in Kosovo to fight a war."[48] As will be shown below, there was considerable reluctance in the ranks of US decision-makers, especially in the Pentagon, to contemplate such a step. By the second month of bombing there was still no concrete plan of operations for a ground campaign. Hence, the question to ask is why the United States was willing to revise its position on deploying ground forces in hostile territory after months of rejecting this notion.

The most convincing explanation is that the United States accepted the ground option only as a supreme measure in order to safeguard its own prestige and that of NATO. For two months, the United States had pinned its hopes on the bombing campaign, which was supposed to soften Milošević into submission, as it had in Bosnia. However, by the end of April, Kosovo had been ethnically cleansed, with 800,000 Albanians pushed into FYROM and Albania, and another 500,000 displaced from their homes.[49] Unless the Albanian refugees returned to Kosovo and their homes were rebuilt by October, they would have faced the prospect of freezing to death in the harsh Balkan winter. This left NATO with only six months in which to find a solution to the refugee problem. By the end of May, if Milošević continued to resist, the alliance would have had only two months to stage an invasion before winter would have set in—since it would have taken at least an additional two months to put into place the logistics of the operation from scratch. Had the United States failed to return the refugees to the province, or had thousands of Kosovars perished in the winter of 1999, its prestige would have suffered severely—the intervention could no longer be presented as a showcase of successful leadership in the post–Cold War world. Therefore, abject failure in Kosovo was not out of question, despite the disparity of the forces involved.[50]

This consideration helps explain why, even before the month of May, the United States had quietly given up its objective of coercing Milošević to sign the Rambouillet agreements, which after all had been the ostensible rationale for the intervention in the first place. To quote Daalder, "Our goals by April...are no longer to prevent him from conducting atrocities against the Albanians or to degrade his capacity to do so. Now our goal becomes to have refugees return."[51] Therefore, the United States was willing to settle for any solution that would have had the Kosovars returned to the province.

However, as the list of targets that could be bombed inside Yugoslavia grew shorter, as Milošević showed no signs of yielding, and as time elapsed in the clock-race to have the refugees return, the United States eventually accepted that only a ground campaign could deliver the victory its prestige so badly required.

The tilt toward a ground option could be traced to the aftermath of the NATO Summit in Washington of April 23–25 celebrating NATO's fiftieth birthday, when the US government formally asked the Supreme Allied Commander in Europe (SACEUR) General Wesley Clark to draw plans for invasion. The NATO Summit was an effort to show that the alliance will stand by its commitments in Kosovo. The declaration the summit issued began with the words: "The crisis in Kosovo represents a fundamental challenge to the values for which NATO has stood since its foundation...We will not allow this campaign of terror to succeed. NATO is determined to prevail."[52] Subsequently, by early May the possibility for ground operations was no longer ruled out. On May 20, Clark presented the president with plans for a force of 175,000 troops, out of which 100,000 US troops would enter Kosovo from Albania. He also stated that a decision on whether to invade or not should have been reached no later than June 10, if the operation was to be mounted at all. By his own admission, by that time Clinton had reached the conclusion that a ground offensive would be necessary.[53]

On June 2, Berger wrote a memo to the president that recommended the ground offensive as the only option left. According to Berger, this conclusion was already in Clinton's mind: "He had made a decision that he was not going to lose and that he was prepared for a ground invasion." The very same day Berger met with a number of Washington insiders and presented them with a laconic agenda of US goals in Kosovo. Point one read: "First, we will win. Period. Full stop. There is no alternative." Coming on the heels of this already very forceful statement, point two argued that "winning means what we've said it means." Finally, after point three, which reaffirmed that the air campaign was working, point four completed the circle by saying that: "Fourth, the president has said that he has not ruled out any options. Go back to 1: We will win."[54]

The official reason cited by Berger for this turnabout was the approaching winter and its possible impact on those Kosovars still trapped in the province.[55] Yet the issue at stake was more than just the fate of the Kosovars: after all if the United States had been preoccupied foremost with their safety it could have used troops from the first hours of the intervention, or at the very least once it was clear that airpower alone would not stop Milošević from widespread ethnic cleansing. Rather, the United States was concerned with what would happen to its prestige, if it was seen as failing to defeat the regime in Belgrade. Evidence that this was the case comes from Berger himself, who while developing the points, remarked that the perception of defeat "would do serious, if not irreparable harm to the US, NATO, and European stability."[56]

As a matter of fact, the length to which the United States was prepared to go to protect its own prestige went even beyond a ground option for Kosovo. All along, during the intervention, concern for both its own prestige and NATO's had permeated the decisions of the United States. Yet, by early June, there were signals that the United States was even willing to act without NATO, if need be. The danger of a split in NATO had appeared in May because of the refusal of the German government to any involvement on the ground. This position meant not only the unwillingness of the German government to contribute any grounds troops—in order to do so, Chancellor Gerhard Schröder would have needed to secure the Parliament's approval and odds of success were minuscule—but also a German threat of vetoing any NATO land offensive, which was seen as the only way the Social-Democrat–led government could stay in power.[57] The US unconditional commitment to victory in Kosovo could thus have required action outside the context of NATO, if the United States would not have been able to persuade Germany to support the invasion. Of course, as Daalder and O'Hanlon point out, "No one can really know how NATO would have reacted to a strong US-British push for a ground invasion of Kosovo," on account of Milošević's surrender on June 3. It is possible that NATO would have fallen in line. But if it did not, this did not necessarily mean the United States would not have proceeded on its own. As Berger confided, "A consensus in NATO is valuable. But it is not a sine qua non. We want to move with NATO, but it can't prevent us from moving."[58] This only shows how much the United States had come from the days in which it was preaching cooperative security as engagement and new world order. Not only had the UN Security Council been discarded—the United States was now willing to do what it takes to achieve results, even at the risk of acting alone, or with a proto-coalition of the willing. Prestige was not the only possible reason for the United States' decisions to intervene and then to escalate against Milošević. For structuralism, the US motive was ensuring the security of the Balkans in the face of a conflict that could have engulfed Greece and Turkey. Conversely, for exceptionalism, the bombing was warranted by the United States' lasting commitment to human rights, which were put in jeopardy by the Serb ethnic cleansing of Kosovars. Finally, revisionism contends that the intervention was the result of the drive to champion global economic and political openness so as to advance the interests of US domestic elites, not in the least those of the military establishment. In what follows, these contrasting interpretations will be weighed against the prestige model so as to determine which one represents a better fit for the Kosovo intervention.

A New Powder Keg in the Balkans?

In his speech to the nation on March 24, 1999, Clinton mentioned the security rationale by proclaiming that the US objective in Kosovo consisted in diffusing a "powder keg at the heart of Europe that has exploded twice before this century with catastrophic results."[59] Before long, skeptics made their voices heard. John Lewis Gaddis summed up the expert opinion regarding "the powder keg" metaphor by remarking that the parallel with the two World Wars did not hold up to scrutiny. In the case of the two World Wars, he argued, the threat to the Balkans came from great powers: Austria-Hungary and Nazi Germany. In 1999 Kosovo, by contrast, the threat came from a small power, Yugoslavia (the federal union of Serbia and Montenegro), which did not have the means to challenge the balance of power in Europe, much less globally.[60]

Gaddis was right in that no US decision-maker seriously envisaged the prospects of World War Three erupting over Kosovo. The best evidence to this effect is that the operation went ahead in disregard of the possibility of Russian military retaliation on behalf of their Serb religious brethren. The United States did not reconsider its decision to intervene even after an April 7 statement by Yeltsin, which threatened NATO with "a minimum of a European war or maybe even a world war," and its resolve held firm even when, once a cease-fire had been reached in June, Russian troops rushed into Kosovo occupying the airport in the provincial capital Pristina.[61] As to the threat posed by Yugoslavia itself to the security of the United States, this was negligible. Unlike in the two World Wars, the foe was decisively outgunned and isolated.

Yet the security implications of Kosovo should not be dismissed so summarily, since they could have involved not the United States per se, but rather its allies in the Balkans. Clinton specifically mentioned the long-standing rivalry of Greece and Turkey. "Eventually," said Clinton, "key US allies could be drawn into a wider conflict." This view was elaborated by Berger on March 25: the United States' national interest was at stake in Kosovo, because the security of South-Eastern Europe was threatened and, therefore, a wider conflict in that area would have sooner or later involved the United States as well.[62] In this line of thought, the repressive tactics employed by Yugoslav forces against the KLA would have caused widespread instability throughout the Balkans that might have ended up in a full-blown war between Athens and Ankara. At a first glance, the danger of a Greco-Turkish war sparked by the events in Kosovo may have seemed "farfetched."[63] There was nevertheless a plausible argument to be made for such concern.

As Scowcroft admitted when explaining US foreign policy in Bosnia, "We were heavily national interest oriented, and Bosnia was of national interest concern only if the war broke out into Kosovo, risking the involvement of our allies in a wider war." Moreover, Secretary of State Eagleburger, while continuing Baker's policy of noninvolvement in Bosnia, took the measure to warn Milošević over Christmas 1992 that an escalation of the war in Bosnia by a Serb attack on Kosovo would provoke the military involvement of the United States. For his part, Christopher entertained a similar view: any conflict in Kosovo "would bring into the fray other countries in the region—Albania, Greece, Turkey" and this conflict could degenerate "into a world war."[64] Consequently, on two occasions, in February and July 1993, Christopher repeated Eagleburger's Christmas warning to Belgrade.[65]

How could Kosovo have triggered a confrontation between Greece and Turkey? The central element in this scenario was the neighboring FYROM. Macedonia had a historical grievance against Greece due to the Greek occupation in 1913 of the harbor of Salonika (actual Thessalonica, the second largest city in Greece after Athens).[66] The declaration of independence of Macedonia in 1991 was thus seen by Greece as a threat to its national integrity, more so because the leadership in Skopje was at pains to create something approaching a national conscience in a divided society that numbered besides Slavs a large and unruly Albanian minority. To do so, it invented the myth of a Macedonian people stretching back to the days of Alexander and Philip of Macedon, as illustrated by the adoption of the emblem of Philip's sun on the national flag. That was, nevertheless, an inopportune connection, since Greece perceived Macedon to be an essential part of the Greek heritage. Furthermore, given that Macedon is estimated roughly to correspond to the region of Greek Macedonia, the flag was seen by Greece as an attempt at changing borders.[67] Athens was incensed as well by the widespread talk in Skopje of a "Great Macedonia," which would have extended to the Aegean and comprised Thessalonica.

In retaliation, Greece obstructed the European Community's recognition of FYROM for two years. When it was eventually forced by European pressure to concede recognition, Athens hit back by putting into place a one-year economic blockade of Skopje, which, coupled with the UN sanctions imposed at the time on Yugoslavia, ran havoc on the Macedonian economy. Greece lifted its blockade only after international pleas and after being given Macedonian insurance that the republic name would be changed to FYROM, that the offending flag would be modified, and that Skopje would denounce any intention to alter existing borders. But by 1999, these matters were still not settled conclusively, since Skopje maintained that FYROM represented only an interim compromise name.[68]

For Athens it was not so much FYROM that it had to fear, but rather Skopje's growing association with Greece's hereditary enemy and fellow NATO member Turkey. FYROM had signed a treaty of military cooperation with Ankara and had extended recognition to the Turkish controlled republic of Northern Cyprus. Hence, Greece feared the possibility of encirclement by a string of Turkish client states, and these fears were worsened by the intensification of Albanian nationalism inside FYROM.[69] The Albanian ethnic group has undergone one of the highest demographic increases in Europe in the last quarter of the century.[70] This development had, as a result, modified the population balance in several parts of the Balkans, most dramatically in Kosovo and in FYROM. It was estimated at the time, though more recent statistics have shown the claim as inflated, that perhaps as many of 40 percent of the two million people that comprise the population of FYROM were of Albanian origin.[71] Furthermore, this large minority was highly politically active, pressing for autonomy since the vote on the independence of the republic (which they boycotted). Since the region the Albanians inhabit inside FYROM is contiguous to Kosovo and to Albania proper, the prospects of a Muslim-dominated greater Albania loomed ominously for both Belgrade and Athens.

Hence, if in 1999, 300,000 Albanian refugees together with a great number of KLA fighters had crossed the border into FYROM, they would have seriously affected the stability of the republic by transforming the Albanians there into a bare majority.[72] This prospect would have been even more menacing to Greece than the one of a revisionist Macedonia, since the Albanians could have also counted on the support of their kin in Tirana, and with Turkish and Islamic help constituted an altogether much more formidable threat. Greece actually warned Albania since 1993 against endorsing the actions of nationalists in Kosovo, by stating that in the eventuality of Albanian autonomy there, it would have sought the same status for the Greek minority in Albania proper, effectively issuing a masked threat of military intervention.[73] Basically, in this line of thought, Milošević's repression of Albanians in Kosovo could have ended up affecting the security equation in the Balkans so badly that it would have triggered Greek intervention, which might have provoked in turn the involvement of Turkey. Hence, a hypothetical case could be made by structuralism that the United States was determined by strategic necessity to put an end to conflict in Kosovo in its incipient stages.

But, while this structuralist argument may not be as far-fetched as it is commonly assumed, it still does present two major weaknesses. First, even if one assumes that NATO acted in Kosovo in order to lessen the security concerns of Greece, it is hard to imagine from Athens' perspective how Greek security could have been enhanced by the US proposal of an autonomous Kosovo, with the possibility of a referendum on independence after three years. Actually, this would have constituted a highly alarming step for Athens, since it would have created an Albanian center of power on its northern border, the very thing it wanted to avoid. To have catered to Greek concerns, the best course of action would have been to allow the Serb forces to eradicate the KLA. In effect, polls in Greece at the time of the NATO intervention showed that 95 percent of Greeks disapproved of the action, 94 percent of them distrusted Clinton, and 63.5 percent had a good opinion of Milošević.[74] It is difficult to imagine how such figures could have been justified if NATO was seen as acting in Greece's best interests. The objection that US intervention in Kosovo might have been designed to cater to Turkish security concerns over losing their FYROM ally also does not withstand scrutiny: if the Kosovo Albanians would have been permanently relocated to FYROM, Ankara could have found the regime in Skopje even more accommodating.

Second, apart from the Christmas warning, of which more will be said below, there was no US perception of a security crisis in the Balkans. The United States could not have developed concerns for the stability of the Balkans overnight. If regional security was indeed the goal justifying the three months of bombing, one would have to find indications of such concern in the months and years preceding the Kosovo intervention beyond the declarations of Eagleburger and Christopher. Yet such signs are conspicuously lacking. There was no mention of Kosovo either in the Dayton accords or in the negotiations process leading to the agreement. Moreover, in August 1998, the US ambassador to NATO Alexander Vershbow sent a cable that read that sooner or later the United States would have to deploy troops to Kosovo, because "we have too much at stake in the political stability of the South Balkans to permit the conflict to fester much longer." Greece and Turkey were specifically mentioned in the cable. Vershbow was consequently urging the creation of a joint American-Russian task force to be deployed in Kosovo, which would have defused the crisis. However, the United States took no initiative in response to Vershbow's telegram. Had the United States shown any serious concern for conflict in the Balkans it would have pressed, at the very least, for the reinforcement of the existing UN peacekeeping force in FYROM UNPREDEP, or asked for a mandate expanding UNPREDEP's role of surveillance of the border with Yugoslavia. Such action was all the more warranted, since by July 1997, violence had broken out between Slavs and Albanians inside FYROM.[75] In the context of the impeachment process of Clinton, and of the al Qaeda bombings in Nairobi and Dar es Salaam, the security of the Balkans took a distant second place.[76]

Evidence to this effect also comes from US policy regarding Albania. The year 1997 witnessed widespread social convulsions in Albania, which were directly responsible for the emergence of the KLA as a viable fighting force. The government of Sali Berisha had allowed the perpetuation of pyramid schemes, totaling about two billion dollars. Ultimately, these collapsed, wiping out the savings of tens of thousands of Albanians. The result was that for all intents and purposes in March 1997 the Albanian state disintegrated. Mobs took to pillaging the army's weapons stocks (it was estimated that more than one million weapons had been stolen), and the country descended into lawlessness as the armed rebels marched on unopposed to the capital. In the words of Albanian Justice Minister Spartak Ngjela: "All structures of the state have failed. In this moment, we are a natural state, if you know your Hobbes."[77] The United States did not respond to the alarming crisis in Albania.[78] The result was that many of the weapons and ammunition stolen found their way north into the hands of the KLA and enabled it to conduct large-scale operations against Belgrade.[79]

This leaves the problem of the Christmas warning. However, by 1998, US officials themselves were confused about whether the warning was still applicable. The political bottom line was that on each of the four occasions when the Serb forces intervened in Kosovo during 1998, there was no invocation of the Christmas warning as a justification for military action. As Daalder put it: "It was very clear from the moment the violence started that the Christmas warning was off the table as far as Sandy Berger, as far as the president is concerned, and as far as Madeleine Albright is concerned. She may have wanted it on the table, but there was a clear decision not to have it on the table."[80] There are indications that even the original "Christmas warning" had been a bluff all along. Eagleburger's Undersecretary of State Arnold Kanter answered a question as to how much truth there was in the original Christmas warning by saying, "To tell you the truth, this is a very hard question. I really don't know."[81]

This passive attitude toward the Balkans not only undermines the structuralist claim that the United States intervened in Kosovo out of security concerns, but also weakens claims that the United States could have been the victim of misperception.[82] One may make the point that the United States intervened in Kosovo because it genuinely thought it saw the ingredients of a Greco-Turkish conflict, even if in fact there were very few or none. But if so, one would have a pattern of US involvement every time the prospect of instability in the Balkans was raised. Hence, the United States should have seen in every major convulsion in the region during this time the specter of a war opposing Athens and Ankara. However, such concerns were noticeably absent: simply put, US concern with Kosovo had little to do with security considerations.[83]

SAVING THE KOSOVARS?

By contrast to structuralism, exceptionalism accounts for the US intervention in terms of ending the human rights abuses in Kosovo. The early 1990s had witnessed a plethora of arguments in favor of humanitarian intervention, which referred to the right, and even the obligation, of great powers to act to prevent gross violations of the rights of individuals or of ethnic and religious groups by a government. This international practice allegedly marked a sizable evolution in the views of statesmen: while during the Cold War remarkably few states claimed they employed force in the service of a humanitarian cause even when such a claim was plausible, in the post–Cold War, humanitarian justifications were invoked among other contexts in Iraq, Somalia, Bosnia, Rwanda, and East Timor. Consequently, there are grounds to also interpret the bombing of Yugoslavia as an instance of humanitarian intervention motivated by a desire to put an end to abuses perpetuated against the Kosovars. By the end of April, 800,000 ethnic Albanians had been pushed into FYROM and Albania, and another 500,000 had been displaced from their homes.[84]

This is the conclusion Daalder and O'Hanlon reach: "Upholding rights and alleviating humanitarian tragedy are worthy goals for American national security and policy. Doing so reinforces the notion that the United States is not interested in power for its own sake but rather to enhance stability and security to promote certain universal principles and values."[85] Other analysts agree with this humanitarian assessment, though they are much less sanguine regarding the wisdom of the policy, seeing Kosovo as "an incoherent policy driven by moral impulses and mushy sentiments, one that hectors and scolds other nations to obey our sanctimonious dictates and ineffectively bombs or sanctions them if they don't" or, to quote Kissinger, as "virtue run amok."[86]

Yet these exceptionalist accounts have to contend with three difficulties. First, if the Clinton administration was motivated by values it is not clear why it postponed intervention for so long, or why decision-makers such as Berger and Cohen, who had first rejected intervention then came to embrace it. Second, exceptionalism has problems for accounting for the modus operandi of the intervention. US leaders pinned their hopes on using airpower against the Serbs, even though it was dubious from the beginning that airpower alone could prevent ethnic cleansing. Moreover, the United States kept rejecting ground deployment even after it had become painfully clear that reliance on airpower was not effective in stopping the onslaught on the ground. Third, a human rights frame of mind contrasts with the treatment of the Kosovar refugees in FYROM and Albania.

Moral revulsion alone cannot explain the launching of a campaign of this magnitude. Had this been the case, humanitarian considerations should have dictated intervention earlier on, once news transpired of the repressive tactics used by Belgrade against the Kosovars. More than 300,000 people had fled their homes in 1998, though most had returned once the fighting had stopped. Yet, as seen from above, suggestions by Albright that the situation in Kosovo might have come down to using force against Yugoslavia, had failed repeatedly to sway the other principal decision-makers from February to December 1998. Therefore, it is dubious that humanitarian arguments succeeded in convincing skeptics in the cabinet and in the Pentagon to rally around Albright. A particularly strong sense of moral outrage over the massacre of Račak cannot be invoked as a possible answer since Cohen and Berger see Račak as a catalyst, and not a game changer. Cohen for instance said that it did not change his thinking that force should be a last resort, but that it was "galvanizing" in that it convinced the United States that it had enough of constant offenses by Milošević.[87] Moreover, for all its rhetoric during the bombing campaign, the administration was not keen on embracing humanitarian intervention as a doctrine. Clinton introduced the proviso of both interests and values being at stake before intervening, and even Albright, deemed the chief advocate of armed humanitarianism, sounded a caution note against assuming that the United States would defend human rights worldwide: "Some hope, and others fear, that Kosovo will be a precedent for similar interventions around the globe. I would caution against any such sweeping conclusions. Every circumstance is unique. Decisions on the use of force will be made by any president on a case-by-case basis after weighing a host of factors." As Daalder and O'Hanlon themselves conclude: "Far from heralding a new age of interventionism, the war in Kosovo highlights the difficulty of pursuing such a course."[88] Apparently, virtue was not running amok in Washington after all.

Exceptionalism faces even more formidable challenges because the NATO military tactics indicate that the well-being of the Kosovars, while an important consideration, represented, nonetheless, a secondary priority on the US agenda. In order for the NATO operation to satisfy the requirements of a humanitarian intervention, one should be able to first and foremost prove a humanitarian intention. Thus, one should find evidence of the prevailing intention on the part of the United States to safeguard the Kosovars from potential harm by Serb forces. However, the United States envisaged only an air campaign against Yugoslavia, without a simultaneous protective deployment of ground troops within Kosovo. Arguably, one could still support the view that the air campaign war still posed a deterrent threat to Milošević. There are such clues in the first days of bombing. For instance, Clinton's speech of March 24 mentioned that the action was aimed at hindering a major offensive that Milošević was planning against the Kosovars. "We act," said Clinton, "to protect thousands of innocent people in Kosovo from a mounting military offensive." This message was reinforced by several statements to the same effect such as the one by the Pentagon that "the primary goal of the air strike would be to arrest the ability of the Serbs to brutally attack the Kosovar Albanians."[89]

But if this was the goal at hand, it was pursued by woefully inadequate tactics, since it soon became evident that high-altitude bombing could not thwart the highly mobile Serb troops and militias from forcing the Albanian population out of Kosovo. The United States could only acknowledge this grim reality—by April 1, a NATO official quoted by the *New York Times* was providing a full backtrack by stating that "we said from the outset that we couldn't prevent atrocities and crimes against humanity with just air campaigning." NATO Secretary General Javier Solana similarly argued that "we may have no means to stop [the violence against Albanians], but we have shown we have the will to try."[90] However, if so why had the United States been so blind to the possibility of Serb retaliation against the Kosovars? Daalder and O' Hanlon argue rather awkwardly that "remarkably, some officials appear to have ignored the basic fact that NATO airpower would simply not be physically able to stop Milosevic's onslaught against the Kosovars. NATO leaders collectively ignored the distinct possibility that Milosevic might actually intensify his efforts once NATO bombs began to fall."[91]

In fact, evidence suggests that the United States was aware that Yugoslavia would lash out at Kosovars, and that, despite this knowledge, did not take any special measures to protect them from harm. While it is possible that the United States was wrong about the numbers of victims of Serb ethnic cleansing, it cannot claim it had no inkling that Belgrade was going to conduct ethnic cleansing in Kosovo. Both US and German intelligence reports had predicted a massive crackdown starting in February 1999 and the director of the CIA George Tenet had briefed the president and his advisors on this topic.[92] While stating that the dimensions of the forced exodus of Kosovars had caught him by surprise, Berger still acknowledged that the United States had expected hundreds of thousands of refugees. Furthermore, Italian Prime Minister Massimo D'Alema had asked Clinton before the campaign against Serbia started what the plan was if Milošević did not balk and the refugee numbers swelled to 300,000.The answer from Clinton was that the alliance will continue to rely on bombing.[93]

A still stronger piece of evidence showing that US decision-makers realized the risks to the Kosovars and still pressed ahead with a bombing campaign comes from Clark's memoirs, in which the former SACEUR recalls a discussion with Albright on March 6, three weeks before bombing began. In the conversation, Clark predicted that once the bombing begins, "almost certainly they [the Serbs] will attack the civilian population. This is what they are promising to do." Albright then asked whether the United States can do anything to prevent reprisals against the Kosovars. Clark's response was blunt and, as events turned out, quite accurate: "We can't. Despite our best efforts the civilians are going to be targeted by the Serbs. It will just be a race, our air strikes and the damage we cause them against what they can do on the ground. But in the short term, they can win the race." In the long run, Clark thought that NATO's superior capabilities would prevail, but that "it's not going to be pleasant." Clark went on to elaborate on the more important rationale for the intervention: not saving the Kosovars, but US and NATO prestige. When Albright presses him whether the United States should still go ahead with the bombing despite the high probability of Serbian retaliation against the Kosovars, Clark answers: "We have to [go ahead]. We put NATO's credibility on the line. We have to follow through and make it work."[94] Based on this exchange, one could argue that the United States believed that any damage the Serbs inflicted on the Kosovars in the first days of the campaign would be reversible, particularly considering the belief the war was going to be short. But such an argument is at odds with the requirements of humanitarian intervention, for which the people one claims to protect cannot be disposed of as expendable assets so as to safeguard prestige.

Furthermore, if humanitarian considerations were overriding, why did the United States continue to stick for more than two months to a tactic that had failed to protect the supposed beneficiaries of the intervention? The decision to continue with only the air campaign was not a temporary blunder, but a deliberate choice. The main advantage of pursuing an intervention only by air was not that it helped defend the vulnerable Kosovars, but that it ensured a low number of US casualties. Accordingly, the three explicit objectives of using airpower against Yugoslavia mentioned by Clark do not include the protection of the Kosovars: instead they consisted of not losing aircraft, of affecting Belgrade's political will, and of deterring an attack on NATO's ground forces in neighboring states.[95] The risks of losing planes was further minimized by the decision to fly only missions above 15,000 feet, which, while diminishing the chance of hitting objectives on the ground, also reduced the peril coming from antiaircraft artillery or from shoulder-fired surface to air missiles. Yet, even analysts who have a favorable view of the coercive ability of air power concede that the bombing was unable to affect the expulsion of the Kosovars by Serb forces.[96] The use of ground forces to supplement airpower had been ruled out from the very start of the intervention, notably by Clinton in his war message. What is more, the United States adamantly refused until after the NATO summit of April 23–25 to even consider a ground option in Kosovo, so that by May, the United States still had no concrete plans for land operations within Yugoslavia.[97] Whenever Clark attempted to include a land dimension to the war, he ran into opposition of the Pentagon. The most illustrative episode in this tug-of-war involved the dispatch of Apache helicopters to Kosovo. This could have potentially resulted in bloody confrontations with the Serb military since the Apaches are used only in complement with targeting teams, and therefore in conflict on the ground. After much wrangling, when the Apaches were sent on the Yugoslav front, the Pentagon, invoking bad weather, lack of landing facilities, and accidents, managed to prevent them from flying a single combat mission in Kosovo.[98] The conclusion is inescapable: the bombing of Yugoslavia might not have been the most appropriate tactic to guarantee the security of the Kosovars, but it was the only approach the US political and military establishment was willing to accept. Yet, the same decision-makers were willing, as seen in Berger's July 2's "we will win" statements, to accept the risks of a ground campaign so as to defend US prestige.

Another indication of the low priority of humanitarian considerations comes from the policy toward the Kosovar refugees. Already, by May, the refugees had become a liability because of the deadline to their return imposed by winter. Creating conditions for surviving winter in the tent cities that had emerged at the borders between Kosovo, Albania, and FYROM was itself a task of staggering proportions since this involved setting housing for almost a million persons. Moreover, there was also the problem of the estimated 580,000 Kosovars displaced inside Kosovo. Albania and FYROM could not accommodate further arrivals (FYROM was anyway reluctant to do so because of the ethnic balance of its population). In these conditions, a humanitarian considerations-driven policy may have required evacuating the refugees into the NATO member states. However, the NATO allies were reluctant to engage in such an effort, owing to concerns over being seen as acquiescing to ethnic cleansing, the economic costs involved with moving the refugees, and, the most often-mentioned cause, the possibility of refugees staying on in the West. Western Europe was undergoing an economic recession, where as high as 10 percent of the total work-force was unemployed in France and Italy. Germany had already spent an estimated $1 billion on the 750,000 refugees from the Bosnian war and had no wish to assist further arrivals.[99] The allies finally agreed to take out of the region 70,000 refugees from a grand total of 900,000.[100]

For its part, the United States refused to exceed the quota of 20,000 Balkans refugees that the Congress had imposed and initially chose, out of all possible relocation places, the base at Guantanamo. The reason for this odd location was that, since Guantanamo constitutes Cuban soil, the refugees could not have claimed the right of asylum into the United States. The proposal met with a wave of protests from US human rights groups, who were concerned that the base seemed more like a "POW camp" than a suitable relocation facility for Miloševíc's victims. One human rights activist (presciently as it turned out) said the whole base was surrounded "by concertina wire. It's like a jail." In the end, the United States agreed to drop the Guantanamo relocation plan, but only on condition the accepted refugees would be returned to Kosovo as soon as the situation normalized.[101]

To conclude, these arguments do not deny that the intervention in Kosovo had a humanitarian component—the United States certainly believed it had right on its side in acting to end and then to reverse Miloševíc's abuses. But humanitarianism was not so important as to have determined the intervention in the first place or the decision to escalate intervention into a ground campaign.

KEEPING THE DOOR OPEN IN KOSOVO?

Revisionism sees Kosovo as an example of the militarization of US foreign policy. Thus, Kosovo is representative of the tendency to transfer authority to modern proconsuls, military leaders who assume responsibility for decision-making in a certain area—in the case at hand, Clark, who acted both as supreme allied commander and as CINC of the US European Command (CINCEUR). Hence, Clark was the single most responsible actor for the intervention because he miscalculated the extent of the opposition that Miloševíc would put up. Nevertheless, the decision to fight over Kosovo, while a possible error of judgment, cannot be seen as an aberration in the overall US strategy, as it was demanded by the logic of preserving the principle of openness in the key European region, by force if necessary.

As Bacevich puts it, "The United States fought over Kosovo not to protect Kosovars, but to forestall the intolerable prospect of European backsliding... If Operation Allied Force did not rise to the level of a great moral victory, it was a necessary strategic one, an example of the work that goes along with running an empire."[102] Similarly, Johnson sees Kosovo as proof that "the Pentagon monopolizes the formulation and conduct of foreign policy."[103]

However, the Pentagon's leaders represented by Secretary of Defense Cohen and by Joint Chiefs of Staff Chairman Hugh Shelton were by far the decision-makers most opposed to intervention. Not only did the Pentagon fight tooth and nail against the bombing of Yugoslavia, on the grounds it did not conform to the Powell doctrine, but it also did its very best to resist Clark's demands for a land war, as illustrated by the Apache episode. By the end of the campaign, relations between the Pentagon and Clark were positively venomous. On the one hand, Secretary of Defense Cohen, privately ruing the day he had made him SACEUR, ordered Clark to stop asking for ground troops and to withdraw from the public light, and attempted not to invite him to the NATO summit in Washington. Clark returned the favor by lobbying outside the command chain both Clinton and British Prime Minister Tony Blair. This excess of zeal cost Clark the traditional renewal for a second term of appointment as the supreme allied commander.[104] This leaves one in serious doubt as to how much authority or autonomy a "proconsul" truly enjoys.

An additional weakness of the revisionist argument on Kosovo is that it presents the intervention as run-of-the-mill imperial work. This interpretation is itself rooted in the classical revisionist view of Vietnam: a turbulent regional rogue calls into question the principle of openness on which the US elite has staked its fate. But, by contrast with Vietnam in the Cold War, in 1999 Yugoslavia was not a Communist state, preaching a rival ideology throughout the Balkans; its repression of the KLA did not risk producing a domino effect, resulting in Serb domination of the entire region; and its potential victory did not pose the same economic threat as the success of a Third World regime rebelling against the dominant capitalist state. In fact, by US standards Yugoslavia was both a democracy, albeit of an illiberal kind, and relatively integrated in the global economy. Yugoslavia was in fact the single exception to the "golden arches theory of peace," which argued that no states engulfed by the tide of globalization as represented by the ubiquitous McDonald restaurant could ever go to war, since Yugoslavia was home to 16 McDonalds.[105]

Chapter Conclusion

Structuralism, exceptionalism, and revisionism fail to explain convincingly, by comparison to the prestige model, the US intervention in Kosovo. In Kosovo, the United States did not attempt to bolster the security of its territory or of its allies, to champion noble principles, or to satisfy the quest for higher profits and political clout of US elites. Instead, the United States aimed foremost at preserving and vindicating its prestige in the face of repeated challenges by Miloševíc.

5

THE INDISPENSABLE NATION
AND US UNILATERALISM

Unilateralism is identified frequently as a component of George W. Bush's foreign policy.[1] Nevertheless, unilateralism antedates the Bush presidency, being already at work during Clinton's second term in office in the refusal to sign in 1998 the Statute of Rome that created the ICC; in the endorsement of NMD (National Missile Defense) in 1999, even though it violated the existing ABM Treaty; and in the interventions without Security Council authorization against Iraq and Yugoslavia.[2] George W. Bush thus inherited a unilateral foreign policy that he simply carried through to the next step: the rejection in his first three months in office of the ICC, followed by the abrogation of the ABM Treaty in December 2001, and the invasion of Iraq in March 2003, to mention only the most prominent items on an otherwise much longer list.[3] Therefore, the growing US unilateralism at the cusp of the millennium supplements its proclivity to use force, resulting in a substantially more assertive policy from the early post–Cold War.

Is unilateralism the appropriate term for designating the above-mentioned measures embraced by Clinton and George W. Bush? Given the protestations, especially from Bush officials, that US behavior was not unilateralist, the question is warranted.[4] If one defines unilateralism as the rejection of any international partnership, unilateralism might not have been in play. Under this rigid definition, the US-led intervention over Kosovo, undertaken under NATO auspices in collaboration with 18 other members, or Operation Desert Fox jointly conducted with Great Britain do not qualify as unilateral.[5] Moreover, it could be argued that, if one were to distinguish between unilateralism, bilateralism, and multilateralism, with the latter representing "an institutional form that coordinates relations among three or more states on the basis of generalized principles of conduct," US policies could be described better as bilateral than as unilateral.[6]

However, these definitions would turn unilateralism into a straw man. The former definition requires that a unilateralist state must act permanently alone, which has rarely if ever been the case. To exemplify, the nineteenth-century United States, even though politically isolationist, was also heavily involved in trade relations with Europe, Latin America, and the Caribbean, and did not shun pursuing extensive diplomatic ties with other nations. As for the latter definition, which raises the alternative of bilateralism, it also reduces to almost nil the cases of unilateralism, because the bulk of the strategic, economic, cultural, and diplomatic connections of states would fall in either the bilateral or multilateral categories.

This is why it is more useful to think of unilateralism as a policy that places limits on the extent of international cooperation, and of multilateralism as a policy that removes such limits or expands and deepens cooperation. In other words, unilateralism and multilateralism stand for degrees of cooperation in a spectrum ranging from perfect cooperation (acting together) to perfect independence (acting alone).[7] The closer a policy gets to perfect cooperation, the more grounds there are to call it multilateral. Conversely, the more a policy approaches perfect independence, the more it is justified to describe it as unilateral. In this sense, a state's foreign policy can evolve from multilateralism toward unilateralism over time and vice versa. Accordingly, to determine at any given time whether a state's policy is unilateral or multilateral, one should measure it both against the two ideal types of perfect cooperation and of perfect independence, and also against the state's previous policy in this regard. Therefore, the point about US unilateralism at the cusp of the millennium is not that Washington acted without partners, but that it became increasingly less cooperative than it had been before. The United States became more reluctant to offer concessions or consult with other states, employed international institutions less frequently, and withdrew from several international agreements.[8]

This unilateralism was the result of an increasing preoccupation of US decision-makers with the symbolic challenges from free-riding states, that is, allies and partners that shirked their logistic, financial, or diplomatic support to the Pax Americana. These challenges affected US prestige in several ways. First, free-riding prevented the United States from enjoying privileges it considered as its due reward. In view of its unique responsibility as the dominant power, the United States considered it was also owed a larger amount of deference than other states, in the form of rights or dispensations from common obligations. This amounted to saying that the rules could not apply equally to the state that ensured the existence and enforcement of the rules. Whenever other states were not forthcoming in granting it privileges, the United States saw itself as justified in resorting to unilateralism to secure its demands.

Second, free-riding also had an indirect effect, by preventing the United States from addressing problems, which, if left unattended, would have cast doubts as to its effectiveness. The US claim to represent the dominant state in the system is based not just on its supremacy in capabilities, but also on its effective performance in the top spot. As seen in chapter three, a trade-off was present between effectiveness and cooperation, in the sense that in order to preserve consensus, problems were addressed by compromise. Thus, the United States ended up being blamed for not doing enough as a leader, even though its passivity was often the result of the desire to show consideration toward its allies and partners. As a result, whenever its initiatives were held back by other states, the United States found it more expedient to circumvent the opposition instead of fruitlessly attempting to persuade it of the suitability of its proposals. In so doing, the United States would have preferred that other states joined its camp, but their endorsement was no longer a sine qua non for action. Hence, unilateralism would have delivered demonstrable public results, and such public shows of effectiveness would have bolstered US prestige.

Finally, free-riding was interpreted as a form of *lèse-majesté*. As seen in chapter two's discussion of Aristotelian categories of offense, free-riding was seen as conveying both spite—frustrating US endeavors—and insolence—because the states in question refused to acknowledge US superiority and, by implication, its right to special treatment. The free-riding states' offense was considered all the more severe since it was interpreted as an ungrateful attack on the state that ensured international conditions that also benefitted them. Thus, unilateralism was also a way for the United States to retaliate against such transgressions.

Of course, US unilateralism could be interpreted alternatively through the prism of pragmatic considerations. As Krauthammer argued, "Unilateralism is the high road to multilateralism," meaning that once the United States chartered the course to follow, other states had no other resort but to follow along, since opposition would have availed them little, and support would have ingratiated them with Washington. Therefore, an argument could be advanced that the more assertively the United States acts, the more others are likely to cooperate by acquiescing to US terms: "No one wants to be left at the dock when the hegemon is sailing."[9] In this sense, assertiveness is motivated by instrumental rather than by psychological motives. However, such an argument presents problems at the levels of both logic and empirical accuracy.[10]

There are many conceivable scenarios where US assertiveness as a means to cooperation could and did fail.[11] Other states may have irreconcilable differences with the United States, preventing them from falling in line, whether these differences are strategic (Russia in Kosovo) or stemming from domestic politics (Germany and Turkey in the invasion of Iraq). Furthermore, other states may want to signal their own prominence by being the ones to stand up to the United States (France in 2003); or even if they cooperate, they may place limits and conditions on the extent of their cooperation so as to maximize their own benefits while apparently placating Washington (China's policy on North Korean sanctions; Pakistan in the war on terror). Finally, other states may seek better terms by manifesting an initial opposition rather than giving an automatic consent (Russia in the ABM talks); or, again, they may seek to bind the United States into accepting general rules of conduct (the ICC negotiations). In these circumstances, resorting to a *fait accompli* would harden rather than mollify the opposition. In effect, as will be seen below, each time the Clinton and the George W. Bush administrations stuck to their favored position with the expectation that other states would eventually give them their blessings, they found out that the resistance had not weakened in the slightest. Nor has US assertiveness in one scenario led to increased international cooperation on other future contested issues. Thus, it is possible to advance the same argument that was invoked for reputation in chapter two. As both assertiveness as a means to cooperation and reputation are instrumental theories, for them to be valid the policy has to make sense materially, yet there is evidence to consider them as strategic suboptimal behavior. Moreover, for both, emotions are excluded from the decision-making process, which represents a cool-headed calculation of costs and benefits. Hence, it is theoretically more advantageous to interpret ambiguous statements through a prestige lens, because prestige is the more persuasive account in explaining why multilateralism was jettisoned.

FROM THE INDISPENSABLE NATION TO THE BUSH DOCTRINE

The US status as the dominant power had become by the late 1990s the fulcrum of unilateralist policies, best seen in the doctrines of foreign policy by posse, of the indispensable nation, and of the Bush doctrine.

Accordingly, Richard Haass, a Republican statesman and the future director of Policy Planning in the State Department from 2001 to 2003, argued in the late 1990s that, as the world leader, the United States did not need to seek authority and support from an overwhelming coalition. Instead, the United States, acting as the sheriff, would recruit partners ("the posse") wherever it could find them, improvising coalitions on a case-by-case basis rather than as a permanent fixture. As Haass phrased it, the posse approach "differs from alliances or institutionalism in its eschewal of formal organizations and not requiring broad or complete consent." The United States should have imposed its views by keeping other countries' contributions limited or, indeed, symbolic. If "posses" were custom-made, there was no danger that the United States would ever run into opposition, since it would have taken care to include only states extending it unconditional support. Therefore, unilateralism was presented as a legitimate avenue of action in order to get things done. While Haass rejected the notion that foreign policy by posse was unilateralist, because ostensibly other states were involved as the posse, the doctrine was the explicit ancestor of the George W. Bush formula of "coalitions of the willing." Actually, Haass used the two terms interchangeably.[12] By 2001, he was referring to the posse approach as "multilateralism à la carte," even though he had earlier on expressly identified unilateralism with an "à la carte approach to alliances and international arrangements."[13]

Meanwhile, the doctrine of the indispensable nation was the joint creation of President Clinton and of his aide Sidney Blumenthal and was used repeatedly throughout the 1996 presidential campaign, most notably in the second inauguration speech in January 1997. "The world's greatest democracy will lead a whole world of democracy…America stands alone," said Clinton, "as the world's indispensable nation."[14] The "indispensable nation" also figured in Secretary of State Madeleine Albright's concluding statement at the Senate Foreign Relations Committee confirmations hearings in January 1997, when she described herself and the senators in audience as "representatives of the indispensable nation."[15] However, the most famous enunciation came in the context of the Iraqi crisis of February 1998, when Albright proclaimed that: "If we have to use force, it is because we are America; we are the indispensable nation. We stand tall and see further than other countries into the future."[16] In her memoirs, Albright explains this rhetoric as a tool for domestic consumption, whose aim was to steer wavering support for US global responsibilities.[17] Nevertheless, the indispensable nation reflected a broader interpretation. To quote Blumenthal: "'Indispensable nation' was his [Clinton's] response to foreign threats after Bosnia...These phrases were no mere slogans. The words mattered."[18]

This suggests that the indispensable nation doctrine was meant to define the US role in post–Cold War international politics. As Blumenthal recalls, the origin of the idea was the need to reinvent US foreign policy in the aftermath of the war in Bosnia, which had marked the first major US departure from relative restraint. "The position of the United States," writes Blumenthal, "was unique in world history. With the collapse of the Soviet Union there was no competing power. No European nation equaled the United States, nor did the European Union. If anything, the disgraceful behavior of Britain and France in dealing with the Bosnian crisis had made it clear that Europe could not assume military responsibilities without the United States."[19] Albright's February 1998 statement also expressed this point: the United States was the only country that foresaw the danger coming from Iraq, and that was prepared, as a responsible leader, to act to address it. Hence, a more persuasive interpretation of the indispensable nation is that it started from the premise that the United States was the only state in the world capable of ensuring effective management, and this is why its participation was vital to the success of any international initiative. It was to this extent that US leadership could not be dispensed with. As a result, if the United States was saddled with exceptional responsibilities, it could not have been held hostage to the consent of lower-ranked polities, or to the same restrictions that applied to them.

The same unilateralist message was at the heart of the Bush doctrine.[20] The George W. Bush team never made a secret of its belief that "the course of this nation does not depend on the decisions of others."[21] Particularly in the aftermath of the September 11 attacks, Bush stressed that the United States will not wait on other states before acting: "Some governments will be timid in the face of terror. And make no mistake about it: if they do not act America will."[22] If other nations disagreed, Bush had no qualms about going at it alone. As he confessed: "At some point we may be the only ones left [in the war on terror.] That's ok with me. We are America."[23] Thus, as Krauthammer put it, the foreign policy agenda of George W. Bush amounted to a logic of "unabashed unilateralism," which consisted in admitting that the United States was not "merely one among many," but "the dominant power in the world, more dominant than any since Rome." Since it had finally given up on its early post–Cold War attempt of "Prometheus playing as pigmy," the United States could remake the international order as it saw fit "by unapologetic and implacable demonstrations of will."[24] In the logic of Bush and Krauthammer, other countries could tag along, or fall into irrelevance, standing by as the US juggernaut continued its advance. Therefore, Washington could afford to select only those partners it wanted on its team, as exemplified by Secretary of Defense Donald Rumsfeld's statement that "the mission determines the coalition. And the coalition must not be permitted to determine the mission."[25]

In all these doctrines, unilateralism was the natural consequence of dominance. As the number one in the hierarchy, the United States had to take matters in its own hands so as to preserve its prestige.

THE ICC

The United States went into the negotiations in Rome in the summer of 1998 on the Statute of the ICC wanting ironclad guarantees that its citizens, specifically the members of its armed forces, would not be tried by the ICC or any other state's court without its accord, even though the prosecution charges would have consisted of crimes against humanity, war crimes, or genocide.[26] The two major US desiderata in Rome were to change Article 12 of the Statute, referring the manner of ascertaining court jurisdiction, and to circumscribe the role of the office of the independent prosecutor. Regarding the draft of Article 12, the proposal backed by the largest number of states (the so-called Like-Minded Group) provided that the ICC could sit in judgment of a person, if *either* the state where the alleged offense was committed or the state of nationality of the accused gave their assent in this sense. By contrast, the United States proposed that the ICC put a person on trial only if *both* these states agreed or if there was an express permission in this sense from the UN Security Council.[27] In respect to the role of the independent prosecutor, the United States contested his or her right to indict, on the basis of any signatory's referral, those parties who had escaped being put on trial in their home countries, either because the domestic courts would not or could not do so, or because such trials would have been susceptible of bias.[28]

The US stubborn holdout for the modification of Article 12 proved the straw that broke the camel's back in Rome. Previously, the Like-Minded Group had accommodated US objections by giving grounds on jurisdiction, excluding first a German proposal for universal jurisdiction, and then circumscribing a South Korean proposal by eliminating the right to prosecute of the state of nationality of the victim or of the state that happened to have the accused in custody. Further concessions were offered on the definition of crimes that the World Court could investigate by excluding aggression or the use of nuclear weapons and land mines, and on matters of procedure by including several US constitutional provisions, such as the prohibition of double jeopardy or the presumption of innocence.[29] After these concessions, Cherif Bassiouni, the chairman of the drafting committee, summed up the mood of the participants: "Most delegations had bent over backward to accommodate the United States...When the delegations began to grapple with such issues as the ICC's jurisdiction and the independent role of the Prosecutor, the US delegation, which had previously secured broad concessions on many points, adopted an unyielding position. Many delegations were dismayed by this display of diplomatic inflexibility."[30]

The reason for US inflexibility was not concern over the loss of sovereignty. Instead, the United States explicitly requested that special dispensation be made in its case because the possibility of other states putting on trial US servicemen would have hindered its unique ability to impose effective international order. The strongest evidence to this effect comes from the leader of the US delegation in Rome, Ambassador David Scheffer. Scheffer invoked the singular international position of the United States, which imposed the peculiar role of guaranteeing international order, and warranted in exchange particular privileges. As he put it: "The United States has special responsibilities and special exposure to political controversy over our actions...We are called upon to act, far more than any other nation." This being the case, he argued that "it is simply and logically untenable to expose the largest deployed military force in the world, stationed across the globe to help maintain international peace and security and to defend US allies and friends to the jurisdiction of a criminal court the US government has not yet joined...No other country, not even our closest military allies, has anywhere near as many troops and military assets deployed globally as does the United States."[31] For this reason, if Article 12 were to be applied, this might have interfered with the US exercise of management: the United States must "be extremely careful," he warned, "that this proposal [Article 12] does not limit the capacity of our armed forces to legitimately operate internationally...that it does not open up opportunities for endless frivolous complaints to be lodged against the United States as a global military power."[32]

Thus, Scheffer's argument was rooted quite overtly in the conviction that the United States deserved prestige above that of all other states because of its dominant status, and that, as such, could not be held accountable to the same standards of behavior as the average state. As Scheffer contended: "The US is not Andorra!...you can't approach this on the model of equality of all states. You have to think in terms of the inequality of some states." The indispensable nation doctrine was also conspicuously mentioned in this line of thought: "There have been times, there will come others, when the US as the sole remaining superpower, the indispensable power, has been and will be in a position to confront butchery head on...But in order for that to be able to happen, American interests are going to have to be protected and American soldiers shielded."[33]

This view of the ICC as both a nuisance to the exercise of effective US leadership and an outright offense to US prestige was not restricted to the administration, but was also prevalent among its Republican critics. As Bush's future speechwriter David Frum argued: "Not the Congress or the American people but a prosecutor perhaps from Bangladesh, and judges drawn (who knows?) from Ghana, Denmark, Jamaica, Ecuador, Oman and Malaysia will decide whether an American president has gone too far in defense of American interests," with the consequence of "sabotage of America's ability to defend itself and to guarantee the world's peace and security."[34]

As a result, the desire to be treated with exceptional deference as well as an angry sense of *lèse-majesté* led the United States to show vehement opposition to the ICC. While Clinton refused to sign the Statute until the last days of his presidency, George W. Bush denounced the whole treaty as flawed and stated he will not seek its ratification. The United States did not simply abstain from the treaty; it also sought to undermine it by seeking to obtain by means of bilateral pressure what it had been unable to get in Rome: the complete immunity for its armed forces from ICC prosecution. Thus, the United States coaxed other states to sign "bilateral immunity agreements," by which these governments promised not to prosecute US troops stationed on their territory. By 2006, one hundred governments had signed BIAs, with the clear understanding under the American Servicemen Protection Act of 2002 that any state that did not sign would be punished by being denied both military and economic assistance by the United States.[35]

MISSILE DEFENSE

The argument that originally led to the creation of the ABM Treaty had been that, since a viable missile defense would remove the possibility of a second strike by a nation under nuclear attack, such an act could spiral an arms race between the superpowers and make first strikes more likely. For this reason, under the ABM Treaty, the United States and the Soviet Union had agreed to deploy a number of missile interceptors not exceeding 200 for each side to only two locations in each country: the nation's capital and an intercontinental ballistic missile (ICBM) site. In 1974 the ABM Treaty was amended to allow each party a single protected site per nation and one hundred interceptors per site, for the United States this being an ICBM site in Grand Forks, North Dakota.

Hence, the United States could not have developed a national missile defense system without contravening the terms of the ABM Treaty. The very concept of a national missile defense was outlawed in Article 1, which read that "each party undertakes not to deploy ABM systems for the defense of the territory of its country and not to provide a base for such a defense." Therefore, a defense covering the entire US territory was prohibited even if the United States had built no additional base, but only established a nationwide system in North Dakota. Furthermore, the United States was forbidden from deploying missiles interceptors in excess of the two hundred, which it was allowed by the treaty.[36]

As a result, the pursuit of NMD became a case of the United States wanting to have its cake and eat it too, by seeking to build a missile defense while keeping in place the ABM, though in an amended version. So, on the one hand, Clinton stressed that "I have no intention of supporting or initiating a unilateral abrogation of the ABM treaty. I will not do that...I have never initiated, encouraged, sanctioned, or blinked at the possibility that we could unilaterally abrogate the ABM treaty."[37] Yet, on the other hand, giving up on NMD was equally unpalatable. The US reason for building a NMD did not consist solely of physical security concerns, even though the ostensible justification was to guard the United States against a missile launch by a rogue state.

However, for a rogue state to contemplate attacking the United States with nuclear weapons delivered by long-range ballistic missiles was suicide, considering the disproportionate size of the US atomic arsenal. Even though the argument was advanced that, unlike the leaders of the Soviet Union, who were interested in their own survival, dictators such as Saddam Hussein or Kim Jong Il were "madder than MAD," that is, so irrational that they could have decided to attack the United States out of pure malevolence, such irrationality was not the motivation emphasized by the Clinton team.[38] Instead, the administration made the case that the rogue states' development of ICBMs would have limited US ability to successfully intervene around the world, and thus would have prevented the United States from exercising its mission as the indispensable nation. James Steinberg, the deputy secretary of defense, summed up this viewpoint: the development of ICBMs and WMD by a rogue state "might have made us more cautious and less likely to take on challenges."[39]

This interpretation is supported by statements from the three Clinton officials most familiar with NMD: Walter Slocombe, undersecretary of defense for Policy; John Holum, the State Department's senior advisor on Arms Control; and the secretary for defense William Cohen. The goal of NMD, argued Slocombe, was "to render less credible any possible attempts by a rogue state adversary to use ballistic missiles armed with unconventional weapons to coerce the United States into holding back from supporting a friend or ally the rogue state threatens with attack."[40] Holum was equally plain: "What the public opinion balance sheet would have been like if Saddam or Milošević could have threatened to use WMD-armed missiles against the United States if we intervened?" Therefore, said Holum, "We have come to the view that such states [rogues] seek missiles and WMD programs primarily as weapons of coercive diplomacy, to complicate US decisionmaking or limit our freedom to act in a crisis."[41] Finally, Cohen in his 2001 Fiscal Year Annual Report to President and Congress made the point that rogue states armed with nonconventional armed missiles "may threaten or use these weapons in an effort to deter or otherwise constrain US power projection capability."[42] Even George W. Bush, once elected, admitted the relevance of these arguments, stating that rogue states "seek weapons of mass destruction to intimidate their neighbors, and to keep the United States and other responsible nations from helping allies and friends in strategic parts of the world."[43]

Thus, the main role of NMD could be explained either by concerns over the safety of vulnerable allies or/and by concerns over maintaining US effectiveness as the international leader. As Lindsay and O'Hanlon put it: "National missile defense, then, could help the United States remain a global superpower," by helping preserve US freedom of action in response to challenges of rogue states.[44] Indeed, US prestige would have suffered were Washington to find itself deterred from intervening by an otherwise weaker rogue state. Both the ally security and the prestige interpretations are tenable and are not necessarily mutually exclusive.

However, there are certain points that strengthen the prestige interpretation. First, one should keep in mind that the United States sought to safeguard its ability to intervene for *both* defensive and offensive purposes. The United States was not solely concerned about the aggression of a rogue state against an ally on the model of the 1990 Iraqi invasion of Kuwait, but also worried about maintaining its ability to coerce recalcitrant rogues. In other words, the US ability to intervene at will covered a much larger spectrum of intervention scenarios than just ensuring the security of allies.

Furthermore, the threat to allies, the threat to US territory, and the security provided by the NMD were all hypothetical. While this does not rule out the ally security argument, it weakens it by showing both that there was an absence of actual danger and that the remedy solution was potentially faulty. The only realistic scenario in which a rogue could attack an ally involved Pyongyang in the late 1990s (particularly given the launch on August 31, 1998 of the Taepodong I missile, the first ever three-stage missile launched by a Third World state). But while North Korea engaged in periodic showdowns with South Korea, its actions could be conceived as efforts to ensure a better bargaining position. Indeed, a recent study estimates that "every DPRK provocation for the past thirty years has been followed within months (on average 5.9 with the United States . . .) by a period of dialogue and negotiations in which the North got something they needed."[45] Of course, one could invoke the cautionary example of the invasion of Kuwait, but one should remember that at that time Kuwait was not a US ally, that Washington had no commitment to defend the emirate, and that the United States had made no serious effort to warn Saddam not to invade. Furthermore, the European allies who were to be the supposed beneficiaries of the NMD complained that they saw no threat from the rogue states to their security.[46]

Besides, no rogue state at the time had either nuclear weapons or the missile technology necessary to attack the continental United States. Initial intelligence estimates argued that rogue states might have been as far away as 15 years before developing ballistic missiles capable of reaching US territory.[47] These estimates were revised to five years based on the conclusions of the Rumsfeld Commission. But the Commission operated on the explicit basis of the assumption that "absence of evidence is not evidence of absence," which represented a worst-case assessment of possible intercontinental ballistic missile developments, rather than an assessment based on available evidence. As Graham writes, the commission "dealt essentially with what *could* happen, not with what was *most likely* to happen."[48]

Additionally, the United States undertook the building of the NMD, with no confirmation that the technology would work. A host of critics contested NMD on technical grounds, either doubting that the concept that was likened to "hitting a bullet with a bullet" was achievable, particularly in the midcourse phase in outer space, or arguing that interceptors could have been easily countered by decoys. The critics could also rely on practical evidence, since by 2002, the system had managed only one hit out of four tests. Even by 2010, the NMD system had succeeded only eight times in fifteen tests. Yet, despite this ambiguous evidence of the system's usefulness, the decision-makers pressed for its deployment.[49]

Finally, although the initial project for the NMD started up modestly under Clinton, with a deployment presumably aimed at defending the United States against a North Korean launch, it soon became clear that it constituted a more ambitious undertaking. Thus, proponents of NMD argued that a deployment against North Korea was not sufficient to guard both coasts, and that another site was needed on the East Coast. Then, the whole system became oriented not only at stopping a rogue state attack, but also at defeating an accidental or an unauthorized missile launch by China and by Russia. And in a subsequent step, the United States extended NMD to its NATO allies, unveiling plans for a multilayered system, aimed to destroy incoming missiles in all stages of flight. To this extent, NMD was much more than a purely defensive endeavor even on behalf of allies, since it went well beyond guaranteeing that the United States would not be held hostage by a rogue state bent on regional hegemony.[50]

Forced to make an immediate decision on deployment if the ABM system was to become operational in 2005, Clinton washed his hands of the entire issue, by declaring on September 1, 2000 that, given that the latest test of the system had been a failure, the final decision was going to be made by the next president. However, the succeeding Bush administration began by signaling its distaste of the ABM Treaty. If for Clinton the treaty was a cornerstone of stability, for Bush it "enshrined the past."[51] The Bush decision-makers tried to convince Russia that since the Cold War was over, there was no longer any reason to preserve the logic of MAD as laid down in the treaty, so the Kremlin should have no qualms to support the US plans for missile defense under an unspecific new framework. The Bush charm offensive, nevertheless, led to the same outcome. At that point, the United States faced the choice of pulling out from the treaty, or continuing to press for an unlikely Russian change of heart. The concern to get things done simply took over. As Bush put it to his advisors in a meeting over NMD while still in the presidential campaign: "My concern isn't with the treaty, my concern is to get a missile defense. And if the treaty doesn't interfere with that concern, then fine, we'll modify it. But if it does, then I don't care about the treaty."[52] Russia unsurprisingly resisted, which led to the announcement in December 2001 that the United States was going to withdraw from the ABM Treaty.

UNSANCTIONED INTERVENTIONS I: FROM IRAQ TO KOSOVO

Obtaining the prior blessing of the UN Security Council before intervening had been a hallmark of the US experiment with restraint in the early 1990s. Ironically, since it had been the Gulf War that inaugurated the pattern, it was a renewed US confrontation with Iraq that led to its unraveling.

The sanctions had come into place through Security Council resolution 687 of 1991, which among other demands also commanded Iraq to destroy its weapons of mass destruction (WMD) programs including their components, delivery systems, production facilities, and production data, and accept long-time monitoring so as not to reconstitute them. Nevertheless, at the time the resolution was passed, most states, including the United States, saw sanctions as a temporary measure. Since Saddam's days in power seemed numbered, sanctions should have been lifted fast, even as soon as in two years.[53] However, Saddam's unanticipated survival meant that sanctions remained in place, with no end in sight. This did not imply a dearth of US efforts to provoke the unseating of Saddam through covert means. But by 1996, as a result of a failed uprising and of the bitter rivalry between Kurdish groups, the United States had been forced to accept that Saddam's fall was not likely to happen, which resulted in an increasing dependence on sanctions as a means to keep him "in a box."[54]

This situation soon produced a duality of views in the Security Council. For France, Russia, and China, the reason to keep sanctions in place was to ensure the destruction of Iraq's unconventional weapons. Conversely, for the US and Britain, the destruction of Iraq's arsenal was only one of the conditions to be satisfied in order for the sanctions to end. The other requirements of resolution 687 would have had to be satisfied as well, and Baghdad might have had to fulfill additional unspecified conditions relating to its "policies and practices," meaning that sanctions should have been maintained for as long as Saddam stayed in power.[55]

The result was a pitched battle over maintaining versus lifting the sanctions, itself hinging upon the outcome of weapon inspections. By 1995, it was clear that the United States, which had staked its prestige on preserving sanctions in place, was on the defensive. In 1994 UNSCOM (the United Nation Special Commission on Weapon Inspections) announced that the inspections were nearing their end, and in March 1995, Russia, France, and China circulated a draft resolution for lifting the sanctions. By July 1995, UNSCOM seemed set to declare an end to sanctions.[56] It took the defection to Jordan of Hussein Kamel, Saddam's son-in-law and the person in charge of unconventional programs, for Iraq to admit having "found" half a million pages referring to missiles, chemical, and biological weapons—and consequently for sanctions to hang on by a thread.[57] But, after this respite, the problem of lifting them resurfaced by the end of 1997, compounded this time by repeated showdowns between Iraq and weapon inspectors. These crises, in which Baghdad barred or restricted access to sites suspected of harboring various components of the unconventional weapon programs, were purposely designed to weaken the inspections process to the point where UNSCOM could issue a statement confirming that all of Iraq's weapons had been destroyed. On each showdown, Iraq asked for an end of sanctions, threatening to end cooperation with UNSCOM, but ultimately settled for revised rules of inspections, which made it harder to ascertain that Iraq had complied.[58] Hence, if the United States did not react to Iraq's pressure tactics, the weapons inspections process would have been irreparably undermined, with the eventual collapse of the sanctions.

Saddam staying in power was embarrassing for the United States, but to contemplate the prospect of a diplomatic defeat that would have removed sanctions would have been an even worse humiliation. This is why Saddam's defiance could not be allowed to go unpunished. Yet, the United States could not go ahead and punish Saddam as long as he was employing skillfully a strategy of defying Washington and then hiding behind his French, Russian, and Chinese protectors. To illustrate a fairly common pattern, consider the crisis of January 1998.

After Iraq barred access to weapon inspectors, the United States warned that it could not rule out the use of force. In reply, Russia made it clear in a phone call between Russian Foreign Minister Yevgeny Primakov and Albright that the Kremlin was opposed to the use of force. While France and Russia again condemned Iraq's resistance to inspections, they also wanted to become more involved in the control of Iraq's weapons. China backed this proposal by arguing that the UNSCOM teams should be more balanced between the five permanent members; and on January 22, Moscow and Beijing urged the

Security Council to acknowledge that Iraq had fulfilled its obligation to terminate its nuclear weapons program. Moscow then dispatched a special envoy to Baghdad. On February 5, just as the United States sent a third air carrier battle group to the Gulf to supplement its presence there, China repeated its opposition to force and France stated it would not participate in any military action against Iraq. The Russian position was even more radical. On February 4, Russia's President Boris Yeltsin warned that the US actions in the crisis could provoke a world war. This rhetoric was supplemented on February 12 by a warning from Russia's Minister of Defense Igor Sergeyev that strikes could cause untold damage to the military relation between Moscow and Washington. To this, the United States replied that Russia's "nyet" did not mean "no" for the United States and that Iraq could be hit repeatedly until it allowed access to the inspectors. On cue, Moscow and Paris sent their foreign ministers to Baghdad and pressed the UN Secretary General to travel to Baghdad to try to persuade Saddam. The visit by Annan resulted in the announcement of a deal on February 23, which Moscow immediately endorsed. The new agreement between Annan and Saddam involved Iraq's acceptance of the requirement for full, unconditional, and unrestricted cooperation with UNSCOM, but also reaffirmed the need to respect the sovereignty and territorial integrity of Iraq and established that the inspection teams that were to conduct the searches were to be specially appointed and had to include diplomats from states other than the United States.[59] In August, Saddam again barred access to inspectors.

Basically, in each instance, Iraq was escaping punishment and obtaining rewards in terms of inspections procedure. Thus, the Security Council's mandatory assent had become a major impediment to the successful exercise of US leadership. Cunning foes understood well that by playing the United States and its partners against each other, they could have escaped retaliation. In less than a year the United States faced four showdowns with Iraq. Particularly damaging was the November 1998 crisis, when the order of bombing was given twice on successive days and had to be countermanded hastily on both occasions, with the planes already in the air because of to Franco-Russian brokered agreements.[60] Moreover, sanctions seemed on the point of finally crumbling—in December 1998 UNSCOM announced that the whole process could have been wrapped up in six weeks.[61]

By the time of the fifth such crisis in December 1998, the US decision-makers were at the end of their tether. Iraq had turned out into an essential test of US leadership. Prestige required action. As Cohen put it to Clinton: "A failure to act now will eradicate our credibility. Our word is at stake. If we don't carry it out, we're going to be tested in the future."[62] The same argument was employed by Clinton in his message justifying the strikes—Iraq had to be attacked in order to safeguard sanctions; so as to show that the international community led by the United States had not lost its will; and because, "If we turn our back on his defiance, the credibility of US power as a check against Saddam will be destroyed."[63] In the process, the Security Council endorsement became a necessary casualty, even though the United States claimed awkwardly, in the absence of an explicit resolution, legitimacy from the resolution 687 of 1991.[64] Yet, in the four-day bombing campaign of Iraq, codified as Operation Desert Fox, the United States had to take on Saddam with a measly party compared to the grand coalition of 1991—only Great Britain contributed planes. Although a dozen other states backed the United States (notably Germany, Japan, Canada, and Saudi Arabia), China, Russia, and France criticized the intervention. That is to say that Operation Desert Fox marked an evolution of US foreign policy in the direction of unilateralism.

Just as the Iraq crises were unfolding, Milošević was following a similar pattern of noncompliance followed by a last-minute retreat in Kosovo. Again, Russia was providing Belgrade with diplomatic cover: For instance, when in October 1998, the United States threatened Yugoslavia, Yeltsin swiftly sent his foreign and defense ministers to Belgrade where they promptly announced a deal with Milošević. At the same time, Yeltsin personally warned Clinton that the use of force against Yugoslavia was "inadmissible and forbidden."[65] With the benefit of its hard-earned experience over Iraq, the Clinton administration thus decided to sidestep the UN entirely, and instead seek an alternative mandate from NATO, a good example of coalition by posse, recruited for the purpose of going after Milošević, even though, as seen in chapter four, the posse's members had little idea of the full implications of their commitment. This time around, the United States gave up on any pretense that the intervention had been sanctioned by previous resolutions, thus sending a signal that the UN seal of approval was no longer a requirement for intervention.[66] On the plus side, using NATO for diplomatic cover was more manageable than waiting in limbo for unlikely Russian and Chinese consent, and allowed the use of force with minimum delays. Moreover, the United States kept tight control over the intervention, as it provided the bulk of the forces employed against Yugoslavia (740 aircraft compared to 300 allied planes), did most of the fighting, and had military command over the operation. Even though the United States had to secure the nominal acceptance of NATO members for each target (a process that did not always run smoothly), it chose the targets.[67] Hence, the United States was calling in the shots under the new coalition model.

Unsanctioned Interventions II: Iraq Again

Nevertheless, even the formula of a NATO posse proved too restrictive for the George W. Bush presidency. War by coalition still implied agreement among the NATO members on the objectives to be accomplished and tactics to be employed. In the case of Kosovo, the United States often found out that other countries (principally France) opposed its choices by advocating a pause in the bombing campaign, by arguing for conducting bombing only in Kosovo, and by vetoing attacks against bridges and communication centers.[68]

This is why when NATO for the first time in its 52-year history invoked Article 5 in the aftermath of the September 11 attacks, the US response was lukewarm. The same day, Undersecretary of Defense Paul Wolfowitz stated that "if we need collective action we will ask for it. We don't anticipate that at the moment."[69] The United States declined not only NATO's support, but also a French offer to contribute troops to Afghanistan, specifically stating that it was not interested in waging another war by committee. Instead of paying attention to its European allies, the United States recruited its "posse" only from the countries logistically relevant to the operation. Accordingly, before the launching of the attack against the Taliban, Rumsfeld could be found not in Paris or Berlin, but on a tour of Egypt, Saudi Arabia, Oman, Pakistan, and Uzbekistan.[70]

This snub came on the heels of increasing US reliance on *fait accompli* in relation not only to the ICC and the ABM, but also in the case of the Kyōtō protocol on global warming, the Comprehensive Test Ban Treaty, the Chemical Weapons Convention, and the Small Arms Treaty, as well as of its intransigent position that other states should have made up their minds whether they were "either with us or with the terrorists" in the war on terror. This unilateralist pattern alarmed France, Germany, Russia, and China. Iraq was therefore for these powers an occasion to reverse the unilateralist trend by sending the United States a signal that they were not entities whose concerns could be dismissed summarily.[71] Hence they insisted that only the UN Security Council, on which they were represented, was allowed to decide when force should have been used.

Meanwhile, the perspective of the United States was diametrically different. On account of its position as the dominant power, the United States did not need to seek a UN resolution over Iraq. The United States was similarly uninterested in a resumption of inspections in Iraq, because as Vice President Dick Cheney put it in August 2002, "A return of inspectors would provide no assurance whatsoever. A return of inspectors would provide no assurance whatsoever of his [Saddam Hussein's] compliance with U.N. resolutions."[72] Besides, the United States had made up its mind to invade, having already deployed 140,000 troops in the Middle East by spring 2003. To this extent, consulting the UN was regarded as a harmless courtesy, but one in which endorsement was clearly expected at the end. The decision to go back to the UN was not therefore a reversal of unilateralism in US foreign policy. Bush made clear that the choices open to the UN were to back the US position or condemn itself to irrelevance: "All the world now faces a test and the United Nations a difficult and defining moment...are Security Council resolutions to be honored and enforced or cast aside without consequence? Will the United Nations serve the purpose of its founding or will it be irrelevant?"[73]

Once inspections resumed, the Bush decision-makers, as well as a large segment of American public opinion, were increasingly upset by what they perceived to be temporizing tactics from the weapon inspectors, and by the refusal of France and Germany to authorize the use of force in Iraq. Temporization was unacceptable for the United States, since the timetable for military action against Iraq required a start of fighting before the summer heat set in. Consequently, the Bush administration launched a full-blown campaign on the personal credibility of weapons inspectors' leaders Hans Blix and Mohammed ElBaradei, which culminated with the declaration of Cheney that "I think Mr. ElBaradei frankly is wrong...and I think that if you look at the track record of the International Atomic Energy Agency... especially where Iraq is concerned, they have consistently underestimated or missed what it was Saddam was doing. I don't have any reason to believe they are any more valid this time than they've been in the past."[74] Hence, at the time Bush issued an ultimatum to Iraq on March 17, 2003, weapon inspections were still taking place on the ground in Iraq. The inspectors had to be hastily evacuated so bombing could start.[75]

A similar indignant US reaction was shown against France and Germany. As US allies, Paris and Berlin were expected to eventually fall into line. Their refusal to offer support was interpreted as insolence by claiming an unwarranted equality with the dominant United States, the state that guaranteed their security. The US decision-makers' anger was also enhanced by their discovery that France and Germany were not only unsubordinated, but also had marshaled resistance against the US initiative for a second resolution in the Security Council, which was seen as evidence of spite: frustrating US wishes on purpose. Thus, the United States retaliated with ostracism and petty insults of its own.[76] Rumsfeld and National Security Advisor Condoleezza Rice complained that relations with Germany had been "poisoned." Rumsfeld went so far as to compare Germany's lack of support to the recalcitrant foreign policy of Cuba and Libya, and exited the room at a Warsaw NATO reunion when his German counterpart spoke. While he denied that that gesture was an intentional snub, Rumsfeld warned Germany that if in a hole, it should stop digging. President Bush refused to speak to German Chancellor Gerhard Schröder, and turned his back on him in a summit meeting. In February 2003, Rumsfeld dismissively referred to France and Germany as "old Europe," and French officials visiting Washington were met with a cold shoulder, if not with straight rudeness.[77] On one occasion, Undersecretary of Defense Paul Wolfowitz warned a French envoy that not even Chirac's office in the Élysée Palace was safe from Iraqi chemical weapons. French and German efforts to resist a US proposal at NATO for defending Turkey from a presumptive Iraqi attack were catalogued in Washington as "shameful," "inexcusable," and "disgusting." Finally, in a gesture reminiscent of the World War I ban on the word "sauerkraut," in favor of "liberty cabbage," the House of Representatives expressed its denunciation of all things French by changing the cafeteria menu from "French fries" and "French toast" to the more patriotically sounding "freedom fries" and "freedom toast."[78] While some of these reactions may seem in retrospect blown out of proportion or, indeed, ridiculous, they are indicative of an irate frame of mind in which the US sense of rightful prestige had been challenged by French, German, and UN offenses. To this extent, unilateralism was not only a way for the United States to regain its freedom of action, but also to punish the perceived offenders by inflicting upon them commensurate humiliation.

By contrast with this interpretation, for structuralism, unilateralism was the consequence of US disproportionate strength; for exceptionalism, it was the latest manifestation of a venerable tradition of avoiding foreign entanglements; and for revisionism, it represented another means to advance the Open Door.

UNILATERALISM OF STRENGTH?

Structuralism may receive partial confirmation in the case of the NMD, which might have been compatible with ensuring the security of US allies. However, physical security concerns do not explain the US opposition to the ICC, or the conduct of interventions in the absence of sanction from the UN Security Council.

Moreover, for structuralism, the more power a state enjoys, the less it is likely to have to depend on others, as others come to depend on it against their will. Consequently, a dominant state such as the United States is not likely to endorse multilateralism, simply because it does not require the assistance of other states to succeed in its political endeavors.[79] Structuralism does not suggest that the United States should not cooperate under any circumstances with weaker states, but rather that the cooperative relation created will reflect the power disparities underlying it, working to the advantage of the stronger polity. To quote Mearsheimer, "The most powerful states in the system create and shape institutions so that they can maintain their share of world power, or even increase it. In this view, institutions are 'arenas for acting out power relationships.'"[80] For structuralism, by being substantially more powerful than other states, the United States is able to proceed without their blessing. To quote Boot, "Any nation with so much power will always be tempted to go it alone. Power breeds unilateralism. It is as simple as that."[81] In the same vein, for Kagan, the policy of choice of strong states has been always to act without considering or sparing the trodden feelings or interests of weaker polities. "The facile assertion that the United States cannot 'go it alone' is more a hopeful platitude than a description of reality. The problem today, if it is a problem, is that the United States can 'go it alone,' and it is hardly surprising that the American superpower should wish to preserve its ability to do so." By implication, multilateralism represents the strategy employed by the weak (the Europeans) in order to conserve a semblance of influence on the actions of the dominant United States.[82]

Yet, this argument runs into a key difficulty: structuralism treats different types of unilateralism indistinctly. Unilateralism comes in many shapes and forms. To exemplify, unilateralism is different when practiced by isolationists, such as a weak or an ideological pariah state, and when implemented by a nearly omnipotent hegemon such as the Roman Empire. In the former case, the state in question minimizes cooperation, either so as not to become the target or the pawn of stronger polities or/and so as to keep its peculiar ideology unadulterated. In the latter case, the hegemon does not need to consult with others because it knows its decisions will be obeyed with minimal opposition.

This chapter argues that the unilateralism of the United States at the cusp of the millennium reveals a third intermediary type: that of a dominant power that resorts to unilateralism as its fallback option.[83] The United States did not choose unilateralism because it was *too powerful*, but rather because it was not powerful *enough* to impose its point of view by persuasion or coercion on the dissenters. In the context of international institutions, differences in capabilities do not matter as long as every state possesses an equally weighing vote. Hence, regardless of its many other capabilities, for the purposes of institutional decision-making, US power does not necessarily exceed that of other institution members—whether the framework is that of the Security Council, of UN committees, or of NATO. Thus, the only way left for the United States to ensure it will prevail fully in every political context is to cut itself loose from the institutional framework. However, this outcome is not evidence of strength, but rather of angry frustration. Therefore, unilateralism was the only way left for the United States to reassert its prestige as well as to punish its opponents for their obstinacy.[84]

This contravenes the structuralist expectation that institutional outcomes reflect power relations. Had structuralism been right, most states would have supported the United States because they had nothing to gain and everything to lose from mounting a futile resistance against the most powerful state in the system. As Krauthammer put it: "Countries will cooperate with us, first, out of their own self-interest and, second, out of the need and desire to cultivate good relations with the world's superpower."[85] But this confident forecast proved patently wrong. In the cases of the ICC, the ABM Treaty, and the use of force in Iraq and Kosovo, the United States first attempted to shape the decisions taken so as to promote its agenda, but ended up being defeated each time. It was only in the aftermath of these failures that Washington walked away from cooperation.[86]

In the case of the ICC talks, US efforts to persuade other states proved unsuccessful, even though the United States exerted a considerable amount of pressure beyond closed doors, including threatening revising security ties to the chief dissenters.[87] Another US proposal that would have allowed the United States to accept for ten years only those parts of the Statute that it found unobjectionable with the possibility of renewal, was equally rejected by 113 countries, with only China and six other nations endorsing US views. Placed on the defensive, the United States next attempted a last-ditch effort to convince the other participants not to sign the Statute. The United States ended up by suffering what a commentator referred to as "the most serious diplomatic defeat since the end of the Cold War": in the final tally, 120 countries voted in Rome to sign the statute, 21 abstained, and only 6 voted against, placing the United States and Israel in the somewhat surprising company of China, Iraq, Libya, Yemen, and Qatar.[88]

Regarding the revision of the ABM, the United States would have preferred to get Russia's consent. Yet, in practice, it soon became clear that Russia would not be persuaded by US entreaties to be allowed to deploy additional interceptors without additional concessions. The United States could have offered inducements to Russia to sweeten the pill of NMD, such as slashing its own nuclear forces, renouncing further deployments beyond Alaska, swapping the allowed missile site from North Dakota to Alaska, or by giving substance to a Russian proposal for a joint boost-phase system. But in all these areas, the United States also rejected compromise. The joint chiefs of staff pronounced themselves against any reduction in nuclear forces both in May and in August 2000. The joint defense proposal was rejected since it would have implied deploying the system either on Russian territory or on Russian-friendly territory, which would have denied the United States the ability to deal with accidental Russian or Chinese launches, an additional goal of NMD. The United States was also reluctant to accept limitations of NMD, such as base-swapping or the rejection of additional deployments.[89]

To solve this conundrum, the United States sought to bring in the European allies so as to corner Russia, only to discover to its dismay that it was the one isolated. The NATO countries opposed the United States on the grounds that the ICBM threat from rogue states was nonexistent, that NMD was encouraging an arms race with Russia and China, and that NMD risked decoupling the United States from European security. The opposition to the United States went even further—France cosponsored together with Russia and China a UN General Assembly resolution condemning NMD as harmful to international stability. The resolution was endorsed in December 1999, by 80 votes to 6, with 64 countries abstaining. As a result, the US foreign policy completed a full circle, by now counting on Russian assent to sell NMD to the Europeans.[90] Under both Clinton and Bush, the United States adopted a unilateralist tactic of "table and stick" approach (put the proposal on the table and stick to it), hoping Russia would accept the inevitable. Yet this proved wishful thinking, as the declarations of Russian defense and foreign policy officials made it clear that in their view the development of NMD constituted "a cure worse than the disease." It was only after resigning themselves that Russia's opposition to the NMD was impossible to overcome that the US decision-makers announced their withdrawal from the ABM Treaty in December 2001.[91]

In respect to unsanctioned interventions against Iraq and Yugoslavia in 1998–1999, the Clinton administration met with a steady resistance from its fellow Security Council members. While France, Russia, and China were open to passing resolutions, such as resolutions 1154 of February 1998 and 1205 of November 1998, which warned Iraq of severe consequences for noncompliance, they resisted adamantly formulations similar to the celebrated "all necessary means" resolution 678. Moreover, the three countries also resisted any suggestion that the warning resolutions should have been interpreted as sufficient in conferring an automatic go-ahead for military action against Iraq, insisting that an explicit resolution (to which of course they were opposed) was needed. The case of Yugoslavia was not much different, except that the relevant resolutions 1199 of September 1998 and 1203 of October 1998 were even weaker-worded.[92] Thus, the United States was prevented four times each in Iraq in between 1997 and 1998 and in Yugoslavia in between 1998 and 1999, from enacting its threats.

The Bush administration did not fare any better in regard to Iraq in 2002–2003, even though, unlike its predecessor, it took care to make it clear that, disagreement or not, war was inevitable. The United States ran into precisely the same obstacle. France, Russia, and China, joined this time around by Germany, demanded two distinct resolutions, the first on the resumption of weapon inspections, and the second, on an eventual use of force against Iraq, if found in noncompliance. While the United States obtained a unanimous decision on the first resolution (resolution 1441), which again warned Iraq of "serious consequences," the second one proved predictably problematic, due to resistance orchestrated by France and its supporters, who argued that more time was needed for inspections. Hence, until mid-February 2003, the Bush officials argued that the United States had already the authority to act against Iraq from resolution 1441, despite the opposition in the Security Council to this view. It was only British insistence that a second resolution should be sought after all that pushed the United States on a renewed path of confrontation, despite the warning from France that it might not get a majority or might even face a French veto. Even if France had not killed the resolution draft by pledging a veto, the United States could not rely on even a silent majority for its proposal. Out of the other 14 members of the Security Council, only Britain, Spain, and Bulgaria endorsed plainly the US viewpoint; on the side of Paris, Moscow, and Beijing stood Canada, Mexico, and Germany, while Angola, Chile, Guinea, and Cameroon were leaning toward the French position. Hence, while the United States might have been so powerful as to create a *fait accompli*, its resort to unilateralism was an admission of its actual powerlessness to sway the dissenters.[93] In this sense, structuralism fails as an explanation of US unilateralism, because it grounds it in overwhelming strength, rather than in embarrassment and anger at being unable to rally behind it the opinion of the international community.

A PROUD TRADITION OF UNILATERALISM?

For exceptionalism, the United States has always been unilateralist at heart. US foreign policy from 1776 to 1941 may have been mislabeled as isolationism, while actually representing unilateralism.[94] Despite the multiplication of US international commitments since World War Two, it should be noted that the United States still refuses to carry them out unless they fully embody its values and interests. As Schlesinger writes: "Unilateralism? There is no older American tradition in the conduct of foreign affairs…The isolationist impulse has risen from the grave in what has always been its essential programme—unilateralism." Similarly, Lieven traces the origins of the present unilateralism to "a belief in America as a unique city on a hill…since it forms part of the view that if the United States really has no choice at all but to involve itself with disgusting and inferior foreigners, it must absolutely control the process and must under no circumstance subject itself to foreign control or even advice."[95]

Yet, there are significant differences between the US unilateralism of yore and its more recent manifestation. If the United States was unilateralist prior to 1941, it was also adverse to foreign interventionism, particularly to efforts to spread US values around the world. As John Quincy Adams underlined in 1821, the United States should not have gone abroad so as to destroy monsters, which should have prohibited interventions in Iraq and Kosovo. The problem, therefore, is that if Clinton and Bush really had been driven by the unilateralism of yore they would have also scaled down, not up, commitments abroad, as well as curtailed interventionism.[96]

The root of the error is that, like structuralists, exceptionalists conflate several forms of unilateralism under a single category. The unilateralism of yore unmistakably belonged to the covenanted variety, which argued that the fewer political interactions between the United States and the world, the lesser the risk that the US principles of government will be compromised.[97] No such qualms animated the supporters of unilateralism in the Clinton and the Bush administrations, who worried more about preserving Washington's prestige as the indispensable nation.

This is not to say that genuine supporters of the unilateralism of yore were nonexistent on the American political scene: they could be found in the person of Pat Buchanan, and in the ranks of Newt Gingrich's Contract Republicans, who asked for a pullout of the US from current engagements.[98] But neither of these groups was dominant in the Clinton and the Bush presidencies. Although Clinton was forced to coexist with a Republican-dominated Congress since 1994, which pressured the adoption of unilateralist measures, including NMD and the rejection of the ICC, the administration successfully resisted Congress pressure against NAFTA, a bailout for Mexico, relations with China, intervention in Haiti, Bosnia, Iraq, and Kosovo, and signing the Kyōtō Protocol. Moreover, Clinton rejected a 1998 letter signed by Republican leaders claiming that the ABM Treaty was null and void because it had been concluded with the Soviet Union not with Russia.[99] As for Bush, by the time he took office most prominent Contract Republicans had already lost their seats. Moreover, the Bush administration was composed of hawkish conservatives such as Rumsfeld and Cheney, as well as of realists, such as Powell and Rice, who were committed to assertiveness, and of neoconservatives, who had developed their foreign policy agenda of primacy as an alternative to Contract Republicanism.[100]

Moreover, in the eighteenth and throughout much of the nineteenth centuries, the United States had to be cautious, since it was both weaker than the European powers of the day, and the sole liberal democracy in a world of authoritarian monarchies. As George Washington and Alexander Hamilton understood, weak states are all too frequently exposed to abuse by stronger political and military entities. Staying clear of such connections was wise not only at for the purpose of preserving the purity of US democracy, but also for the correlated aim of ensuring the state's survival. To quote George Washington's Farewell Address: "Europe has a set of primary interests, which to us, have none or a very remote relation . . . Hence therefore it must be unwise in us to implicate ourselves, by artificial ties, in the ordinary vicissitude of her politics, or the ordinary combinations and collisions of her friendships or enmities."[101] But if this was the case in the times of Washington and Adams, the United States could not plead such vulnerability when the occupants of the White House were Clinton and George W. Bush. Even Washington had anticipated the possibility of the United States growing so powerful that it could afford to dispense with caution: "The time may well come when we choose our own policy."[102] Therefore, under the propitious circumstances of the post–Cold War, no reason was present for the United States to play the part of a voluntary international recluse. Under Clinton and George W. Bush, the United States was not afraid that it was going to be used as a pawn by other powers, but rather resented their unwillingness to serve as its docile chess pieces.

OPEN DOOR INTERESTS?

Revisionism argues that in order to be able to foster and maintain openness in the world, the United States has to remain unconstrained. The Open Door is propped not only by US propaganda or dollars, but also by the naked threat of military coercion. It is hence natural for the United States to resist arms control treaties or arrangements that limit or raise questions as to the legitimacy of this coercive capacity. If the United States were to lose its military edge, it would also jeopardize its ability to advance the agenda of the Open Door. Hence, the imperatives of promoting openness, maintaining US preeminence in strategic areas, and conserving global military supremacy in perpetuity are mutually reinforcing.[103]

However, revisionism's interpretation of unilateralism is contradicted by the egregious fact that the agreements the United States rejected were the results of the United States' own efforts. It was the United States that had pushed for the creation of a permanent international court to prosecute war crimes and crimes against humanity, after having experimented earlier in the decade with ad hoc tribunals for the former Yugoslavia and Rwanda.[104] Similarly, the United States had strong stakes in the ABM as "a cornerstone of US security." The United States had in fact renegotiated the treaty in 1997 with Russia, in order to differentiate between long-range forbidden missiles and shorter-range weapons (under 3,500 kilometers), which were allowed.[105] Furthermore, the United States was the state that had inaugurated in the context of the Gulf War of 1990–1991 the cooperative formula of the Security Council-sanctioned coalition as the means to address threats to global or regional peace and security.

There is little doubt that the ICC, the ABM Treaty, and the Security Council-sanctioned military missions would have contributed substantially toward enhancing international openness. The United States would have found it easier by adhering to these measures to put misbehaviors on trial, to limit dangerous nuclear proliferation, and to isolate and punish recalcitrant states. Moreover, these endeavors would also have had a public relations role in showcasing the United States as a benevolent hegemon, and would have therefore minimized resistance to what revisionists believe is the US informal empire. Accordingly, viewed from an Open Door perspective, the recent US unilateralism appears as remarkably short-sighted and self-defeating, resulting in a less open environment as well as in increased resentment against the United States.

Chapter Conclusion

The US choice for an assertive policy characterized by unilateralism was motivated by considerations of prestige. If the United States was truly the "indispensable nation," then it could not allow free-riding states to obstruct its course of action and hence expose it as an ineffective leader. Moreover, as the indispensable nation, the United States believed it was entitled to a greater degree of respect than was conferred upon an average state. Finally, the United States sought to punish those states that frustrated its initiatives or/and refused to confer it prestige commensurate to its claims. The problem was that recourse to unilateralism, instead of forcing increased cooperation, produced further dissension, which, in turn, bred more unilateralism. As a result, US foreign policy became more assertive.

6

THE UNITED STATES SUPREME: THE INVASION OF IRAQ

The US decision to invade Iraq was the result of the congruence in the aftermath of the September 11 attacks between the neoconservative movement that provided the second tier of decision-makers, the Bush administration, and the central hawkish conservative players in the cabinet, especially Secretary of Defense Donald Rumsfeld and Vice President Dick Cheney.[1] The chief consideration was maintaining US prestige as a strong international leader.

This is not to suggest that the invasion of Iraq was the result of a conspiracy perpetuated by neoconservatives. This view is manifestly wrong, for several reasons.[2] Neoconservatives never controlled the principal functions in the administration: the most senior neoconservative figure was Paul Wolfowitz, the number two at the Pentagon. Before September 11, the neoconservatives did not meet with any success in promoting their agenda of regime change in Iraq, and, moreover, the formula that they advocated, which was seizing control of an enclave in Southern Iraq and developing there the forces of the Iraqi opposition, was not adopted. The administration also rejected the neoconservative candidate to succeed Saddam, the Iraq National Congress leader Ahmed Chalabi.[3] Finally, suspecting, based on his campaign declaration in favor of a "humble foreign policy" and his reliance on Condoleezza Rice, a known protégé of Brent Scowcroft, that Bush was going to follow the same realist precepts in foreign policy as his father did, the neoconservatives had openly backed as president his Republican counter-candidate John McCain.[4] Hence, there is little substantial evidence attesting to a neoconservative takeover of the Bush administration.

Yet, neoconservatives played a significant part in the invasion of Iraq, not directly, but through their ability to provide a ready-made intellectual framework justifying Saddam's elimination from power.[5] The administration simply subscribed to this view, while disagreeing on tactics such as the enclave plan, nation-building, or the imposition of a Chalabi government. In this sense, the relation between neoconservatives and the Bush administration might be seen as an alliance determined by common concerns over prestige, in which the neoconservatives played the role of the junior partner. Thus, regime change was the product of the eventual triumph, not of the neoconservatives themselves, but of their view of the world, which was especially emphatic on the need to castigate challengers so as to reaffirm US prestige. Therefore, it becomes significant to address how and why the neoconservative views emerged, developed, and ultimately came to define US foreign policy in the aftermath of September 11.

The Neoconservative Call for Greatness

For the neoconservatives, prestige constituted the raison d'être of the reinvented movement in the late 1990s. According to neoconservatives, US dominance is supported by two fundamental pillars: "military supremacy" and "moral confidence." But while the US already controlled the most powerful military in the world, so it was just a question of preserving this lead relative to would-be competitors, "moral confidence," however, was in short supply in Clinton's "tepid times."[6] The result of this alleged absence of vision was that "the 1990s were a squandered decade…The United States held a position unmatched since Rome…The great promise of the post–Cold War era, however, began to dim almost immediately."[7] Thus, the peril came principally from the erosion of the US dominant rank as a consequence of "the declining military strength, flagging will and confusion about our role in the world."[8]

Accordingly, for neoconservatives, the United States, under the first president Bush and particularly under Clinton, had exhibited a dangerous lack of will in playing its assigned part as the dominant power by tolerating the political survival of Saddam and Milošević, by reducing instead of increasing defense expenditures, by engaging instead of containing dictators, and by placing a misguided faith in multilateralism. As Kristol put it: "The [main] danger is American withdrawal, American timidity, American slowness…The danger is not that we're going to do too much. The danger is that we're going to do too little."[9] Prestige was slipping away because, despite its superior status, the United States tolerated brazen offenses from lower-ranked recalcitrant and free-riding challengers. As Wolfowitz argued while

criticizing Clinton's foreign policy, the US global leadership should
have consisted in making sure that "your friends will be protected
and taken care of, that your enemies will be punished, and that those
who refuse to support you will live to regret having done so."[10]

The neoconservatives' solution for remedying this situation
was making sure that the United States not only stayed as the
international number one, but also acted as a proper number one. As
Kagan and Kristol harangued: "The appropriate goal of American
foreign policy is to preserve...hegemony as far in to the future as
possible," and, furthermore, "to preserve and extend an international
order that is in accord with both our interests and our principles."[11]
This desideratum was to be achieved through the enactment of three
measures. First, the United States should have ensured its continued
unrivalled military supremacy by spending more on its armed forces
than any potential rival. The neoconservatives thus contended, echo-
ing the 1992 DPG, that the United States should be able to fight off
not just rogue states, but also if need be the other great powers, and
possibly even coalitions of great powers. Accordingly, the neoconservatives called for a massive 25 percent increase in spending from
$70 billion to $95 billion per year for the army, from $83 billion to
$115 billion for the air force, and from $91 billion to $115 billion
for the Navy and the Marines.[12] Second, the United States should
have restored "a sense of the heroic" and "a moral clarity" to its
foreign policy, by educating Americans to accept the United States'
proper role as global leader and, implicitly, to put up with the financial and military costs of US dominance. Third, and most important, the United States should have abandoned the policy of live and
let live with recalcitrant challengers, favoring them instead of root-
ing them out. As Kristol and Kagan put it: "Because America has
the capacity to contain or destroy many of the world's monsters...
and because the responsibility for the peace and security of the international order rests so heavily on its shoulders, a policy of sitting
atop a hill and leading by example becomes in practice a policy of
cowardice and dishonor."[13] Therefore, the United States should have
followed the precise opposite of Adams' advice: seek out the monsters and prevent them from inflicting further harm to world order,
and implicitly to US prestige as a successful global leader. As Kristol
and Kaplan warned, allowing "successful challenges to American
power will invariably weaken America's created norms," with potential catastrophic consequences soon to reach US shores.[14] To avoid
this outcome, the United States should have punished offenses so
soundly as to send the unambiguous message to any would-be rival

or challenger in Europe, Asia, and the Middle East: "Don't even think about it." Furthermore, the neoconservatives argued that the United States did not require the assent of other states, because while a policeman gets assignments from a higher authority, in international affairs there was no higher authority than the United States.[15] To sum up, the neoconservative agenda was designed to achieve a position for the United States in which its claim to superior prestige would have become prohibitively costly to contest by other actors, whether foes or friends.

These were not just grandiose words. In the summer of 1997, Kagan and Kristol founded the PNAC (Project for the New American Century)—a pressure group reuniting analysts, politicians, and opinion leaders. The PNAC was not a strictly neoconservative enterprise: the list of founding members comprised mainstream conservatives such as Cheney, Rumsfeld, and Jebb Bush. Yet, the PNAC was predicated on the distinct neoconservative tenets that the Clinton administration had been squandering away US prestige, and that the best way to address the mounting word's problems was to reassert US leadership. The PNAC's statement of principles in fact begins with the words: "American foreign and defense policy is adrift. We aim to change this. We aim to make the case and rally support for American global leadership," and concludes by arguing that such a leadership-oriented policy is "necessary if the United States is to build on the successes of this past century and to ensure our security and our greatness in the next." In practice, this meant lobbying in favor of increased defense budgets and eliminating the most outstanding challengers. Topping the list was Saddam Hussein.[16]

Getting rid of Saddam became for the PNAC the equivalent of *delendo est Carthago* for Cato the Elder. From 1997 to 2001, the PNAC pursued an obsessive campaign for regime change in Baghdad, by means of articles, testimony to Congress, and lobbying decision-makers. Iraq took the center stage because it epitomized for the PNAC everything that was wrong with Clinton's foreign policy, as the United States vainly relied on multilateral sanctions to keep the Iraqi regime bottled up, and failed to punish decisively a defiant Saddam.[17] Consequently, as the PNAC put it in an open letter to Clinton on the subject of regime change in Iraq, since "the current policy…is dangerously inadequate," what was needed was "a willingness to undertake military action as diplomacy is clearly failing. In the long term, it means removing Saddam and his regime from power."[18] The means to do this was force, since "only the substantial use of military force could prove that the United States is serious."[19]

This was more a debate about means than ends: the Clinton administration wanted just as much as the PNAC to see Saddam ousted, but it relied on sanctions rather than on force. While the subject of Iraq was breeched in the first cabinet meetings of the George W. Bush administration, the new presidency did not arrive at any decision other than to stick to the policy it inherited from Clinton. As a result, the PNAC did not make any headway in prompting large-scale military action against Iraq even after Bush had come into office. The September 11 attacks, however, provided the neoconservatives with the opportunity to air again their arguments to a far more receptive audience.

SEPTEMBER 11: HUMILIATION, ANGER, AND REASSERTING AMERICA'S PRESTIGE

The answer to why neoconservatives' ideas on the need to effect regime change caught on has to do with the trauma caused by September 11. The terrorist attacks had been resented as a commensurable offense, and triggered an angry desire for exerting retribution. This was fertile ground for an assertive policy predicated on restoring US prestige by punishing recalcitrant challengers.

With the advantage of hindsight on the course of the war on terror, it is all too easy to minimize the traumatic toll September 11 exerted at the time on the psyche of US decision-makers and of the American public. The attacks represented not only the largest-scale terrorist attack in history, but also the most significant loss of American life in combat on US territory since the Civil War. Even Pearl Harbor paled by comparison: it resulted in fewer casualties, 2,403 killed compared to an eventual toll of 2,973, the bulk of the casualties consisted of military rather than civilians (only 68 civilians were killed at Pearl Harbor), and the 1941 attack did not take place in the continental United States.[20] Following September 11, the United States shut down its borders, the National Guard was called in New York and Washington, and two air carrier groups were deployed in New York's harbor—measures that showed that the US territory itself was for the first time in living memory on tangible war footing.[21] The most palpable symbols of US economic and military dominance were either lying in ruins or were otherwise damaged, and the White House itself could have been added to the list. These events were traumatic not only because of their physical impact, but also because they challenged in a painful fashion the existing vision of the world entertained by the United States.[22]

The shock and grief caused by the attacks was soon followed by a sense of outrage at the magnitude of the offense committed against the United States. This was deemed all the more severe as it came in the form of a surprise assault and as it disregarded established rules of war by targeting civilians. The governor of the State of New York George Pataki referred to 9/11 as "an incredible outrage," the Democratic senator of New York Charles Schumer called it "a dastardly attack," the leaders of Congress stated they were "outraged at these cowardly attacks," and the *Washington Times* put on the headline "Infamy." Bush referred to the attackers on various occasions as "barbarians," "cowards," representing "the very worst of human nature," compared them to the fascists, to the Nazi, and to supporters of totalitarianism, and spoke of the attacks as "evil, despicable acts of terror." Unmistakably, the upcoming conflict between America and terrorism was presented as a "monumental struggle of good versus evil."[23]

The root cause of this sense of outrage, as discussed in chapter two, is that an individual, and by extension a group, can be injured not only physically, but also in its sense of self-esteem—in its sense of order and of proper role in the world. As the chapter argued, prestige requires receiving an appropriately respectful treatment, which is an essential condition of self-esteem. This is why an insult may be resented just as much as an actual injury, and why it requires in turn a response that reasserts prestige by showcasing one's right to respect and by effecting retribution on the injury-causing party.[24] In this sense, September 11 was a double offense: first to US physical safety, but also in a symbolic sense to US identity—to its values, its way of life, and its prestige, as the terrorists had attempted to demean the United States by exposing it as weak and vulnerable and thus deflating its claims to superior status. Basically, the point of the attacks was to humiliate the United States, and in so doing, as chapter two mentioned, to assert the superiority of the offender relative to the insulted party.[25]

This interpretation was not lost on US decision-makers. As Bush argued in his very first statements after the attacks, the aim of the terrorists was not solely directed at harming Americans. Instead, "freedom itself was attacked this morning by a faceless coward." This attack on US identity became a leitmotif in Bush's declarations. For instance, on September 13, Bush argued that terrorists "can't stand freedom. They hate our values, they hate what America stands for." On September 15, Bush declared that the United States had been attacked "because we are freedom's home and defender." In his speech in front of Congress on September 20, he made the similar point that the terrorists hated the United States because "they hate our freedoms, or freedom of religion, our freedom of speech, our freedom to vote and assemble and disagree with each other."[26] Furthermore, the US decision-makers perceived the attacks as a contestation of the United States' will to lead, and, by implication, of its right to command superior prestige in world politics. Accordingly, the United States had to meet this challenge by demonstrating publicly it had "what it took" to command such prestige. As Bush put it: "These acts of mass murder were intended to frighten our nation into chaos and retreat, but they have failed...these acts shattered steel, but they cannot dent the steel of our resolve."[27] And he concluded: "The resolve of our great nation is being tested. But make no mistake: we will show the world that we will pass this test."[28] This conclusion was reinforced by Cheney on September 16: "We have to recognize we are the strongest, most powerful nation on Earth. We've got a tremendous set of accomplishments and an enormously bright future ahead of us. There are those in the world who hate us and that will do everything they can to impose pain, and we can't let them win."[29]

Outrage at what was perceived in Aristotelian terms as both a spiteful and an insolent challenge against US prestige produced a tidal wave of anger and demand for retribution among US decision-makers and public alike. These emotions, as seen in chapter two, may be seen a strong indication of the presence of prestige considerations.

Bush spoke of a "quiet, unyielding anger," of the United States as a peaceful nation, "but fierce when stirred to anger," of how "our grief has turned to anger, our anger to resolution," and of how "in our grief and anger we have found out our mission and our moment." The mission consisted in exacting revenge against the perpetrators and any governments that abetted them or gave them safe haven: "Make no mistake, the United States will hunt down and punish those responsible for those cowardly acts." At Ground Zero, the president pledged to the assembled New Yorkers that "the people who have wrecked these buildings will hear all of us soon." He even mentioned that his administration wanted bin Laden "dead or alive." On another occasion, Bush paraphrased a presumed quote from Japanese Admiral Isoroku Yamamoto in saying that the US "will rid the world of evil-doers...they have roused a mighty giant, and make no mistake about it we're determined." Meanwhile, Cheney warned the terrorists and their supporters of "the full wrath" of the United States. A poll conducted by the *Washington Post* on September 12 found that close to 90 percent of Americans were favoring retaliation.[30] Thus, a strong emotional support of a muscular policy of reasserting US prestige represented an excellent opportunity for neoconservatives to press the case of Iraq as a necessary phase of the upcoming campaign against terrorism. The neoconservative vision also carried the day because of the lack of viable policy alternatives. September 11 confronted the United States with an unforeseen scenario that called into question its previous assumptions about likely threats and therefore imposed a wholesale reassessment of US foreign policy objectives. As Bush put it, on 9/11, "Night fell on a different world."[31] The foreign policy of relative restraint that had been experimented by Clinton and George H. W. Bush appeared ill-fitted for that world, since it was seen as having ignored the terrorist threat and could not have accommodated the public call for retaliation. Hence, the moderate strategic options, such as cooperative security or selective engagement, which might have led to a possible scale-down of America's foreign policy in the Middle East, did not find support among decision-makers and opinion leaders. The only realistic strategic option left was an unapologetic new line of assertiveness, whose chief exponents were the neoconservatives.

Effectively, there was little debate on the policy to follow after September 11: the neoconservatives' ideas won the day without a fight. There even was a palpable sense of relief that the many contradictory demands leveled on the US post–Cold War foreign policy had finally been laid to rest. As Rice, the National Security Advisor, put it: "An earthquake of the magnitude of 9/11 can shift the tectonic plates of international politics...The international system had been in flux since the collapse of Soviet power. Now...it is indeed probable— that this transition is coming to an end...this is a period not just of grave danger but of enormous opportunity." Similarly, for Cheney, "When America's great enemy suddenly disappeared, many wondered what direction our foreign policy would take...All of that changed five months ago [on 9/11]. The threat is known and our role is clear now." The administration understood September 11 as a fresh beginning, similar, as Rice put it, to Truman's time in office, when containment had first been articulated.[32] "Moral clarity" and resolve had replaced doubt to the extent that even the diehard realists, such as Rice and Secretary of State Colin Powell, had jumped on the bandwagon of "benevolent hegemony."

Finally, the victory of neoconservative ideas also had to do with the propitious background of continual preoccupation of decision-makers from the time in office of Clinton onward, with the deterioration of US prestige in the face of challenges. Thus, the neoconservatives did not hijack the foreign policy agenda—that agenda already existed—they only provided its sharpest and most cogent definition: that September 11 was the inevitable result of the United States being perceived as a weak leader that deserved minimal respect, and that, hence, the way to deal with this perception was through a public demonstration of strength.[33] Both reputation and prestige could have been at work in these statements, but, as chapter two has argued, since prestige overlaps reputation, and accounts better for strategic suboptimal behavior and for emotions, prestige is on stronger ground in explaining the United States' decision to invade Iraq.

SENDING A SIGNAL OF STRENGTH

Even though the neoconservatives later employed justifications for regime change, such as Saddam's WMD, the connections of Iraq to al Qaeda, and the necessity of promoting democracy worldwide, their immediate reaction in the aftermath of September 11 concentrated on restoring US prestige. In the very first post-September 11 number of *The Weekly Standard* on September 17, the director and deputy director of the PNAC made the case that the real stakes of the attacks had been to drive the United States out from the Middle East. The appropriate response to this challenge was to reassert "our role as the region's dominant power" through "a sustained campaign that addresses not just the problems of bin Laden and other terrorist organizations but the underlying strategic goal that animates them and their allied states." Hence, the United States should have mounted a public demonstration of strength destined at showing its enemies its ability and willingness to preserve its preeminence in the Middle East, and by implication in the world. In the words of Schmitt and Donelly: "Eliminating Saddam," regardless of his involvement in September 11, "is the key to restoring our regional dominance and preventing our enemies from achieving their war aims." Such an action would have restored "the global credibility tarnished in the Clinton years. Both our friends and our enemies will be watching to see if we pass this test." Thus, instead of a national calamity, 9/11 offered an opportunity "to restore American preeminence in a crucial region of the world." Moreover, action would have allowed revenge not only on the perpetrators of the attacks, but also on the challengers in the area writ large: "America can avenge the attack on our cities, restore national honor, and, finally, win the larger war in the Middle East." Three days after the article, the PNAC wrote another open letter to President Bush advocating action not only against al

Qaeda, but also against Saddam. As the letter put it: "Even if evidence does not link directly Iraq to the attack, any strategy aimed at the eradication of terrorism and its sponsors must include a determined effort to remove Saddam Hussein from power in Iraq." This was to be done on the grounds that "failure to undertake such an effort will constitute an early and perhaps decisive surrender in the war on international terrorism."[34]

This reasoning was condensed in the adagio that the weakness shown by the United States throughout the 1990s had made September 11 "inevitable."[35] By implication, further leniency toward challengers would have resulted in an even sharper decline of US prestige: "Had 9/11 been followed by a resurgence of Saddam's power, the United States would have broadcast to the world an even more lethal message: The Americans are weakening. The future belongs to America's enemies. So we had to strike back and hard after 9/11, to prove that terrorism was *not* winning."[36] Thus, the neoconservative logic amounted to saying that after the humiliation of September 11 it was necessary to boost back US prestige, and that overthrowing Saddam was the best means to achieve this goal. To quote Kagan and Kristol, "What signal does it [refusing to confront Iraq] send to fence-sitters in the Arab world, a world that respects the decisive use of power above all, if we seem hesitant now to do the job we should have finished a decade ago?"[37]

This very same argumentation is detectable in statements coming from members of the administration. Thus, Rumsfeld arrived at the conclusion that echoed Perle's that the chief lesson of September 11 was that "weakness is provocative" and that "so is the perception of weakness." Rumsfeld was so convinced of the soundness of this point as to elevate it into a general principle of conduct or so-called Rumsfeld rule, stating: "History teaches that weakness is provocative. Time and again weakness has invited adventures which strength might well have deterred." Rumsfeld repeats this rule several times in his memoirs for emphasis.[38]

Weakness was for Rumsfeld the result of "hesitant, and in some cases feckless" behavior in the post–Cold War, of which he compiled an extensive catalogue: the withdrawal from Somalia, *The Harlan County* incident, the reluctance to punish the alleged Iraqi effort to assassinate George H. W. Bush, the tolerance of Iraqi defiance of UN sanctions throughout 1997–1998, and the absence of military responses to the successive al Qaeda attacks from 1996 to 2000.[39] Rumsfeld came to the conclusion that "we had on a number of occasions seemed to the rest of the world to have been attacked or

hit or somebody killed and the immediate reaction was a reflexive
pull-back." Such pusillanimity, however, led to the decline of prestige since the United States showed it was not willing to reprimand
misbehaviors for their transgressions: "The capability and the will of
the United States helped discipline the world... by virtue of the fact
that people recognized that we had capabilities and were willing to
use them." Hence, due to these successive pullbacks, "A lot of people
in the world had come to conclude that we were gun-shy, that we
were risk averse," so that the US unwillingness to use its capabilities
"encouraged people to do things that were against our interest."[40]
As a remedy, Rumsfeld supported a policy of "leaning forward not
back," i.e. confronting challenges rather than hiding from them.[41]
This forward-leaning inference was actually an almost word-for-word
reproduction of Kagan and Kristol's depiction earlier on in 2000 of
the role of the benevolent hegemon, which in their view involved
a decision between leaning forward and sitting back. The decision
should have been solved in favor of the former option.[42]

Further evidence to the importance of prestige considerations for
both neoconservatives and Rumsfeld comes from the repeated calls of
the secretary of defense for a public demonstration of strength. In the
National Security Council meetings of September 12 and September
15, Rumsfeld and his Undersecretary Wolfowitz argued that "the US
would have to go after Saddam at some time if the war on terrorism
was to be taken seriously." Four days later, on September 19, Rumsfeld
commented in a meeting that while toppling the Taliban was important, it was still not enough. "The United States," Rumsfeld contended, "needed to do more to demonstrate that there were serious
consequences for mounting an attack on the US and show it would
not suffer any unsavory governments that were affiliated with terrorists." As one aide to Rumsfeld remarked: "Rumsfeld was advocating
a demonstration of power."[43] In other words, in the same vein as
the neoconservative proposals, Rumsfeld was arguing that the United
States needed a demonstrative victory that would have proven its credentials as a worthy dominant power. This was to be accomplished
by a series of blows against challengers, even those not directly connected with the September 11 perpetrators.[44]

Cheney's view closely resembled Rumsfeld's. According to his
foreign policy advisors, Aaron Friedberg and Stephen Yates, in the
aftermath of 9/11, Cheney thought that "we had been hit very hard,
and we needed to make clear the costs to those who might have been
supporting or harboring those who were contemplating those acts."
Consequently, he wanted to send out the message that "the world's

last remaining superpower must not stand helpless against the dangers of a state-terror nexus…The United States could not destroy every potential foe, unseat every hostile government, but tackling one would send a powerful message to the rest." While Cheney was worried about the risks of a terrorist attack by unconventional means, his main concern in advocating a wider war on terror was not to ensure the physical security of the United States, but rather to augment its prestige by delivering a decisive victory. Accordingly, what was needed in his view was a "demonstration effect," to show to all that "we were able and willing to strike at someone. That sends a very powerful message."[45]

Of course, substantially more information is necessary on the spread of neoconservative ideas into the ranks of the administration. What can be gleaned from the available evidence is that by the fall of 2001, the administration consciously relied on neoconservatives for policy guidance. For instance, Wolfowitz ordered a study on how to deal with a crisis such as September 11 from a group of experts headed by neoconservative Christopher DeMuth, and incorporating members sympathetic to neoconservative views such as Reuel Marc Gerecht, James Q. Wilson, Fouad Ajami, and Bernard Lewis. The group's report entitled "Delta of Terrorism" argued that September 11 was the symptom of a larger conflict between fundamentalist Islam and the United States, and that in order to win this battle, "a confrontation with Saddam was inevitable." Iran was an equally menacing adversary, but Iraq was easier to address. To quote another member of the panel, Steve Herbits, a personal aide to Rumsfeld, the report's conclusions were that "we're facing a two-generation war. And start with Iraq." Both Cheney and Rumsfeld read the report and declared themselves very pleased with its findings.[46]

WHY IRAQ?

The Bush administration was adamant that the response to September 11 would not be limited to Afghanistan. In other words, a second act was required after the opening salvo against al Qaeda and the Taliban. Thus, on September 13, Wolfowitz spoke of "a campaign, not a single action" to "end" states that were seen as supporting terrorism; and on September 27, 2011, Rumsfeld told the public to "forget about 'exit strategies.' We're looking at a sustained engagement that carries no deadline."[47] This second act became all the more necessary considering the developments in Afghanistan that showed the limitations of that operation as a "demonstration effect." The fall of the Taliban had been anticlimactic, the enemy lacked "a face," and complete victory had eluded the United States since the operation had failed to deliver the capture or killing of Osama bin Laden at the siege of Tora Bora in early December. The military operations thus had assumed the semblance of an extended police search. However, routine patrols and shadowy intelligence operations were not the stuff of victories showcasing US power and success. Hence, a more dramatic second act was needed. Out of all the recalcitrant states that could have been the targets of a second phase of the war on terror, Iraq appeared the most suitable choice, meeting the criteria of vulnerability and prominence in conjunction with a history of defiance, development of WMD, support for terrorism, and continued hostility to the United States even after September 11.[48]

By comparison to other possible opponents, such as Iran, Iraq was relatively militarily weak, so victory was easier to achieve.[49] Feasibility was also on the mind of Cheney, who was of the view that Iraq was a better choice for a demonstration of US prowess than Iran or North Korea, since by comparison it was more vulnerable, as well as visibly connected to the Arab world.[50] A related factor was accessibility. Afghanistan, while the ostensible target for US retaliation since it was sheltering the perpetrators of September 11, was far from an ideal ground to mount a campaign. In fact, one of the arguments advanced by Wolfowitz in the National Security Council meeting on September 15 was precisely that Afghanistan comprised few targets that could have been attacked and presented the risk of US troops getting bogged down into an indecisive campaign in mountainous terrain. By contrast, an operation in Iraq would have been easier to pull off.[51] A similar piece of supporting evidence comes from General Wesley Clark, the former SACEUR. Clark reports a feasibility-driven mentality in the Pentagon, as he was told that "we are going after him [Saddam] anyway...we've never been very good at taking on terrorists, but one thing we can do is take down states, and there's a list of them they [the civilian leaders] want to take out."[52]

The second reason why Iraq was singled out was its prominence among US adversaries. In Clark's words, Iraq (and even more to the point Saddam) had "a face": "Action against Iraq would provide focus against a visible, defined, and widely disliked adversary. It followed the Cold War mind-set of assigning terrorists, a state sponsor, a 'face,' that could be attacked."[53] While al Qaeda represented a secretive opponent, which generated relatively little public interest prior to September 11, Saddam had been built by successive administrations into a nemesis for more than a decade, and had a long of history of defying Washington with seeming impunity.[54] It was a testimony to the place of pride that Saddam occupied on the list of US opponents that in the aftermath of the terrorist attacks, decision-makers including the president seriously contemplated whether Iraq had been involved in their planning or/and execution.[55] Hence, what better showcase for reasserting US prestige than removing the irritant of the troublesome Iraqi regime?

Both Rumsfeld and Rice argue in their memoirs that there were more reasons than just WMD to get rid of Saddam Hussein.[56] These reasons could be summed up under the category of Saddam's long and constant history of defiance. Because this defiance was never punished soundly, and because he had been allowed to remain in power, Saddam had come to believe, as Rumsfeld's put it, that the United States represented "a paper tiger." Rumsfeld points out that Saddam's Iraq was the only country in the world that attacked the US military on a daily basis, totaling no less than two thousand attacks in the space of two years. Moreover, Saddam was the only leader who had gloated at the US pain on September 11.[57] For her part, Rice states that "we invaded Iraq because we had run out of other options," rather than out of concern for Iraq's possession of WMD, or out of desire to bring democracy to Iraq.[58] In other words, the United States had no other effective way left to end Saddam's challenges, other than oust him. As Rice puts it, enumerating the continual Iraqi transgressions: "Saddam Hussein was a cancer in the Middle East." To this extent, the invasion of Iraq was about taking revenge against Saddam as the most visible and well-known contester of the US-imposed order. To quote Rice: "What really should have anchored the argument was the problem of WMD in the hands of Saddam, not just the problem of WMD per se."[59]

Strong evidence regarding the prominence of Saddam as the main reason of antagonism toward Iraq also comes from the US foreign policy record. In the 1990s, Wolfowitz actually had made a strong case that the United States should have admitted explicitly that: "Saddam *is* the problem." Blaming Clinton for his 1993 declaration that Saddam might have been redeemable, Wolfowitz contended that "the United States government has never been able to state explicitly that Saddam Husayn is the heart of the problem. As a result we are left with the subterfuge [of disarming Iraq] to explain the continuation of sanctions."[60]

Indeed, from the end of the Gulf War onward, the United States had invoked Iraq's unconventional arsenal in order to justify getting rid of Saddam by means of sanctions. In May 1991, George H. W.

Bush specifically stated that sanctions will be maintained for as long as Saddam stayed in power. A memo sent the same month by Undersecretary of State Eagleburger to embassies in the chief Gulf War coalition countries confirms that this was official US policy: "All possible sanctions will be maintained until he [Saddam] is gone. Any easing of sanctions will be considered only when there is a new government...We are ready to work with a successor government in Baghdad if the Iraqi people change their government. From the outset, we have made clear that our problem is not with the Iraqi people but with their leadership and especially Saddam."[61] This remained the case during the time in office of the Clinton administration. For instance, in March 1997, Secretary of State Madeleine Albright stated: "A change in Iraq's government could lead to a change in US policy. Should this occur, we stand ready...to enter rapidly into a dialogue with the successor regime. Until that day containment must stay in place."[62] Hence, for Iraq to eliminate WMD was never a sufficient condition for sanctions to be lifted. Instead, the WMD issue was an instrument to justify seeking the overthrow of Saddam.

Even during the 2002–2003 crisis that preceded the invasion, the United States sought to impose terms that demanded the political exit of Saddam and of his family, rather than simple disarmament. For instance, in April 2002, Bush declared in a press conference that "the policy of my government is the removal of Saddam and all options are on the table." Furthermore, the ultimatum of March 17, 2003 did not call for a last-minute Iraqi pledge to disarm, but stated that "Saddam Hussein and his sons must leave Iraq within 48 hours. Their refusal to do so will result in military conflict...It is too late for Saddam Hussein to remain in power."[63] Finally, the ousting of Saddam could not have been prevented whether he disclosed that Iraq possessed WMD, or whether he denied it, since in the first case he would have been exposed as having lied and found in breach of UN sanctions, and in the latter he would have been accused of hiding the weapons.[64] Hence, provided that a different leadership had emerged in Baghdad, Iraq might have well escaped American invasion, WMD or not.

Even more than other conflicts, Iraq represents the "Rashōmon of wars."[65] For structuralism, Iraq was targeted because of the perception that its pursuit of WMD endangered US security. For exceptionalism, regime change was caused by the US missionary impulse on behalf of democracy in the Middle East. For revisionism, the overthrow of Saddam was meant to secure Iraq's oil reserves and regional bases for the pursuit of the Open Door.

An Honest Mistake?

At the time, the key public justification of regime change had to do with Iraq's continuing possession of WMD that posed a threat to the security of the United States.[66] Bush summed up this rationale in Cincinnati in October 2002: "The Iraqi dictator must not be permitted to threaten America and the world with horrible poisons and diseases and gases and atomic weapons."[67] This theme also resurfaced in the State of Union Address of January 2003: "The gravest danger facing America and the world is outlaw regimes that seek and possess nuclear, chemical and biological weapons."[68] Iraq stood accused of being in actual possession of chemical and biological weapons, of reconstituting its nuclear program, and of seeking delivery systems consisting of long-range missiles and unmanned aerial vehicles forbidden by UN resolutions. Bush's war address of March 2003 is clear on this point: "Intelligence gathered by this and other governments leaves no doubt that the Iraq regime continues to possess and conceal some of the most lethal weapons ever devised."[69] Hence, these assertions were presented as more than mere allegations. As Powell argued repeatedly in his presentation in February 2003 to the UN Security Council: "These are not assertions. These are facts corroborated by many sources, some of them sources of the intelligence services of other countries." Furthermore, "we [the US] know" that Iraq represented a clear imminent threat.[70] Wolfowitz was also explicit in linking the decision to war to intelligence: "I don't think we've ever had a war…in which the work of the intelligence community…[has] been as important as this one."[71] Consequently, the decision to invade was presented as based on "fact," "evidence," "documented evidence," which was "bulletproof" and left "no doubt" as to Saddam's capabilities and aggressive intentions.

Considering that the Iraq Survey Group (ISG), the organization in charge of the search for Iraq's unconventional arsenal, admitted that it had found no weapons and that probably none had existed, these statements can be seen in two ways.[72] In one sense, they can be interpreted as an effort to employ false or purposefully exaggerated information in order to sell the invasion to the American people. Alternatively, they can be regarded as evidence of an honest mistake on the part of US decision-makers.[73]

Structuralism supports the latter view in the sense that, while there was no genuine threat coming from Iraq, the US decision-makers firmly believed that there was one, despite contradicting evidence. Threat assessment is a subjective process prone to misperception: an actor may feel imperiled and act to ensure its safety even though no danger is in fact present. In the aftermath of September 11, the Bush administration was understandably susceptible to overstate the likelihood of worst-case scenarios in which the United States would be targeted again by terrorists or by rogue states. To quote Bush: "Because September the 11th made the security of the American people the priority…a sacred duty for the president…Saddam Hussein's capacity to create harm, all his terrible features became much more threatening. Keeping Saddam in a box looked less and less feasible to me."[74] Consequently, for structuralism, the US decision-makers had an incentive to act early on to eliminate even a very remote threat from Iraq. Hence, the overthrow of Saddam Hussein has the markings of a preventive war—caused by the perceived increase in Saddam's ability to threaten the United States, either directly or by transferring unconventional weapons to terrorists.[75] Evidence corroborating this view might be found in the Bush administration National Security Strategy of 2002, which affirms an American right to use force "preemptively" in case an opponent is on the brink of developing WMD and is known to sponsor terrorism.[76]

As a result, the US decision-makers used the available intelligence selectively, a process known as "cherry picking." The Bush cabinet showed signs of both cognitive consistency, by paying particular attention to those reports that fit their preexisting expectation of an Iraqi threat, and of cognitive dissonance by dismissing information that raised doubts on their assessment.[77] In this sense, the US decision-makers exhibited signs of unintentional exaggeration and omission consistent with misperception.[78] A groupthink effect might have also been present, as decision-makers as well as intelligence analysts shared similar assessments of Saddam's capabilities.[79] Finally, another point supporting misperception is the obstinate conviction of US decision-makers that WMD will end up being found in Iraq, a belief that held firm despite the absence of confirming proof.[80]

Nevertheless, this interpretation has to address, besides the earlier mentioned point regarding the established US policy of ousting Saddam regardless of the state of disarmament of Iraq, two additional objections. These refer to: (a) the timing of the decision to invade and of the intelligence ascertaining the presence of WMD; and (b) the intentional misleading by the administration in regard to the most alarming aspect of Iraq's WMD—nuclear weapons.

A TIME TO INVADE

If the US decision-makers had been animated by an authentic fear of an Iraqi attack, then the decision for war should have been most likely taken in the aftermath of the October 1, 2002 unveiling of the National Intelligence Estimate or NIE, the most authoritative product of the US intelligence community, which is compiled out of the estimates of the 15 intelligence agencies. The October NIE, in stark contrast with previous intelligence estimates in February and July 2002 by the Central Intelligence Agency (CIA) and the Defense Intelligence Agency (DIA), painted an alarming picture of the threat from Iraq. This assessment constituted the foundation for the severest accusations leveled by the United States against Baghdad in the fall of 2002.[81] As such, and supposing the administration was guided by intelligence, the NIE should have been crucial to informing decision-making about the risk posed by Saddam.[82]

However, the available evidence points the other way. In fact, the decision to target Iraq was in all likelihood reached in the months following the fall of the Taliban regime, in the interval from November 2001 to January 2002.[83] Before November, the option of a campaign against Iraq had been raised twice in the National Security Council in September, and each time it was ruled out.[84] However, on September 26, Bush officially asked Rumsfeld to look into plans for possible military action against Iraq, inquiring again in November on the state of the planning process.[85] By the time of the State of Union address of January 29, 2002, Iraq had been singled out as the most dangerous component of the axis of evil, which also comprised North Korea and Iran.[86] Gordon and Trainor also write that the State of the Union "was the first hint of what CENTCOM already knew: Iraq would be the next phase in the White House campaign on terror." Paul Pillar, at the time the official responsible for the Near East and South Asia at the National Intelligence Council, which draws up the NIEs, also confirms this information: "Clearly fairly in early 2002 to just anyone working in intelligence on Iraq issues that we were going to war, that the decision had essentially been made." This leaves a conspicuous gap of nearly two months between November and January, when, although no information is available on a principals meeting on Iraq, the decision to invade must have been taken.[87]

Confirming evidence from February 2002 onward shows an irrevocable US commitment to attacking Iraq even before any alarming proof of WMD was issued. In February, the Pentagon began to prepare in earnest plans for an invasion of Iraq after presenting a first draft to Rumsfeld. The following month, Bush dropped by a meeting between Rice and a group of senators and delivered an unambiguous message: "Fuck Saddam. We are taking him out." The same month, on a visit to Capitol Hill, Cheney told senators that the question was no longer whether the United States would attack

Iraq, but only when the offensive was going to proceed.[88] By the first week of July, Richard Haass, the director of the Policy Planning at the State Department, who had raised objections against the invasion was told by Rice "essentially that the decision has been made, don't waste your breath."[89] On July 23, a British principals meeting took place in London, where the director of MI6 Sir Richard Dearlove (code name "C") reported back on a recent meeting with his counterpart, CIA director George Tenet. "C" told the British leaders that in Washington "military action was now seen as inevitable. Bush wanted to remove Saddam through military action, justified by the conjunction of terrorism and WMD. But the intelligence and facts were being fixed around the policy."[90]

This alternative timeline does not absolutely rule out misperception as an interpretation, but weakens it significantly by contesting the view that it was solely faulty intelligence analysis that forced the hand of US decision-makers into war with Iraq. Thus, the straightforward connection assumed between mistaken intelligence and faulty decision-making needs to be revised, perhaps in favor of a loop effect, in the sense that it was decision-making in favor of invasion that created a strong demand for intelligence confirming the presence of WMD, which means that intelligence officers were encouraged to place priority on more alarmist or speculative analyses of Iraqi weapon programs.[91] This might have been then taken as confirming proof to what the US decision-makers thought they knew already about Iraq.[92] In Pillar's words: "Official intelligence analysis was not relied on in making even the most significant national security decisions... intelligence was misused publicly to justify decisions already made."[93] However, even in the case of such a loop effect, structuralism would have to prove the preexistence of beliefs among US decision-makers as to the danger posed by Saddam's WMD independent of the outcome to be explained, that is, the pressure to generate supportive intelligence. Presently, such evidence is far from strong since the policy record suggests, in accordance with the above discussion of the prominence of Saddam as a challenger, that the WMD issue had been traditionally employed by US decision-makers so as to provide a rationale for seeking regime change in Baghdad.

LIES, DAMNED LIES, AND INTELLIGENCE

The point of misperception is not that decision-makers state something that turns out to be untrue, but that they genuinely believe in so doing that their statement represents the truth. To make a false statement in full knowledge of its falsehood, however, is not an honest mistake, but a lie. This is to say that misperception might explain the "cherry picking" of intelligence to fit the version of events preferred by the administration, but it cannot account for the purposeful misuse of intelligence that had been known as being untrue. This is why, while misperception may be invoked to justify US claims regarding Iraq's chemical and biological weapons, it fails to explain the claims regarding Iraq's nuclear program.

Iraq stood accused of having acquired uranium ore from Niger and of importing aluminum tubes, which could be used for building rotors for a centrifuge to enrich uranium with the purpose of building an atomic bomb. This was the most incriminating evidence justifying immediate regime change. The administration went on the record by saying that if not stopped, Iraq could have obtained an atomic bomb in as soon as one year. To quote Cheney: Iraq posed a "mortal threat" to the United States since "we now know that Saddam had resumed his efforts to acquire nuclear weapons...Many of us are convinced that Saddam will acquire nuclear weapons fairly soon."[94] Bush brought the nuclear danger even closer in Cincinnati: "If the Iraqi regime is able to produce, buy, or steal an amount of highly enriched uranium a little larger than a single softball, it could have a nuclear weapon in less than a year."[95] "Saddam is determined to get his hands on a nuclear bomb," warned Powell. "He is so determined that he has made repeated covert attempts to acquire high-specification aluminum tubes from 11 different countries. These tubes are controlled...precisely because they can be used as centrifuges for enriching uranium."[96]

These allegations help explain why the United States decided to attack a regime it believed was armed with WMD, which could have decided to lash out against the invaders or their allies.[97] However, assuming that Iraq, while seeking nuclear weapons, was not ready to field them, an offensive to disarm it would have carried less risk of sustaining heavy casualties.[98] Moreover, the window of opportunity for action was closing rapidly: the sooner the attack would have been under way, the lesser the chances that Iraq could have finalized its nuclear projects. From this point of view, invading Iraq was a race against the clock. As Bush put it, "Facing clear evidence of peril, we cannot wait for the final proof—the smoking gun—that could come in the form of a mushroom cloud."[99] One should also keep in mind that the nuclear issue has peculiar resonance with the US public: between 1990 and 1998, controlling nuclear proliferation ranked in polls as the number one US foreign policy goal.[100] Yet, it is precisely the intelligence on the Iraqi nuclear programs that has been exposed as having been doctored.

The aluminum tubes accusation had been contested, starting a week from Bush's UN speech in September 2002, by experts who pointed out their unsuitability for building centrifuges.[101] As the top expert of the Department of Energy summed it up: "It would have been extremely difficult to make these tubes into centrifuges. It stretches the imagination to come up with a way."[102] This assessment was shared by the expert community as well as by the March 7, 2003 report of the UN weapons inspectors. As the IAEA report put it: "It was highly unlikely that Iraq could have achieved the considerable redesign needed to use them in a revived centrifuge programme."[103] Even assuming that Iraq had managed to use the tubes for centrifuges, it could have built only 1,000 machines, and for producing one atomic bomb a year one needs at least 3,500 machines. (At its peak, Iraq's nuclear program in the 1980s never had operated more than 550 machines.) Even if Iraq could have managed such a feat, there would have been delays that would have pushed back the estimate of a deployable nuclear weapon from one year to between five and seven. The NIE thus had to inflate the number to no less than 25,000 machines to arrive at a suitable timeframe for the claim of an Iraqi bomb available in one year to be warranted.[104] Despite this contested information, which even Powell acknowledged privately, ultimately the US decision-makers employed it as verified and uncontestable evidence of Iraq resuming its nuclear efforts. To quote Powell in his UN presentation: "Let me tell you what is not controversial about these tubes…all the experts who have analyzed the tubes in our possession agree that they can be used for centrifuge use." Bush argued as well in the State of Union address of 2003 that "our intelligence sources tell us that he [Saddam] has attempted to purchase high-strength aluminum tubes suitable for nuclear weapons production."[105]

Meanwhile, the documents that attested the sale of 500 tons of yellowcake from Niger to Iraq were proved to have been visible forgeries.[106] In February 2002, the United States dispatched at Cheney's request former diplomat Joseph Wilson to Niger to investigate the claims of the sale. Wilson reported to both the State Department and the CIA that "it was highly doubtful that any such transaction had ever taken place."[107] The US intelligence community showed caution as well: while the State Department's Bureau of Intelligence and Research was "highly dubious" of the claim, the other agencies consulted for the NIE concluded that they did not know the status of the transaction. The report on the sale of uranium from Niger, though it was mentioned in the British cabinet dossier of Iraq in September 2002, was considered so tenuous by the CIA that Langley struck it out from the draft of the speech Bush was to deliver in Cincinnati, on the grounds that both the transaction and the quantity of uranium involved were doubtful.[108] The National Intelligence Council itself (the body responsible for the NIE) concluded prior to the State of the Union Address that the Niger accusation was "baseless and should be laid to rest."[109] Nonetheless, the accusation still appeared in Bush's State of the Union address in the so-called Sixteen Words: "The British Government has learned that Saddam Hussein has recently sought significant quantities of uranium from Africa."[110] The accusation also appeared in a Rice opinion piece in January 2003, as well as in a State Department rebuttal of the Iraqi declaration of WMD in mid-December 2002, which casts doubts on the allegation being a slipup.[111]

How the Sixteen Words made the speech is still unexplained, considering that the CIA had to approve the wording beforehand, and had already objected twice to the use of the Niger evidence. The ulterior spin effort by the Bush administration was to argue not to have had any indication that the Niger accusation was a fake, thus throwing the blame on the CIA. As Rice put it: "May be someone knew down the bowels of the agency, but no one in our circle knew that there were doubts and suspicions that this might be a forgery."[112] However, by the time of the State of the Union, the information on Niger had been made privy to the Pentagon, the State Department, the National Security Council, and the vice president.[113] In fact, Powell refrained in following weeks from using it in his presentation at the UN. In March, the IAEA finally gained access to the documents and exposed them as having been forged.[114]

The two lies show that the US decision-makers did not merely fall prey to their convictions about WMD, but also, at least occasionally, engaged in the conscious vamping up of evidence in order to make the threat appear much more serious than it actually was. This point is also corroborated by the "Wolfowitz indiscretion," in which Wolfowitz stated that "for bureaucratic reasons, we settled on one issue weapons of mass destruction, because it was the one reason everyone could agree on." The interpretation is also backed by Rice's discussion with Powell on a suitable justification for attacking Iraq. Rice thought that the WMD issue was the only one that had "legs" because the connection between al Qaeda and Iraq seemed weak and improvable, and the issue of Saddam's abuses against Iraqis did not resonate with the US public.[115] The risks posed by WMD, by contrast, were an issue of intense preoccupation to the US public. Furthermore, this issue could be settled by the invocation of authoritative intelligence, which would have been difficult to refute given that only the administration was privy to its full content and that there were few means of independent verification of its claims.[116] Intelligence therefore had the cachet of quasi-scientific proof, which had an objective validity beyond dissenting opinions or beliefs.

An additional piece of evidence against misperception is that the intelligence in regard to Iraqi nuclear weapons paled by comparison to the information available on North Korea's. In June 2002, information surfaced of a large North Korean uranium enrichment program, including the purchase of "tons" of aluminum tubes as well as the acquisition of Pakistan's designs of centrifuges from the A. Q. Khan network. Furthermore, on October 4, 2002, days before the Cincinnati speech, when confronted by US officials with this evidence, Pyongyang all but confirmed the allegations. The First Vice Foreign Minister Kang Sok Ju, "the dominant figure in the North Korean foreign policy apparatus," told US Assistant Secretary James Kelly that not only was Pyongyang entitled to nuclear weapons, but it also had a right to have even more powerful weapons. This was widely interpreted both by the delegation and by the administration as a de facto admission of enriching uranium. (This secret program was unveiled in 2010.) Yet, despite the North Korean smoking gun, the United States concentrated its attention on Iraq, where the evidence was far weaker. While the president was denouncing Iraq in Cincinnati, North Korea was not mentioned at all.[117]

Hence, while substantially more archival evidence is needed to determine the degree of misperception that affected US decision-makers, and while genuine concerns about WMD may be part of this story, the available information goes to suggest that the rationale for invasion was far more complex than an honest mistake regarding an Iraqi threat to US physical security.

A LIBERTY DOCTRINE FOR THE MIDDLE EAST?

In the aftermath of the futile search for WMD in Iraq, the exceptionalist argument that the invasion had been caused by zeal on behalf of the promotion of democracy gained new credence.[118] In November 2003, Bush introduced the idea of the "great challenge" of bringing democracy to the Middle East as an alternative to military dictatorships or fundamentalist theocracies—with Iraq as a crucial test. "Iraqi democracy will succeed," said Bush, "and that success will send forth the news from Damascus to Tehran that freedom can be the future of every nation. The establishment of a free Iraq at the heart of the Middle East will be a watershed event in the global democratic revolution."[119] In early 2006, Bush announced an even more ambitious goal: "Our nation is committed to an historic, long-term goal—we seek the end of tyranny in the world." Democracy was presented as the main weapon to combat terrorism: "Ultimately, the only way to defeat the terrorists is to defeat their dark vision of hatred and fear by offering the hopeful alternative of political freedom and political change."[120] Thus, Iraq represented square one of a "domino theory in reverse," which argued that the transition of Iraq to full-fledged democracy would have encouraged the development of democratic regimes throughout the Middle East.[121] This result would have been achieved through (a) the means of successive US regime change interventions; (b) the intimidation of dictators that could see the fate that awaited them; and especially (c) the capturing of the hearts and minds of Muslims by providing them with the example of a successful Iraqi democracy.

Nevertheless, had the spread of democracy to the Middle East been the chief reason to invade, the US decision-makers would have insisted on democracy rather than on WMD in justifying the invasion; and, considering the stakes of the success of Iraqi democracy, they would have devoted substantial attention to shepherding Iraq's democratic transition. However, the US decision-makers were considerably skeptic of making the case for invasion based on the promotion of democracy: as the earlier quotes from Wolfowitz and Rice show, the issue was not seen as having "legs."[122] Rice insists in her memoirs that democracy was not a reason in determining invasion: "We did not go to Iraq to bring democracy any more than Roosevelt went to war against Hitler to democratize Germany, though that became American policy once the Nazis were defeated."[123] Actually, the administration did not warm up to democracy promotion until 2004, when the searches turned out no Iraqi WMD.[124]

This timing is odd, because how can democracy possibly win over the rival ideology of Islamic fundamentalism when its most fervent proponents are hesitant to argue its case openly? One could not seriously envision the transformation of the Middle East into a zone of blossoming democracies unless the toppling Saddam was accompanied by a suitably massive and sustained propaganda effort, aimed at portraying the action in the context of a wider US regional effort. But the propaganda effort began only belatedly.

Furthermore, if the purpose of the invasion of Iraq was to put in place a democracy that would constitute a model for the entire Middle East, then the administration should have devoted more attention to issues such as restoring order in occupied Iraq to prevent looting and violence, dealing with the remains of the Baath party and of the Iraqi army, repairing the destroyed infrastructure, and preparing a road-map of measures to be implemented before the transition of power to an Iraqi authority. However, the available evidence shows that the US decision-makers did not spend much time on these issues. This was not "because the government did no planning but because a vast amount of expert planning was willfully ignored by the people in charge."[125]

The most significant such planning effort was conducted by the State Department Future of Iraq Project under the direction of Thomas Warrick. Nevertheless, the institution that eventually emerged as the linchpin of the efforts to administrate Iraq in the aftermath of the overthrow of Saddam was the Pentagon, which created for this purpose the ORHA (Office of Reconstruction and Humanitarian Assistance). Even though the Pentagon's nominee to head ORHA, retired general Jay Garner, wanted to use the State Department's blueprint, Rumsfeld and the Office of Special Plans vetoed both the collaboration and the presence of Warrick on Garner's administration team.[126] By that time, war was only weeks away. As Garner put it: "This is an ad hoc operation, glued together over about four or five weeks' time." ORHA thus went into Iraq with little preparation besides the expectation that the United States would be greeted as liberator, that order could be restored speedily, and that transition will result in elections in four months' time. On the ground, ORHA had to cope almost instantly with the anarchy that followed the collapse of Saddam, including the suspension of basic services such as electricity, the looting of every government building, and widespread violence. ORHA also lacked the resources to carry out its task, including troops, radios, working phone lines, translators, and vehicles. Garner was replaced in a matter of weeks with Ambassador Paul Bremer, who dissolved the Iraqi army and forbid the employment of former Baath party members in government positions—policies that created in a week 450,000 enemies of the United States.[127]

This abhorrence of nation-building was also in evidence in the assumption of a "Wizard of Oz" moment, where after Saddam was gone, institutions would remain functional. This view was endorsed foremost by the Pentagon because it supported Rumsfeld's overall goal of relying on technology, not manpower. In this logic, the United States should not have had to police Iraq because such an endeavor was too costly, and could have been delegated to the Iraqis themselves.[128] Thus, the Pentagon not only refused to contemplate the obstacles that democracy promotion could encounter in Iraq, but also did not care much about the process itself, undermining the exceptionalist claim that democracy promotion was the reason for toppling Saddam.

Oil and Bases Rights?

From a revisionist angle, the invasion of Iraq has a cynic explanation: oil.[129] Regime change in Iraq allowed access to its considerable oil wealth—Iraq was at the time thought to control the world's second largest oil reserves after Saudi Arabia.[130] These calculations could not have been lost on a cabinet filled with former oil executives, such as Bush, Cheney, and Rice, or on an administration with strong ties to the Saudi oil industry. As Unger puts it, "Never before had the highest levels of an administration so nakedly represented the oil industry."[131] At the very least, as the president of the Petroleum Research Foundation put it: "If we go to war, it's not about oil…But after Saddam, it becomes all about oil."[132]

Nevertheless, if oil had been the rationale for invasion, regime change should have occurred much earlier on, either in the Gulf War or in Operation Desert Fox. The alleged insatiable US thirst for oil also does not fit the sanctions pattern that cut off Iraq from the global market from 1991 to 2003, since by far the easiest way to ensure continued oil flows would have been to rehabilitate Saddam.[133] This is not to say that oil did not affect the strategic picture at all—but it did so in very different ways from the revisionist argument. Oil was seen as one of the key capabilities available to whichever government happened to be in charge in Baghdad. Hence, if Saddam was allowed to escape sanctions and resume oil exports, the US view since 1991 onward was that he would use the revenues to rebuild his military and resume his bid for controlling the region.[134] Conversely, the US decision-makers were convinced that a new regime would have used oil exports to pay for the reconstruction of Iraq as a regional power.[135] True enough, Saddam's occupation of Kuwait, and later on, his survival in power did call into question the principle of US supremacy in a region key to the global economy.[136] Yet, this argument cannot account for the change in policy from Clinton's keeping Saddam in a box to Bush's regime change, even though the same Open Door imperative allegedly applied. That is to say that, while revisionists believe in a continuity of policy from Clinton to Bush toward Saddam, they cannot explain the escalation to full-scale invasion by reference to just Open Door motives.

A potentially stronger revisionist argument is based not on oil, but on the US need for military bases in the Middle East.[137] One of the principal concerns of US decision-makers in the 1990s had been to find alternatives to basing troops in Saudi Arabia.[138] Even before the troops were deployed, there was considerable dissent inside the Saudi kingdom, including the royal family, as to the desirability of their presence. As the home to the Two Mosques of Mecca and Medina, Saudi Arabia was reticent to be the host of US non-Muslim troops. However, Saddam's survival in 1991 meant the perpetuation of US military presence in Saudi Arabia, which soon exposed the monarchy to criticism not only from extremists such as Osama Bin Laden, but also from clerical figures on its own payroll.[139] Moreover, Washington was sensitive to the risk of attacks on Saudi territory, as in the 1996 Khobar Towers attack.[140] In this sense, the overthrow of Saddam would have removed the reason for the presence of US troops in Saudi Arabia while finding an even more suitable geopolitical location in Iraq. Indeed, by May 2003, the last US combat troops had left Saudi Arabia.[141]

However, the decision to scale-down US deployment in Saudi Arabia had followed the showdowns with Iraq in 1997 and 1998, in which Riyadh hesitated to allow the United States to use the bases in its territory for attacking Saddam. Therefore, the United States had already decided well prior to the invasion to relocate its troops and weaponry to Qatar, which became the regional hub for American forces in 2001.[142] Certainly, while Iraq was better placed geopolitically than Qatar, securing it as a base at the cost of war was not profitable, given that the United States already had a perfectly viable alternative, without counting the naval and air bases in Bahrain and Turkey. More importantly, the United States had withstood the mounting Saudi concerns over its military presence for more than 12 years. Given the presumed extent of US influence, why would Washington have believed that it was easier to invade Iraq than to coerce the Saudis into continuing to accept its military forces in the kingdom? Since Saudi Arabia is home to the world's largest oil reserves, the maintenance of American troops to protect the fields should have been in the revisionist logic of utmost priority.

Chapter Conclusion

The invasion of Iraq is less attributable to the motives emphasized in the existing literature, that is, US concerns over WMD, democracy, and oil. The decision to invade owes more to the preoccupation of the Bush decision-makers over the deteriorating prestige of the United States in the aftermath of September 11, manifested in the conviction that weakness was provocative and that the United States needed to mount a demonstration of strength. The neoconservative weltanschauung, which constantly preached a foreign policy of greatness, and, as such of assertiveness, was ideally suited to the requirements of mounting a strong response to this prestige injury. Iraq was chosen as a test ground for this policy, both because military operations were seen as feasible and because of the prominence of Saddam as a challenger.

7

THE FUTURE OF US FOREIGN
POLICY: RESET GAME

Barack Obama's mandate began with an effort to distance himself from the excesses of his predecessor. The Bush administration itself had all but admitted the conclusion of the Bush revolution, due foremost to the multiplying costs of the unanticipated insurgency in Iraq, which ended up producing ten times the casualties of the war to oust Saddam.[1] The wider Bush agenda in the Middle East was abandoned; the United States involved its NATO allies in operations in Afghanistan; opened up a multilateral dialogue to convince North Korea to give up its nuclear weapons program; and mended relations with Russia, China, France, and Germany. Furthermore, the fall of 2008 produced the most serious economic crisis since the Great Depression, which diminished the resources available for an assertive US foreign policy.[2]

The initial Obama foreign policy agenda was characterized by the buzzword of "reset," which Vice President Joseph Biden used to describe conciliatory efforts toward Russia. However, the very concept begged the question: reset to what exactly? As it turned out, the policy that the Obama team had in mind showed clear similarities to the model of restraint experimented by George H. W. Bush and Clinton. Yet, for all its interest in restraint, the Obama administration remained vulnerable to the same dilemma that had bedeviled its predecessors. On the one hand, once the United States implemented restraint, it found itself in a weaker position to address challenges to its prestige. But if, on the other hand, it took assertive measures against challengers, the material costs of foreign policy spiked up. Thus, each option presented the United States with advantages and sizable drawbacks. The clearest formulation of this constant post–Cold War dilemma between costs in prestige versus material costs came from none other than Osama bin Laden. Just before the US attacked Afghanistan, bin

Laden told Mullah Omar that the United States "is currently facing two contradictory problems: a) if it refrains from responding to jihad operations, its prestige will collapse, thus forcing it to withdraw its troops abroad and restrict itself to US internal affairs…b) on the other hand, a campaign against Afghanistan will impose great long-term economic burdens, leading to further economic collapse."[3] By the onset of the financial crisis, when it was estimated that the full costs of the Iraq war ran as high as $720 million per day or $500,000 a minute, the material side of the dilemma appeared the more pressing, and, as a result, the benefits of endorsing restraint once again loomed large.[4] But, as the Obama team was about to discover, in its urge to cut costs, the United States ran from the Scylla of economic expenses once again straight into the jaws of the Charybdis of prestige losses.[5]

Restraint Reloaded

Evidence of a penchant for restraint does not come only from Obama professing being a realist and an admirer of the foreign policy of George H. W. Bush and Scowcroft.[6] The statements and policies of the early administration also confirm an interest in a thriftier foreign policy. Thus, in February 2009, Obama announced a pullout of all combat forces from Iraq until August 2010, to be complemented by a full withdrawal by the end of 2011.[7] While Obama wanted to end old wars, he also did not intend to become involved in new ones. In his inaugural speech, he pledged to extend a hand to those recalcitrant leaders who would be willing to unclench their fist.[8] Accordingly, in March 2009, Obama sent a congratulatory message to the people of Iran on the occasion of the festival of Nowruz marking the Iranian New Year, in which he was the first US president to refer to Iran by its official name as the Islamic Republic of Iran. Obama announced his commitment to diplomacy to solve the issues between the two countries and followed through with a private letter sent to the supreme leader of Iran, Ayatollah Ali Khamenei, in which he pledged improved relations in return for an end to Iran's nuclear program.[9] Obama also extended an olive branch to North Korea, shrugging off missile and nuclear tests in early 2009, dispatching former president Clinton on a visit to Pyongyang in August, and sending a private letter to North Korean ruler Kim Jong Il in December of the same year, promising economic concessions and diplomatic normalization in return for denuclearization.[10]

Restraint was also evidenced by a steady US rhetoric of multilateralism. Thus, in his Nobel Peace Prize acceptance speech, Obama pledged, in stark contrast with the preventive war doctrine of George W. Bush, to respect the role of international institutions. As he announced, "America—in fact, no nation—can insist that others follow the rules of the road if we refuse to follow them ourselves. For when we don't, our actions appear arbitrary and undercut the legitimacy of future interventions, no matter how justified."[11] Meanwhile, Obama's National Security Strategy unveiled in May 2010 echoed the Clinton notions of comprehensive engagement, deep cooperative relations, and strengthening international institutions, which were presented as the linchpin of the US-led global order.[12] In perhaps the most developed articulation of the administration's new approach, Vice President Joseph Biden stated in February 2009 that the new administration was "determined to set a new tone not only in Washington, but in America's relations around the world." Biden elaborated that the new tone meant that "we'll work in a partnership whenever we can, and alone only when we must. The threats we face have no respect for borders. No single country, no matter how powerful, can best meet these threats alone." He then proposed a great bargain, which for all intents and purposes was not much different from the quid pro quo of restraint versus cooperation characteristic of the new world order: "So we'll engage. We'll listen. We'll consult. America needs the world, just as I believe the world needs America. But we say to our friends that the alliances, treaties and international organizations we build must be credible and they must be effective. That requires a common commitment not only to listen and live by the rules, but to enforce the rules when they are, in fact, clearly violated. Such a bargain is the bargain we seek."[13]

Another clue to Obama's interest in restraint was the renewed use of the UN and of international institutional frameworks for assembling diplomatic and logistic support for US foreign policy.[14] In each of the three areas examined in chapter five, the administration moved toward compromise. Although the United States continued not to be a nominal member of the ICC, it became in 2010 an observer to the Court, and offered support for the Court's investigations. In relation to missile defense, the United States scrapped in 2009 the Bush plans to deploy missiles in Poland and the Czech Republic, to the great relief of Russia. (However, a year later, the administration made public its intention for missile deployment in Romania and Bulgaria.) The most significant step was taken in relation to internationally sanctioned interventions. When the United States intervened in Libya, in part at the request of Paris and London, it was careful to secure the prior blessings of not only the UN Security Council, but also of NATO, the Arab League, and the Organization of African Unity; and when it imposed sanctions on Iran in 2010, it did so in conjunction with measures implemented by the UN and the EU. When such international consensus was not forthcoming, as in the case of the uprising in Syria, the administration refrained from pressing the matter.

These efforts to reset the United States toward restraint do not mean that US foreign policy had come on full circle. Many differences existed between the early 1990s and 2009, not in the least since in the latter interval the United States struggled with a serious economic crisis and was involved in a long-term war. To that extent, and with the benefit of two decades of learning, the Obama administration was much less prone to illusions about the absence of challenges to US prestige, about the automatic support of allies and partners to its initiatives, and about the ability of negotiations to convince recalcitrant actors to comply.[15]

Nevertheless, that the Obama team had found inspiration in precisely the tenets of the new world order and of engagement showed just how very limited was the US menu of choice in respect to foreign policy. Once the United States became disenchanted with the assertiveness of the Bush revolution, the only alternative left was to go back to experimenting with restraint, even though there were preciously few indications, and quite a few doubts, that the experiment would work this time around.

From the Mountains of Afghanistan to the Shores of Tripoli

In the aftermath of the invasion of Iraq, Afghanistan had been relegated to an issue of secondary concern. As Admiral Mike Mullen, chairman of the Joint Chiefs of Staff during the second George W. Bush administration put it to Congress in 2007: "In Afghanistan we do what we can, in Iraq we do what we must. There is a limit to what we can apply to Afghanistan."[16] Accordingly, the United States had left nation-building in the charge of its NATO allies, while maintaining a force of 25,000 troops in the country.[17] However, this relative neglect meant that the Afghan Taliban resurfaced as a formidable challenger.[18] The Taliban attacks against coalition forces multiplied on a yearly basis: for instance, 2005 witnessed 1,558 attacks, but the number increased in 2006 to 4,542, and went up in 2007 by a further 27 percent. 2008 witnessed a further spike, with 151 US soldiers killed by comparison with 111 in 2007, and an estimated 40 percent increase in the number of civilian Afghan casualties. By the advent of the Obama presidency, the Taliban, while not in command of Afghanistan's major cities, were controlling large sways of the countryside. As a result, the NATO allies became increasingly reluctant or resentful to foot the bill of a protracted war in Afghanistan and threatened to end their deployments.[19] In short, on the pattern of the 1990s, if the United States refused to address a problem substantially, it only grew worse as time went by.

The United States sought to rectify the situation through a combination of engagement with Pakistan and a moderate surge in the troops deployed in Afghanistan. To this end, Obama announced in March 2009 sending 17,000 troops and 4,000 trainers to Afghanistan to supplement the 32,000 troops the United States already had de-ployed. This measure, meant as a momentary detour into assertiveness, however, begot only further assertiveness. In August 2009, General Stanley McChrystal, the commander of US forces in Afghanistan, made a request for an additional deployment on top of the March one, warning that "failure to provide adequate resources...risks a longer conflict, greater casualties, higher overall costs, and, ultimately a critical loss of political support. Any of these risks, in turn, are likely to result in mission failure." Furthermore, McChrystal made clear that the deployment was needed within "the next 12 months" or "risk an outcome where defeating the insurgency is no longer possible."[20] After much soul-searching, the Obama presidency decided on a smaller deployment of 30,000 troops, compared to the option of a 40,000-strong force endorsed by the Pentagon. Additionally, the deployment was publicized as a temporary expedient to be reassessed in July 2011. At that time, the presidency announced the surge troops' withdrawal by summer 2012, to be followed by a full withdrawal of combat forces as well as of the international forces by the end of 2014.[21]

Nevertheless, despite efforts to keep a lid on its dimensions, the surge decision suggests that the Obama presidency is no less concerned than its predecessors by the implication of perceived failures for US prestige. In the principal decision-makers' meeting on September 30, 2009, a clear conviction reigned that the United States should not just exit Afghanistan, because doing so would have conveyed the impression of defeat. As National Security Advisor James Jones argued: "If we're not successful here...people will say the terrorists won...Any developing country is going to say, this is the way to beat [the United States] and we're going to have a bigger problem."[22]

The point to notice here is that the surge decision was not caused as much by strategic considerations to defeat the Taliban in the field as by psychological concerns of being seen as the losing side. For the Obama decision-makers it was fairly clear, despite McChrystal's prior warning of an outcome where defeating the militants was no longer possible, that the point had already been reached. The argument that the Taliban could not be defeated was made repeatedly on October 8, October 30, and November 11 by Jones, Biden, Secretary of Defense Robert Gates, and by Commander in Chief of CENTCOM (the military command responsible for the Middle East) David Petraeus.[23] Moreover, the United States was not so concerned about the strategic stakes of Afghanistan as to commit to its defense indefinitely and with unlimited troops resources. Yet the perception of losing Afghanistan would have hurt US prestige as an effective world leader, and for this reason, assertive action had to be undertaken to impress an image of overall success over what was an unwinnable stalemate.

In effect, Obama's strategy for Afghanistan made no mention of defeating the Taliban. Instead, it stated that the goal was "to deny the Taliban the ability to overthrow the Afghan government."[24] The key US objective in Afghanistan had become to create the perception that the Taliban momentum had been reversed, hence to create the perception that they were not the side wining the war. Only then would the United States have been able to transfer the mission's burden to the newly formed Afghan army and police. Thus, the Afghanistan surge constitutes an exercise in saving face, that is, minimizing prestige losses, and shows how, when pitted against considerations of prestige, restraint loses out.[25]

A similar outcome occurred in the 2011 US intervention in Libya. On the surface, this constitutes a much clearer instance of humanitarian intervention than Kosovo, because this time Washington, which had been asked by France and Great Britain only to provide a no-fly zone, undertook two weeks of strikes on the justification that a no-fly zone would not have stopped the slaughter on the ground.[26] But humanitarian considerations, while certainly important, were not the only factor affecting the administration's decision. Another significant concern was that if the United States allowed Gadhafi to hunt down insurgents house to house in the city of Benghazi, its claim to international leadership was going to be weakened by its demonstrated inability to discipline misbehaviors. This passivity in the face of defiance would have loomed large in the context of the economic recession because it would have shown that owing to already existing commitments, the United States was reluctant to take on additional ones. As Obama put it to his advisors, "If we don't act, if we put brakes on these things it will have consequences for US credibility and leadership, consequences for the Arab Spring, and consequences for the international community." This message was then repeated in his speech at the National Defense University—for Obama, "to brush aside America's responsibility as a leader... would have been a betrayal of who we are."[27] Of course, even in the case of Libya, the material costs were not neglected—so that the United States after two weeks transferred the responsibility for military operations to Paris and London.[28] Nonetheless, if economic costs had trumped prestige considerations, there should have been no intervention at all.[29]

THE ATOMIC TWINS

Comparable trade-offs between prestige and material costs loom in the cases of Iran and North Korea. In both, a state is developing or has already developed a nuclear capability, which, while at the moment not posing a direct threat to the United States, constitutes sizable worries to the proliferator's neighbors and limits the US ability to exercise world leadership.[30] Both Tehran and Pyongyang would prefer normalized relations with Washington: neither country has diplomatic ties with the United States, and North Korea still has to sign a peace treaty ending the Korean War officially. However, neither country is willing to offer concessions on its nuclear program, which is seen as a guarantee of the continued survival in power of its political regime. Hence, any concessions would have to come from the United States' end.

For its part, the United States would prefer a restrained policy of live and let live, which may give way eventually to a political détente. The material costs of military action against either regime are prohibitive. A report by the Federation of American Scientists in November 2012 contemplated six scenarios of confrontation with Iran, with global economic price ranges in between $325 billion for a blockade to $1.7 trillion for a full-scale ground invasion.[31] Meanwhile, a military confrontation with North Korea is likely to result in hundreds of thousands of casualties. Aside from its nuclear capability and a sizable chemical weapon arsenal, North Korea has massed thousands of artillery pieces in striking distance of the South Korean capital Seoul, leaving by some estimates only a 45-second warning before the shells, of which hundreds of thousands can be fired per hour, hit their targets.[32]

On the other hand, the development of nuclear weapons is regarded as a major challenge to the US-imposed international order and, as a result, the US goal is not just to reach a modus vivendi with

Iran and North Korea, but also to eliminate their nuclear arsenal and related production facilities.[33] Of course, security is a nonnegligible consideration in both contexts.[34] Yet, these scenarios bring back to mind the discussion of the rationale for NMD in chapter five: the United States is concerned both about the security of its allies and about the impact on its ability to carry out intervention throughout the system, and, consequently, on its prestige as the international leader.[35] Which is why, while the United States would prefer to show restraint for material reasons, its commitment to denuclearization constrains it to take action in the face of Iranian and North Korean recalcitrance or see its prestige as an effective world leader reduced. As seen in chapter two, the United States is more likely to lash out against challengers when the challenge comes from a recalcitrant state, when the offense is particularly blatant, and when the challenge is cumulative over time. Arguably, all of these conditions are present in the Iranian and the North Korean scenarios, which points toward an increased policy of assertiveness in the form of gradually tougher sanctions and even of possible displays of US military might.

In effect, the initial restraint policy favored by the Obama administration had by 2010 given way to increased assertiveness. Iran had balked out of a 2009 deal allowing the swap of its low enriched uranium for nuclear fuel and it was discovered that it had built another uranium-enrichment facility near the city of Qom, besides the known locations of Natanz and Ispahan. Meanwhile, North Korea proceeded in March 2010 to sink a South Korean warship, killing 46 sailors, to shell the South Korean Yeonpyeong island, and to then formally unveil a uranium-enrichment program.[36] In each case, the United States responded with sanctions, while leaving room for even more assertive policies.

Thus, the United States imposed, in cooperation with the UN and the EU, strong sanctions on Iran. The US-EU sanctions are especially biting, as they put into place a European embargo on Iranian oil (the EU being the destination of a fifth of Iran's oil exports); they prohibit financial transactions with Iranian companies associated with the nuclear program, which includes most Iranian banks; ban travel for Iranian officials; and, in relation to the United States, also institute sanctions on foreign companies doing business with Iran's oil industry.[37] However, as sanctions take their toll only over the long haul, the United States is aware that they may be a futile effort to arrest an Iranian program only years away from nuclear capacity. In December 2011, Secretary of Defense Leon Panetta stated that an Iranian nuclear weapon was "unacceptable" and that the United States "will take whatever steps necessary to stop it."[38] This message was delivered even more emphatically by Obama in March 2012: "Iran's leaders should understand that I do not have a policy of containment; I have a policy to prevent Iran from obtaining a nuclear weapon. And as I have made clear time and again during the course of my presidency, I will not hesitate to use force when it is necessary to defend the United States and its interests."[39]

Sanctions were also imposed on North Korea. UN Security Council resolutions 1718 and 1874 put in place an arms embargo, a freeze of assets, an inspection of cargo entering and leaving North Korea for signs of nuclear smuggling, as well as travel bans on North Korean officials. However, counting on the free-riding of China, its main economic partner, Pyongyang has continued its course of defiance, thus increasingly making stepped-up assertiveness a more attractive option for the United States.[40] In effect, as these lines are written, the United States is preparing to put into effect further sanctions in retaliation of a third North Korean nuclear test in February 2013. US decision-makers are now aware that engagement of North Korea does not pay: as a study by Cha has shown, every single North Korean provocation from 1984 onward has resulted in dialogue in which Pyongyang has secured concessions. Moreover, North Korea has employed engagement to buy time to develop both a nuclear arsenal and a long-range missile program.[41]

THE PAKISTANI BIND

The Obama administration's practice of restraint entailed taking prestige costs not only from recalcitrant challengers, but also from free-riding actors, with Pakistan perhaps the worst such offender. Just as in the case of recalcitrant challenges, such prestige losses resulted in a renewed course of assertiveness.

Although Pakistan receives up to $2.2 billion of US aid annually to fight terrorism, its efforts in the aftermath of its joining the US-led coalition have been half-hearted and solely directed against al Qaeda militants.[42] Pakistan has constantly ignored the Taliban fighters that had poured in across its border from Afghanistan after their defeat in 2001. This was not the result of benign neglect. Pakistan lives under the double threat of external destruction by its larger Indian rival and of implosion due to the ethnic diversity of its population. In order to address these issues, Pakistan has been relying since the 1970s on a common Islamic identity and (especially in Kashmir) on the military instrument of Islamic insurgent groups. Moreover, Pakistan has an abiding interest in avoiding encirclement by pro-Indian forces, which requires it to secure the presence in power in Kabul of an ally or a client regime. As such, Pakistan had strongly supported the Taliban in the 1990s as a proxy in Afghanistan. Extending sanctuary and even logistic support to the Taliban is a way to preserve them as a valuable instrument for the advancement of Pakistani interests. However, the Taliban's location in Pakistan makes it exceedingly difficult for the United States to crush their insurgence across the border in Afghanistan, since its troops cannot conduct military operations inside sovereign Pakistani territory without Islamabad's consent. Meanwhile, the Pakistani military leadership, which has the authority to act against the Afghan Taliban inside its own borders, declines to do so.[43]

Admittedly, since 2004, the Pakistani military has conducted several campaigns against militants, notably a major offensive in the Swat Valley in 2009.[44] But the targets of these efforts are not actually those groups involved in insurgency in Afghanistan. Rather, they represent the Pakistani version of the Taliban. Many of theses militants had fought on the side of the Taliban in 2001 and have engaged in a drive to overthrow the Pakistani establishment ever since the government has assaulted their center in the Red Mosque in Islamabad in July 2007.[45] Hence, while Pakistan is fighting its own insurgency, it continues to, at best, turn a blind eye, and, at worst, actively give support to the groups using its territory as a springboard for attacks into Afghanistan and India.[46]

Nor is this the sole US complaint against Pakistan. In 2004, it was unveiled that the father of the Pakistani nuclear project, Abdul Khadeer (A. Q.) Khan, had been operating for years an extensive network of nuclear smuggling operating through Dubai. Thus, the Khan network smuggled technical plans, centrifuge components, and even nuclear material, with the customer list comprising Iran, Libya, and North Korea. While A. Q. Khan was placed under house arrest by Islamabad in 2004 after being pardoned by President Musharraf, the extent to which his activities had been known or sanctioned by the Pakistani intelligence remains ambiguous.[47]

The Obama team started up by describing the fight against the Taliban as an Afpak problem, thus extending beyond Afghanistan into Pakistan, and demanding a larger regional solution. At first, this solution took the characteristic form of engagement, in which there were hints of a bargain involving a settlement with India in return for an end to tolerance toward militants. But because of Indian reluctance to give ground, the initiative came to naught. By 2010, even the rhetoric of Afpak was abandoned over Pakistan's objections at being treated as part of the Afghan problem.[48] But US restraint did not result in improved cooperation.

Faced with continuous Pakistani resistance and feet dragging, the United States resorted again to unilateralism in the form of targeted killings by drones. Initially, the United States sought to preserve formal multilateralism by informing their Pakistani counterparts before strikes were conducted, only to discover that the targets were being forewarned. As a result, the United States moved to conducting attacks, with no prior warning of the Pakistani side.[49] These attacks multiplied from 19 strikes in 2008 to a height of 90 strikes in 2010, then to 54 in 2011, and 34 in the first eight months of 2012.[50] US unilateralism is also detectable in the conduct of the raid that killed Osama bin Laden. The Pakistani side was not informed of the action until the special forces had already exited its territory, and no authorization was ever requested.[51]

Just like the unilateral measures of Clinton and George W. Bush, these Obama forays into assertiveness have not resulted in the free-rider's compliance, but only in more opposition. In turn, this stubborn resistance has justified the need for further unilateral policies. To exemplify, in response to the bin Laden raid, the Pakistani Parliament officially condemned the operation, asked for a review of counterterrorist cooperation with the United States, and demanded an immediate end to drone strikes. The United States then punished Islamabad by freezing $800 billion of its annual aid package.[52]

While the security aspect is not negligible in US-Pakistani relations, it does not surpass prestige concerns. As seen from the above, the United States has given up on the objective of a comprehensive victory over the Taliban, so that the lack of cooperation by Pakistan on military matters less in securing an unachievable strategic objective. However, the Pakistani refusal to submit to US wishes is an impediment to the effective exercise of US leadership, and also represents defiance of an upper-ranked actor. Prestige therefore prompts an assertive policy response that the Obama administration would have avoided otherwise.

POSITIONAL CHALLENGER IN THE MAKING?

A similar evolution toward assertiveness took place in US relations with China. Despite Obama's efforts to enlist China as a partner in its neo-new world order project, to the point where there was speculation about the emergence of a G2 world economic (and possibly political) directorate or of a Chimerica (China plus America) combined economic system, relations between Washington and Beijing eventually took a turn for the worse in his first four years in office. By January 2011, Secretary of State Hillary Clinton was stating that the US relationship with China "is not a relationship that fits neatly into the black and white categories like friend or rival" and that "there is no such thing as a G2."[53]

From the point of view of the United States, the sources of friction between the two countries come at least in part from China's free-riding, that is, its shirking its contribution to the US-ensured global order of which it is a chief beneficiary. The "responsible stakeholder" argument, made by Undersecretary of State Robert Zoellick, was predicated on this precise point: as "the dragon emerged and joined the world," it had "a responsibility to strengthen the international system that has enabled its success," by working with the US to address challenges.[54] Nevertheless, China has constantly limited, conditioned, or avoided altogether providing its share to the maintenance of international order, which has also affected US prestige as an effective international leader. The list of US complaints comprises old grievances such as China's human rights records, copyright infringement, and China's refusal to curb down its carbon gas emissions; and also a flurry of new ones, such as the overvaluing of the Chinese yuan by reference to the US dollar, which gives an edge to Chinese products in competition to America's, US access to China's market, and China's export limitations of rare earth metals. Chinese foreign policy also makes the list, as the United States is unhappy about the opposition of China to international action against recalcitrant governments in Pyongyang, Tehran, and, more recently, Damascus.[55]

The current Chinese bouts of free-riding had a clear prestige underlining, as China sought to convey the message that a declining United States deserved less deference from a rising Beijing. In effect, a recent report made the case that a significant reason for the growing strategic distrust between Washington and Beijing comes from the latter's perception that the former is in decline, while its own capabilities have increased to the point of warranting great power status, which entitles it to additional prestige.[56] Thus, the Chinese press cover of Obama's visit to China in November sought to create the impression that the US president had come as a supplicant to China. In subsequent international talks in December 2009 in Copenhagen, China offended the United States, by sending to meet with Obama a lower-ranked official, who then repeatedly interrupted talks to get instructions from superiors. Moreover, in order to get a deal and talk to the Chinese prime minister, the US president and the secretary of state had to burst uninvited into a private session of Chinese, Brazilian, and Indian leaders. This behavior was widely viewed by the US camp as an elaborate and deliberate Chinese insolent insult.[57]

China may well emerge to constitute not just a symbolic challenger, but also a positional one, which may overtake the United States economically, and may become a competitor in the military field, and in terms of influence in the Asia Pacific region, thus displacing Washington as the dominant power in the international hierarchy. Of course, the United States would seek to preserve its supremacy (and the accompanying prestige), which would also lead to increase assertiveness. As its economic and military capabilities developed, Beijing has stepped up both the rhetoric and the action in regard to activities by other parties' warships within the confines of its exclusive economic zone, stretching 200 nautical miles from its shores, even though these activities, if not hostile, are allowed under the UN Convention on the Law of the Sea. Furthermore, China has emphasized the protection of its sea-lanes, by taking action outside the economic exclusive zone in the disputed territories in the South China Sea (the Spratly Islands) and in the East China Sea (the Senkaku or Diaoyou Islands). So far these actions have comprised the prohibition of fishing, the arrest of Vietnamese fishermen, and the conduct of patrols and military exercises. Finally, China has been vocal in criticizing US military exercises in the China Sea.[58]

The United States has responded to these Chinese symbolic and possibly positional challenges through increased assertiveness of its own. Thus, at the July 2010 ASEAN meeting in Hanoi, Clinton signaled the US commitment to ensuring free navigation in the South China Sea. In September of the same year, Assistant Secretary of State Kurt Campbell restated the US abiding interest in the freedom of navigation in the area, its right to conduct to military exercises there, and its intention "to step up its game" through a "consequential, long-term investment and commitment" to Asia Pacific, which he described as the "fulcrum of history."[59] This commitment then became official when the Obama administration announced in late 2011 its "pivot to Asia" initiative, which means that henceforward Asia Pacific is going to be considered as a region of particular significance for US foreign policy and warrant an extensive commitment of US military resources, even under the conditions of economic austerity. As Obama put it to the Australian Parliament in November 2011 describing the United States' "top priority" in the region: "We are a Pacific power and we are here to stay...So let there be no doubt: In the Asia Pacific in the 21st century, the United States of America is all in." This discourse was soon followed by the unveiling of a US-led Trans-Pacific Strategic Economic Partnership, comprising nine states, among whom are Singapore, Australia, Malaysia, and Vietnam, and possibly extendable to Japan; the deployment of US forces to Australia and of additional ships to Singapore; and the extension of naval defense cooperation with the Philippines and of security collaboration with India and Indonesia.[60]

The conclusion to be drawn is not that the United States has vowed to pursue the containment of China, but rather that the relations between the two countries are more tense than they used to be, even though manifold economic and security incentives exist for cooperation. For certain, Asian security is a nonnegligible aspect of the US foreign policy pivot to Asia. But this is not necessarily the exclusive consideration, as the United States is equally preoccupied with making sure it remains the uncontested dominant power in the region. Thus, the pivot to Asia is really about remaining and being acknowledged as the international number one, a point acknowledged by Campbell in his 2010 declarations: according to the assistant secretary of state, the United States means " to play an important and indeed dominant role in the Asia-Pacific region for the next, forty, thirty, fifty years."[61] Hence, in order to conserve its prestige as the dominant power, the United States is willing to put up with the increased economic costs of a substantially more assertive foreign policy toward China.

CHAPTER CONCLUSION

As Obama's experiment with restraint predictably ran into the same sort of symbolic challenges that had plagued the original version of the policy, the United States has begun to reconsider the advantages of the previously discounted policy of assertiveness. It is true that the administration attempted to keep a lid on the dimensions of its foreign involvement. But to the extent that a decision for involvement was made, considerations of economic costs lost out every single time when pitted against prestige. Symbolic challenges forced the United States to revert to assertiveness, whether in the form of use of force, threats to use force, the pledge and undertaking of commitments, or/ and unilateralism. Thus, the result of these measures is at present a foreign policy hybrid of assertiveness practiced on the cheap.

8

CONCLUSION

If there is a common denominator in the US foreign policy in the post–Cold War, this consists in the emphasis of the role of world leader. Reference to the need for continual exercise of global leadership by the United States or to the related motif of US greatness as the international leader figures in every single State of the Union Address delivered by a US president for more than two decades from 1990 to 2012. Thus, from George H. W. Bush's forewarning proclamation in 1991 that "today, in a rapidly changing world, American leadership is indispensable," to Clinton's announcement in 1995 that "our security still depends on our continued world leadership for peace and freedom and democracy," to George W. Bush's conclusion in 2006 that "the only way to control our destiny is by our leadership—so the United States of America will continue to lead," to Obama's 2009's point that "as we stand at this crossroads of history, the eyes of all people in all nations are once again upon us—watching to see what we do with this moment, waiting for us to lead," every post–Cold War president has paid homage to the US position as number one. The most recent address in 2012 is also a case in point, as it mentions "the renewal of American leadership" and "that America remains the one indispensable nation in world affairs."[1]

Why does world leadership weigh so heavily on the US leaders' psyche? The most convincing answer is that the status and prestige associated with being the dominant power are of considerable importance for US decision-makers and public alike as a key source of national self-esteem. It is only by comparison with other groups, in this case other states, that a social actor is able to receive confirmation of its social worth. Thus, being number one is a source of US pride.[2] This is not just a conjecture, as in a period of recession no less, more Americans prefer for the United States to remain number one with little growth, than to be number two to China in a scenario where their income would double. Clearly, as Aron once put it, "Man does not live by bread alone."[3] Self-esteem is a fundamental psychological requirement as well, and prestige, which is to say the manifestations of deference by other actors, represents the means to secure it. As a result, individuals and groups constantly require prestige and would take measures to defend against its loss.

While the United States was never in jeopardy of losing its number one rank in the post–Cold War, it constantly faced manifold symbolic challenges to its prestige, which, if left unaddressed, would have raised questions as to its right of leading the world, as well as would have proven humiliating. The vast majority of these challenges fell into the category of insolent offenses, in which the challenger, to paraphrase Aristotle, robbed the United States of the honor that was its due by refusing to show it appropriate deference as world leader. These challenges came both from recalcitrant actors who openly contested the international order, and in so doing could not help but defy the United States, and from free-riding states, who, while benefitting from the US-imposed order, sought to minimize their contributions to its maintenance. In order to protect its self-esteem, the United States reasserted its prestige through demonstrations of will and punishment of the challengers. In the process, preserving prestige in the face of challenges proved incompatible with the attempts at restraint, which were discarded in favor of an increasingly assertive foreign policy.

The findings confirm these hypotheses. As chapter three shows, the US experiment with restraint was short-lived and unsatisfying. The US decision-makers mistakenly assumed following the Gulf War of 1991 that they would preside over an unprecedented period of peace and prosperity, with little fear of new recalcitrant challenges and with the wholehearted help of its international partners. However, the illusions of order, cooperation, and peace under the budding globalization of the early 1990s were never fully translated into practice. Instead, the post–Cold War years, understood as a "holiday from history" compared to the half century of confrontation with the Kremlin, proved a troublesome interval. As James Woolsey, the director of the CIA in the first Clinton administration, put it in his 1992 confirmation hearing: "We have slain a large dragon. But now we live in a jungle filled with a bewildering variety of poisonous snakes and in many ways the dragon was much easier to keep track of."[4] In the post–Cold War, if a challenge occurred, this became the United States' responsibility, as the only superpower left and as the self-proclaimed world leader. Every time the United States did not act, its passivity was susceptible of being viewed as pusillanimity and opened up Washington to accusations of having abdicated its role as a dominant power. This was not conjecture, as chapter three shows: the accusation was in fact leveled by Chirac in the aftermath of the fall of Srebrenica, when the French president claimed that the position of world leader was now vacant.[5] Consequently, the post–Cold War timeframe witnessed a US obsession with avoiding the impression of vacillation, which led to repeated demonstrations of political and military success, destined to prove to the world US mettle as world leader.

In Kosovo, as chapter four elaborates, the problem was the cumulative effect of successive instances of Yugoslav disobedience on US prestige, coming on the heels of a similar experience in Bosnia. If the United States could not stand up to a petty Balkans dictator, how could it possibly entertain pretensions of maintaining order in the world? For this reason, the United States sought a military confrontation with Miloševíc, designed to prove beyond doubt its credentials as the indispensable nation. When the expectation that Yugoslavia was going to cave in after a few days was not borne out by facts, the United States persisted with bombing, because achieving victory in the sense of returning the Kosovar refugees to the province was crucial to safeguarding US and NATO's prestige. This is also why by May 1999 the United States was even willing to consider a ground offensive in Kosovo, a prospect it had opposed tooth and nail since the start of the crisis. In Kosovo, the United States shed the reluctance to employ force on a large scale, which had been a mainstay of its earlier foreign policy. Moreover, the United States sought retribution against Miloševíc in the aftermath of the bombing campaign, working toward his political exit and extradition to The Hague.

Prestige accounts as well, as seen in chapter five, for the unilateral turn in US foreign policy. In its mission to ensure order as the world leader, the United States sought both improved effectiveness, which was restricted by the opposition or feet-dragging of allies and partners, and being awarded exemptions from the responsibilities of ordinary states. Furthermore, the United States sought to punish those partners and allies that not only shirked contributing to the maintenance of international order, but also blocked US endeavors. Hence, the United States demanded (a) guarantees that its troops stationed abroad would not be the subject of prosecution by the ICC; (b) that the United States would be allowed to deploy a NMD system in violation of the ABM Treaty so as to prevent the possibility of being deterred from intervention by rogue states that threatened to develop nuclear weapons and intercontinental ballistic missiles; and (c) that its requests to use force would receive the blessings of the UN Security Council. However, on all these points, the United States was defeated by the resistance of other international actors. It faced two options: either persist with a multilateral approach, even at the risk of often being condemned to passivity when international agreement could not be reached; or take matters in its own hands and face its partners with a *fait accompli* at the risk of provoking their discontent. As such, the first option had backfired, with Bosnia, Iraq, and Kosovo being the most poignant examples. The United States thus turned to the alternative avenue of unilateralism. It refused to sign the ICC statute, withdrew from the ABM Treaty when Russia refused to modify the treaty to allow for NMD, and did away with the requirement of a UN Security Council authorization to use force.

Finally, as chapter six shows, the invasion of Iraq was conceived as a showcase of US leadership, made necessary by September 11. The Bush administration, in particular Rumsfeld and Cheney, and its neo-conservative supporters wanted to send a message to the effect that the United States could not be provoked with impunity and that it was the rightful world leader, not only because of its power, but also because of its will in making use of it. In this respect, Afghanistan was ill-suited as the grounds for a "demonstration effect:" it was a remote and mountainous terrain, where operations would have bogged down into a police search for the faceless al Qaeda and the Taliban, which did not seem significant enough foes. Saddam Hussein was, by contrast, the most prominent of the challengers the United States had to face in the post–Cold War. His regime had nowhere to hide, and action against it would have been "a cakewalk." Therefore, bringing Saddam down would have been the ultimate vindication of US prestige. In so doing, the Bush administration would have achieved the national greatness the neoconservatives clamored for: the implications for any challenger would have been unambiguous: "Don't even think about it."[6]

Alternative Accounts of Assertiveness

How do structuralism, exceptionalism, and revisionism fare by comparison to prestige in accounting for post–Cold War US foreign policy?

Structuralism emerges as the most formidable theoretical competitor to prestige as an explanation for US assertiveness. Security makes a plausible case for the US intervention over Kosovo, caused by fears of a wider conflict that could have engulfed the Balkans. This is particularly based on the Christmas warning to refrain from military operations in Kosovo. However, by 1999, the Christmas warning was no longer on the table: throughout 1998 the United States had tolerated four Serb offensives in Kosovo. The United States also did not pay attention to the risk of a conflict in the Balkans extending to Greece and Turkey, by remaining uninvolved in the Albanian crisis of 1997 and by avoiding a preventive deployment in FYROM in 1998.

Concerning the US resort to unilateralist measures, structuralism has a possible valid point in portraying the pursuit of NMD as caused by concerns over the security of allies in face of coercion by rogue states. But this point has to be qualified since the allies did not believe they were at risk from rogue states, the United States had no reliable information that missile defense would work, and the deployment allowed not only defensive, but also offensive operations by the United States. In relation to the wider phenomenon of unilateralism, structuralism posits it to be the consequence of unrivalled US power. However, the record points not to overwhelming US strength, but to US weakness as the root of unilateralism. The United States only chose unilateralism as a second-best option after its efforts at persuading other states failed.

Structuralism is on its strongest ground in the case of the invasion of Iraq, which it explains by reference to US concerns over Saddam's possession and development of WMD. Even if no WMD programs were found in Iraq, structuralism holds that US decision-makers thought they were in fact present. However, misperception cannot be invoked regarding the element that represented the most significant justification for regime change: the alleged Iraqi effort to develop nuclear weapons. The leading pieces of evidence invoked by the US officials—the aluminum tubes and the uranium from Niger—have been demonstrated as false, and were nonetheless used in the public case for invasion. The misperception theory is also weakened by the timing of the decision to invade, which was taken independently of the available intelligence on Iraqi WMD, as well as by the US policy record from 1991 onward, which was concerned not with disarming Iraq, but instead with overthrowing Saddam. To this extent, structuralism provides only an incomplete answer as to why Iraq was invaded.

Exceptionalism or the desire to promote democracy in the world appears overstated in the three case studies. In Kosovo, although the bombing campaign is often presented as an instance of humanitarian intervention, the United States paid little attention to the impact of Serb retaliation against the Kosovars. The Clinton decision-makers had anticipated such a reaction from Belgrade and took no measures to prevent it. Once Milošević began to empty the province of its Albanian inhabitants, the United States continued to pursue the intervention through high-altitude bombing, which, even if ineffective in curtailing ethnic cleansing, posed no danger to NATO pilots.

The exceptionalist account of unilateralism in the late 1990s is counterintuitive, because it is the covenant approach rather than democracy promotion that emerges as the better fit for the US policy of going at it alone. Even the covenanted interpretation is not fully convincing, since the US reaction was not motivated by the concern to maintain the purity of US principles, as in the times when the United States was an ideological outsider and a vulnerable state.

Concerning Iraq, exceptionalism mounts what is an ex post facto case for a reverse domino theory, in which the Middle East was going to be transformed into a zone of democracy, with Iraq as the first domino. Yet, this project emerged as the alternative justification for the invasion only after no WMD were discovered in Iraq. In fact, US decision-makers were skeptic of the potential of democracy in selling the war to the public, even though a genuine commitment to democratization of the Middle East should have required a strong propaganda effort on behalf of democracy. Furthermore, some of the key Bush decision-makers, foremost Rumsfeld and Cheney, had little interest in the development of Iraqi democracy and, consequently, ignored the process of transition required by democratization.

Revisionism stands on the thinnest ground when accounting for US policy in the post–Cold War. Kosovo had little to do with the Open Door, as Yugoslavia was more open to globalization than either FYROM or Albania, and Belgrade was only interested in a Serb nationalist project, not in disseminating a message of resisting the United States. The vaunted militarization of the US empire also fails to convince: if anything the Pentagon was the branch of the US government most opposed to intervention and to a ground campaign in Kosovo. Furthermore, revisionism has difficulties in explaining US unilateralism. If the US goal is to promote global openness to US products of capital by sponsoring international treaties and institutions that enhance the American empire's power and legitimacy, a choice to undermine them becomes unfathomable. Revisionism's best case is by far Iraq, regarding both oil reserves and the potential for military bases. However, oil was not the chief US motivation to overthrow Saddam: if so, such action could have been carried on in the 1991 offensive, or the United States would not have had to rely on international sanctions for 12 years. As to basing rights, revisionism does not address the reasons for which the United States did not pressure Saudi Arabia into continuing to harbor its troops instead of launching a cost-ineffective invasion, nor does it take into account the US basing rights in Qatar.

The structural emphasis on power, the prominence of exceptionalist values, and the revisionist attention to domestic concerns for economic openness, are all necessary, although not sufficient components of any rigorous account of US foreign policy in the post–Cold War. However, the inclusion of prestige considerations in such a mixed model is also necessary to make sense of the logic of the US actions in this interval.

THEORETICAL IMPLICATIONS AND POLICY RELEVANCE

These conclusions contribute to the growing scholarly interest in status and prestige by demonstrating the relevance of prestige considerations for a unipole at the height of its power. At this point, the literature is focused overwhelmingly on the prestige demands of rising powers to the neglect of implications of prestige for dominant powers, which, however, should be equally, if not much more, interested in averting prestige losses.[7] The case of the United States in the post–Cold War, which, because of the extent of its unparalleled dominance in the last four centuries, represents a mandatory subject of discussion, redresses this omission.

A further contribution of my argument is that it refines our understanding of the role of prestige in explaining conflict under unipolar conditions. The literature assumes that because its position is beyond question, the unipole will not face any prestige challenges unless it suffers substantial declines in capabilities and performance relative to a competitor state.[8] Yet, prestige may be called into question not solely by positional challenges, where a rising state is on the verge of surpassing the dominant power, but also by symbolic challenges, where no such risk exists, but questions are being raised as to the right of the unipole to be dominant based on the perception of its effectiveness.

Unipolarity may be peaceful as well as stable, but only as far as great power relations are concerned. Indeed, the unipole and the second-in-rank great powers are likely to minimize confrontation, since conflict will not result in the improvement of the latter's status.[9] However, unipolarity is not likely to be peaceful in relation to confrontations between the unipole and recalcitrant challengers. This is not so, as the structuralist argument goes, because the unipole is concerned for its security or for the status quo, for which there is little concrete evidence.[10] Instead, the unipole is constrained to act so as to demonstrate its effectiveness and, in so doing, preserve its prestige vis-à-vis the other actors in the system. It is even possible that unipolarity supposes a multiplication of symbolic challenges, because the unipole has to live to higher expectations of effectiveness than ordinary states, because it requires a higher level of deference from more states than would be the case of a regular dominant power, and because of the multiplication of the responsibilities it assumes as the only state capable of addressing global issues.

The theoretical contribution of this volume also lies in its argument in favor of understanding prestige as a goal pursued by states in world politics for psychological satisfaction rather than as a means for obtaining instrumental rewards in terms of security and power. Considering prestige as a goal in its own right provides theoretical value added in two ways. First, prestige is on a much stronger ground than instrumental views in accounting for suboptimal strategic behavior, that is, when states choose policies that do not pay off materially or produce increased material costs. This certainly does not mean that prestige is the only variable that could lead to suboptimal strategic behavior—domestic politics, misperception, and ideology are often invoked in this respect. However, as seen from the discussion of alternative theories, these factors played only a limited part by comparison to prestige in affecting US suboptimal strategic behavior in the post–Cold War. Therefore, while prestige does not claim to account for all suboptimal policies, it still represents an important explanation for the occurrence and pervasiveness of this type of strategic behavior.[11]

Second, the instrumental views of prestige miss the role played by emotions in foreign policy decision-making. By contrast, prestige, understood as a psychological goal, is built on the premise that emotions help determine the priority of pursuing various state goals, and that, occasionally, they lead decision-makers astray by making them pay less attention to the adverse material consequences of the policies considered.

My most important conclusion in terms of policy relevance is highlighting the inherent limitations of a foreign policy of restraint from the point of view of satisfying US prestige requirements. Restraint is frequently urged on US decision-makers by scholars and public opinion leaders on account of keeping a lid on economic costs, strengthening cooperation, augmenting US soft power, and avoiding backlash by removing semblances of threats and bullying. The alternative of assertiveness is deemed to have the opposite effect of increasing material costs, diminishing international sympathy, and increasing opposition to US leadership, factors that, if unaddressed, may lead to decline, and to demotion.[12] The point I raise is not that such recommendations of restraint are necessarily wrong, but rather that they are unfeasible, since they do not take into account the need to secure US prestige in the eyes of the American people, as well as in the eyes of the world.

The many advocates of restraint are correct in that assertiveness represents a suboptimal strategic behavior.[13] Even though assertiveness is neither the root cause nor the sole determinant of the ongoing recession and of the lopsided US budget and trade deficits, its sizable financial costs, nevertheless, contribute to this overall development. A Congressional Report estimated that by March 2011, the direct and indirect costs of the war on terrorism was 1.283 trillion dollars; while some analyses raised the prospect that only the operations in Iraq, Afghanistan, and Pakistan would run eventually to an excess of three trillion dollars.[14] This latter estimate would place the costs of the wars at about the same level as the annual total US expenditures of 3,599 trillion dollars, and about a fifth of its 15.20-trillion-dollar 2011 GDP.[15] The soft power costs are no less significant. By 2003, the US public global image had plummeted in polls even among allies.[16] In 2003, majorities in 15 EU countries went so far as to indicate the United States as the principal cause of world instability, ahead of the alleged "axis of evil" trio of Iraq, Iran, and North Korea. Similarly, in 2006, a PEW poll conducted in 15 countries found that more people around the world worried about US power than about Iran's nuclear program.[17] And even if these costs may be seen as tolerable for the unipole, assertiveness is yet to produce offsetting material benefits.

However, the lofty price tag of assertiveness should not imply that restraint is a cost-free option—the practice of restraint involves a no-less hefty prestige bill. A state that practices restraint signs on a voluntary policy of meekness, as it refrains from employing force, takes the objections of allies and partners to heart, abstains from embarrassing them by acting without their support, and reduces its political and military commitments to other states' security and welfare. Nevertheless, in so doing, the restrained state denies itself the instruments to respond to challenges to its prestige, both because it foregoes employing punitive force and because it is constrained by the need to secure the assent of other states before acting.

Hence, for a restrained state it is difficult to issue warnings to the effect of "don't tread on me," if there are no consequences to such trespasses. Not responding to challenges is, on the one hand, humiliating, and, on the other hand, socially awkward since it implies that the aspersions concerning the right of the state to superior position and deference may be justified. This may not be an issue for states that are anyway low-ranking in the international hierarchy and are therefore unable to contemplate action beyond hopeless protests. But in the case of a dominant state, responding to perceived offenses is a requisite of preserving one's high rank, the deference of others, and implicitly one's sense of self-esteem. As Aristotle has argued, there are psychological and even possible social demotion costs for not answering symbolic challenges: "For those who are not angry at the things they should be are thought to be fools...for such a man is thought not to feel things nor to be pained by them, and since he does not become angry, he is thought unlikely to defend himself; and to endure being insulted and to put up with insults to one's friends is slavish."[18]

One could object that not putting up with insults/challenges may result further down the road in improved security by deterring future offenses or/and by persuading opponents that it is more prudent to comply rather than cross the dominant power. However, as I have argued repeatedly, it is considerably difficult to separate reputation or leadership from prestige owing to an inevitable overlap. According to the literature, the tangible benefits of a foreign policy are largely hypothetical. As Mercer argues, "It is wrong to believe that a state's reputation for resolve is worth fighting for," or as Tang contends, "Too many wars have been waged for the sake of defending honor, prestige, reputation and credibility."[19] My findings confirm that a firm stance or the punishment of a challenger by the United States in the post–Cold War did not result in any noticeable lessening of future challenges or in any improvement of the US leverage in imposing its will on opponents.

However, the volume disagrees with the conclusion of reputation studies that because it does not result in verifiable material benefits, a foreign policy of prestige is a useless pursuit. If this were the case, policy-makers would have internalized the lesson of its counter-productivity over millennia. What I suggest therefore, is that decision-makers seek prestige principally not out of material utility concerns, but rather because of its psychological and social payoff both for themselves as representatives of the state, and for the wider public. As Kissinger has argued, "No serious policymaker could allow himself to succumb to the fashionable debunking of 'prestige,' or 'honor,' or 'credibility'."[20] Nor are US policy-makers likely to.

Therefore, the issue that so far has been neglected by recommendations of restraint is that the United States does not have only security, economic, and soft power considerations to live up to, but also prestige concerns that need to be addressed by its foreign policy. Of course, there are important additional arguments to be made in favor of assertiveness—for example, that US disengagement from the world would lead to a worsening of regional and global security, a proliferation of authoritarianism and human rights abuses, and a reduction in global economic and cultural exchanges.[21] However, the United States refrains from pulling away from the world not just because it is concerned with what would happen to the world, but also and mainly because of the erosive effect such a pullout would have on its own prestige. No matter how sincere the efforts of sympathetic foreign policy-makers may have been in the post–Cold War, the US experiment with restraint turned out sour, because of the constant reoccurrence of provocations that continually pulled back the United States into overseas matters. A similar evolution to the early 1990s is discernible, as chapter seven shows, in Obama's foreign policy. Thus, an examination of US foreign policy in the last two decades shows a clear propensity toward strategies at the assertive end of the foreign policy spectrum. Hence, restraint may be commendable, but it constitutes an unsustainable option, given the United States' supreme position in international hierarchy.

A Smart Policy of Prestige

The United States should avoid being oversensitive to prestige challenges. Not even the United States has the resources to respond to every perceived offense to its prestige around the world. Accordingly, the US decision-makers should be careful not to keep grudges whenever an avenue of rehabilitation is workable, and challengers signal they are willing to mend their ways. An irascible US foreign policy, which sees offenses at every turn, would serve only to increase the costs of dealing with challengers, would alienate allies and well-wishers, and would generate more sympathy and, possibly, even support for US opponents. Furthermore, a response that is ill-considered risks causing the impression of defeat or of failure, which would undermine rather than strengthen US prestige. But on the other hand, the United States should not put up with defiance, whether from recalcitrant actors or free-riding states. As September 11 has shown, there are challenges that the United States has to answer.

Different offenses deserve different responses: from forgiveness to shrugging the offense off, signaling diplomatic displeasure, mounting counter-propaganda efforts, shunning the offender, imposing economic sanctions, and mounting military responses of varied intensity from the conduct of exercises to strikes and intervention. In this sense, even an assertive United States should discriminate between challenges and challengers. This trend is already present in US foreign policy, as seen in the greater forbearance shown toward powerful partners such as Russia and China, and in the stronger responses in those contexts where the material costs of the response are cheaper (Somalia, Kosovo, and Libya). However, the avoidance of costs should not necessarily be the only consideration on the table, as this may lead to (a) over-involvement in areas that otherwise present few material interests; or/and (b) an abrupt end of the mission before objectives are fully secured. The magnitude of the perceived offense should also be taken into account, as should be the specific background of the challenger, and of the international context at that moment, as well as the ability to devote appropriate resources and to garner domestic and international support. Trying to achieve the best of both worlds and mount public shows of strength with insufficient means is a recipe for future embarrassment, as was seen in the 1990s in Somalia and Kosovo and, more dramatically, in the 2000s in Afghanistan and Iraq. Hence, if the United States cannot help being assertive, it should, nonetheless, be assertive in a smart way.

NOTES

1 INTRODUCTION

1. US Department of Defense, *Soviet Military Power* (Washington: Department of Defense, 1990), p. 21.
2. Grand strategy is "both as a conceptual road map, describing how to match identified resources to the promotion of identified interests, and a set of policy prescriptions." Colin Dueck, *Reluctant Crusaders: Power, Culture, and Change in American Grand Strategy* (Princeton: Princeton University Press, 2006), pp. 9–11; also see Richard Betts, *American Force: Dangers, Delusions, and Dilemmas in National Security* (New York: Columbia University Press, 2012).
3. The post–Cold War refers to a timeframe beginning in 1989 and continuing to the present. For different timelines ending in 2001 and 2003, see Hal Brands, *From Berlin to Baghdad: America's Search for Purpose in the Post–Cold War World* (Lexington: University Press of Kentucky, 2008); Derek Chollet and James Goldgeier, *America between Wars: From 11/9 to 9/11* (New York: Public Affairs, 2008).
4. Chollet and Goldgeier, *America between Wars*; Brands, *From Berlin to Baghdad*; ; Barry Posen and Andrew Ross, "Competing Visions for US Grand Strategy," *International Security* 21 (Winter 1996/1997): 5–53.
5. Ivo Daalder and James Lindsay, *America Unbound: The Bush Revolution in Foreign Policy* (Washington: Brookings Institution Press, 2003); Philip Gordon, "End of the Bush Revolution," *Foreign Affairs* 85 (July/August 2006): 75–86; Melvyn Leffler and Jeffrey Legro, eds., *To Lead the World: American Strategy after the Bush Doctrine* (Oxford: Oxford University Press, 2008); Daniel Drezner, "Does Obama Have a Grand Strategy?" *Foreign Affairs* 90 (July/August 2011): 57–68.
6. Robert Gilpin, *War and Change in World Politics* (Cambridge: Cambridge University Press, 1981), pp. 23–4; Fareed Zakaria, *From Wealth to Power: The Unusual Origins of America's World Role* (Princeton: Princeton University Press, 1998).
7. Nicholas Spykman, *America's Strategy in World Politics: The United States and the Balance of Power* (New York: Harcourt, Brace, 1942), pp. 3–7.

8. Barry Buzan, *United States and the Great Powers: World Politics in the 21st Century* (Cambridge: Polity Press, 2004), pp. 68–71; Stephen Brooks and William Wohlforth, *World Out of Balance: International Relations and the Challenge of American Primacy* (Princeton: Princeton University Press, 2008).

9. Paul Kennedy, "The Eagle Has Landed," *Financial Times*, February 2, 2002.

10. Robert Jervis, "The Remaking of a Unipolar World," *Washington Quarterly* 29 (Summer 2006): 7–19; Robert Jervis, "Unipolarity: A Structural Perspective," *World Politics* 61 (January 2009): 191; John G. Ikenberry, Michael Mastanduno, and William Wohlforth, "Unipolarity, State Behavior, and Consequences," *World Politics* 61 (January 2009): 1–27.

11. Barry Posen, "Pull Back: The Case for a Less Activist Foreign Policy," *Foreign Affairs* 92 (January/February 2013): 116–28; Christopher Layne, "America's Middle East Strategy after Iraq," *Review of International Studies* 35 (January 2009): 5–25; Richard Rosecrance and Gu Guoliang, eds., *Power and Restraint: A Shared Vision for the US-China Relationship* (New York: Public Affairs, 2009); Barry Posen, "After Bush: The Case for Restraint," *American Interest* 3 (November/December 2007): 6–32; Stephen Walt, *Taming American Power: The Global Response to US Primacy* (New York: W. W. Norton, 2005); John G. Ikenberry, ed., *America Unrivalled: The Future of the Balance of Power* (Ithaca: Cornell University Press, 2002); Christopher Layne, "From Preponderance to Offshore Balancing: America's Future Grand Strategy," *International Security* 22 (Summer 1997): 86–124; Eugene Gholz, Darryl Press, and Harvey Sapolsky, "Come Home America: The Strategy of Restraint in the Face of Temptation," *International Security* 21 (Spring 1997): 5–48.

12. Richard Ned Lebow, *A Cultural Theory of International Relations* (Cambridge: Cambridge University Press, 2008); William Wohlforth, "Unipolarity, Status Competition, and Great Power War," *World Politics* 61 (January 2009): 28–57; Deborah Larson and Alexander Shevchenko, "Status Seekers: Chinese and Russian Responses to US Primacy," *International Security* 34 (Spring 2010): 63–95; Thomas Volgy, Renato Corbetta, Keith Grant, and Ryan Baird, eds., *Major Powers and the Quest for Status in International Politics: Global and Regional Perspectives* (New York: Macmillan, 2011); Thomas Lindemann and Erik Ringmar, eds., *The Struggle for Recognition in International Politics* (Boulder: Paradigm, 2011).

13. Richard Ned Lebow, *Why Nations Fight: Past and Future Motives for War* (New York: Cambridge University Press, 2010), p. 113.

14. Wohlforth, "Unipolarity, Status, and War," p. 29.

15. Volgy et al., *Major Powers*; Larson and Shevchenko, "Status Seekers."

16. Alexander George and Andrew Bennett, *Case Studies and Theory Development in Social Sciences* (Cambridge: MIT Press, 2005),

pp. 205–10, 215; James Fearon, "Counterfactuals and Hypothesis Testing in Political Science," *World Politics* 43 (January 1991): 178, 180.

17. Posen and Ross, " Competing Visions."
18. The United States has continually tilted in the post–Cold War toward assertiveness, because cooperative security and primacy represent the most assertive strategies. By comparison, isolationism, offshore balancing, and selective engagement have not been seriously considered.

2 US PRESTIGE AND ITS CHALLENGERS

1. Barry O'Neill, *Honor, Symbols and War* (Ann Arbor: Michigan University Press, 1999), pp. 193–4; Daniel Markey, "The Prestige Motive in International Relations," Unpublished doctoral dissertation (Princeton University Department of Politics, November 2000), p. 156; Brian Turner, *Status* (Minneapolis: University of Minnesota Press, 1988), pp. 1–8.
2. Reinhard Wolf, "Respect and Disrespect in International Politics: The Significance of Status Recognition," *International Theory* 3 (February 2011): 105–42.
3. Honor covers both internal honor, or natural self-worth, and external honor, or the acknowledgement of this claim. Julian Pitt-Rivers, "Honor and Social Status," in *Honor and Shame: The Values of Mediterranean Society*, ed. J. G. Peristiany (Chicago: University of Chicago Press, 1966), p. 21. The Chinese concept of "face" is a rough equivalent for honor. Hsien Chin Hu, "The Chinese Concepts of Face," *American Anthropologist* 46 (January 1944): 45–64.
4. Turner, *Status*, p. 5.
5. See esp. Weber, "Class, Status, Party," in *From Max Weber: Essays in Sociology*, ed. H. H. Gerth and C. Wright Mills (New York: Oxford University Press, 1946), pp. 180–95; Erving Goffman, *Interaction Ritual: Essays in Face-to-Face Behavior* (Chicago: Aldine, 1967), pp. 70–1.
6. Thomas Lindemann and Erik Ringmar, eds., *The Struggle for Recognition in International Politics* (Boulder: Paradigm, 2011); Robert McGinn, "Prestige and the Logic of Political Argument," *The Monist* 56 (January 1972): 100–16.
7. Fred Hirsch, *Social Limits to Growth* (Cambridge: Harvard University Press, 1978), pp. 27–31, 36–41, 52; Robert Frank, *Choosing the Right Pond: Human Behavior and the Quest for Status* (New York: Oxford University Press, 1985); Randall Schweller, "Realism and the Present Great Power System: Growth and Possible Conflict over Scarce Resources," in *Unipolar Politics: Realism and the State Strategy after the Cold War*, ed. Ethan Kapstein and Michael Mastanduno (New York: Columbia University Press, 1999), pp. 48–9.
8. Roger Gould, *Collision of Wills: How Ambiguity about Social Rank Breeds Conflict* (Chicago: University of Chicago Press, 2003), pp. 42–9.

9. For a review of political philosophy and prestige, see Markey, "Prestige Motive," pp. 11–70; Richard Ned Lebow, *A Cultural Theory of International Relations* (Cambridge: Cambridge University Press, 2008), chap. 3; for evolutionary biology arguments, see Stephen Peter Rosen, *War and Human Nature* (Princeton: Princeton University Press, 2005), chap. 3; Alan Booth, Greg Shelley, Allan Mazur, Gerry Tharp, and Roger Kittok, "Testosterone, and Winning and Losing in Human Competition," *Hormones and Behavior* 23 (1989): 556–71; Robert Wright, *The Moral Animal: Evolutionary Psychology and Everyday Life* (New York: Vintage Books, 1995), pp. 239–46.

10. Michael Hogg and Dominic Abrams, *Social Identifications: A Social Psychology of Intergroup Relations and Group Processes* (London: Routledge, 1988), chap. 2; Henri Tajfel and John Turner, "Social Identity Theory of Intergroup Behavior," in *Psychology of Intergroup Relations*, ed. William Austin and Stephen Worchel (Chicago: Nelson-Hall, 1986).

11. Lebow, *Cultural Theory*, p. 63. A related argument consists in the psychological safety (ontological security) of the self from uncertainty, as opposed to physical security, which consists of the safety of one's corporeal body from harm. Jennifer Mitzen, "Ontological Security in World Politics," *European Journal of International Relations* 12, no. 3 (2006): 341–70.

12. Leon Festinger, *A Theory of Cognitive Dissonance* (Stanford: Stanford University Press, 1957); Robert Jervis, *Perception and Misperception in International Politics* (Princeton: Princeton University Press, 1976); Jeff Greenberg, Sheldon Solomon, Mitchell Veeder, Tom Pyszczynski, Abram Rosenblatt, and Shari Kirkland, "Evidence for Terror Management Theory II: The Effects of Mortality Salience on Reactions to Those Who Threaten or Bolster the Cultural Worldview," *Journal of Personality and Social Psychology* 58 (1990): 308–18; Jean Piaget, *The Child and Reality: Problems of Genetic Psychology* (New York: Grossman, 1973).

13. Rosen, *War and Human Nature*, p. 73.

14. Robert Frank, *Luxury Fever: Why Money Fails to Satisfy in an Era of Excess* (New York: Free Press, 1999); Johan Huizinga, *Homo Ludens: A Study of the Play Element in Culture* (New York: Roy Publishers, 1950), p. 50.

15. K. Fliessbach, B. Weber, P. Trautner, T. Dohmen, U. Sunde, C. E. Elger, and A. Falk, "Social Comparison Affects Reward-Related Brain Activity in the Human Ventral Striatum," *Science* 318, no. 23 (November 2007): 1305–8.

16. E. J. Mishan, *What Political Economy Is All About?* (Cambridge: Cambridge University Press, 1982) p. 149; Schweller, "Realism and Great Power System," p. 50.

17. See Benjamin Valentino, "Survey on Foreign Policy and American Overseas Commitment," available at http://www.dartmouth.edu/~benv/files/poll%20responses%20by%20party%20ID.pdf.

18. Frank, *Choosing the Right Pond*; Tajfel and Turner, "Social Identity Theory."
19. Jacob Burckhardt, *The Civilization of the Renaissance in Italy* (London: Penguin Books, 1990), pp. 98–110, 272–89; Eugène Terraillon, *L'Honneur: Sentiment et Principe Moral* (Paris: Librairie Félix Alcan, 1912), pp. 9–10, 20–1, 46–7, 75–7, 132–3.
20. Alexander Wendt, "The State as a Person in International Theory," *Review of International Studies* 30, no. 2 (2004): 289–316.
21. Tajfel and Turner, "Social Identity Theory," pp. 11–4.
22. John Turner, "Social Identification and Psychological Group Formation," in *The Social Dimension: European Developments in Social Psychology*, ed. Henri Tajfel (Cambridge: Cambridge University Press, 1984), vol. 2, pp. 518–38, 528.
23. Robert Cialdini, Richard J. Borden, Avril Thorne, Marcus Randall Walker, Stephen Freeman, and Lloyd Reynolds Sloan, "Basking in Reflected Glory: Three (Football) Field Studies," *Journal of Personality and Social Psychology* 34, no. 3 (1976): 366–75; Robert Cialdini and K. Richardson, "Two Indirect Tactics of Image Management: Basking and Blasting," *Journal of Personality and Social Psychology* 57 (1980): 626–31"; Mark Deschesne, Jeff Greenberg, Jamie Arndt, and Jeff Schimel, "Terror Management and the Vicissitudes of Sports Fan Affiliation," *European Journal of Social Psychology* 30 (2000): 813–35.
24. Daniel Druckman, "Nationalism, Patriotism, and Group Loyalty: A Social Psychological Perspective," *Mershon International Studies Review* 38 (1994): 43–68; Paul Stern, "Why Do People Sacrifice for Their Nations?" *Political Psychology* 16 (June 1995): 217–35.
25. Liah Greenfeld, *Nationalism: Five Roads to Modernity* (Cambridge: Harvard University Press, 1992), p. 487. However, as is shown below, domestic pressure is not the only reason for decision-makers to pursue prestige.
26. Furthermore, decision-makers may be more prestige-sensitive than the average citizen because they are visible symbols of the group, because of their own experience in seeking acknowledgment through public office, and because they may compare their prestige to that of foreign leaders with whom they have frequent interactions. Reinhard Wolf, "Recognition and Disrespect between Persons and Peoples," in *Struggle for Recognition*, ed. Thomas Lindemann and Erik Ringmar, p. 46; Alastair Iain, Johnston, *Social States: China in International Institutions* (Princeton: Princeton University Press, 2008), pp. 95–8.
27. Wendt, "State as a Person," p. 314.
28. Wolf, "Respect and Disrespect," p. 116.
29. Evelyn Lindner, *Making Enemies: Humiliation and International Conflict* (Westport: Praeger, 2006); William Ian Miller, *Humiliation and Other Essays on Honor, Social Discomfort, and Violence* (Ithaca: Cornell University Press, 1993).

30. Charles Flynn, *Insult and Society: Patterns of Comparative Interaction* (London: Kennikat Press, 1977), p. 40.
31. Aristotle, "Rhetoric," in *Complete Works of Aristotle: The Revised Oxford Translation*, transl. W. Rhys Roberts (Princeton: Princeton University Press, 1984) pp. 2195–7.
32. Lebow argues that from ancient Greek times to the recent present "affronts to honor and thus to self-esteem, have been at least as great a source of war as threats to material well-being and security." Lebow, *Cultural Theory*, p. 131.
33. Jerome Neu, *Sticks and Stones: The Philosophy of Insults* (New York: Oxford University Press, 2008), pp. vii, 9–10, chap. 2, esp. pp. 45–8; also see Thomas Conley, *Toward a Rhetoric of Insult* (Chicago: University of Chicago Press, 2010), pp. 100–1.
34. O'Neill, *Honor, Symbols, and War*, pp. 108–12, 146–52.
35. The essence of honor or prestige consists of "the keen sensitivity to the experience of humiliation and shame…honor is that disposition which makes one act to shame others who have shamed oneself, to humiliate others who have humiliated oneself…at root honor means 'don't tread on me.'" Miller, *Humiliation*, pp. 84–5, 116–7.
36. Anthropological studies confirm that, even though there are other possible responses to insults such as shrugging them off or even suicide, responding to perceived insults through violence is a common feature of societies that place a high premium on honor. Modern society, while reducing individual violent responses such as the duel and the vendetta, still punishes insults in varied forms of libel, calumny, blasphemy, group defamation, or hate speech. Flynn, *Insult and Society*, pp. 21–4; Neu, *Sticks and Stones*.
37. Oded Löwenheim and Gadi Heimann, "Revenge in International Politics," *Security Studies* 17 (2008): 685–724; Peter Liberman, "An Eye for an Eye: Public Support for War Against Evildoers," *International Organization* 60 (Summer 2006): 687–722.
38. For a similar argument that in addition to material gains, policies also present a psychological payoff, see Robert Jervis, "Rational Deterrence: Theory and Evidence," *World Politics* 41 (January 1989): 183–20, esp. pp. 202–3. Jervis entertains the possibility that conduct that satisfies the criteria of psychological utility may be nonetheless rational, even though leading to less than optimal material results.
39. Stephen Brooks and William Wohlforth, *World Out of Balance: International Relations and the Challenge of American Primacy* (Princeton: Princeton University Press, 2008); Robert Jervis, "Unipolarity: A Structural Perspective," *World Politics* 61 (January 2009): 188–213.
40. William Wohlforth, "Unipolarity, Status Competition, and Great Power War," *World Politics* 61 (January 2009): 38–40. The view that the ambiguity of rank breeds violence is also seen in accounts of interpersonal and of ethnic conflict. Gould, *Collision of Wills*, chap. 3; Donald

Horowitz, *Ethnic Groups in Conflict* (Berkeley: University of California Press, 1985), pp. 24–32, chap. 4, esp. pp. 179–81.

41. As Monteiro argues, the United States has been at war for 13 out of the 22 years of the post–Cold War, representing 25 percent of the total time in history the United States spent at war. Numno Monteiro, "Unrest Assured: Why Unipolarity Is Not Peaceful," *International Security* 36 (Winter 2011): 9–40.

42. Positional in this sense should not be mixed up with the theory of positional goods mentioned earlier on.

43. Evan Luard, *Types of International Society* (New York: Free Press, 1976), chap. 7.

44. William Wohlforth, "Stability of a Unipolar World," *International Security* 24 (Summer 1999): 24–5.

45. CIA World Fact Book, http://www.cia.gov/library/publication/the -world-factbook; Stockholm Peace Research Institute, http://www .sipri.org; Wohlforth, "Stability of a Unipolar World"; Brooks and Wohlforth, *World Out of Balance*; Barry Posen, "Command of the Commons: The Military Foundation of U.S. Hegemony," *International Security* 28 (Summer 2003): 5–46.

46. Jack Levy, *War in the Modern Great Power System, 1495–1975* (Lexington: University Press of Kentucky, 1983), pp. 10–7, 17.

47. To quote Gilpin: "Although prestige is largely a function of economic and military capabilities, it is achieved primarily through victory in war. The most prestigious members of the international system are those states that have most recently used military force or economic power successfully and have thereby imposed their will on others." Robert Gilpin, *War and Change in World Politics* (Cambridge: Cambridge University Press, 1981), pp. 32–3.

48. Robert Jervis, *The Meaning of Nuclear Revolution: Statecraft and the Prospect of Armageddon* (Ithaca: Cornell University Press, 1989), pp. 187–90.

49. Quoted in Paul Kennedy, *Rise and Fall of Great Powers: Economic Change and Military Conflict From 1500–2000* (New York: Random House, 1987), p. 133.

50. Hans Morgenthau, *Politics among Nations: The Struggle for Power and Peace* (New York: Knopf, 1967), p. 79.

51. Lebow, *Cultural Theory*, pp. 69, 441. The term "parvenu power" is Lebow's. On Germany's anger at being denied world power recognition, see Michelle Murray, "Recognition, Disrespect, and the Struggle for Morocco," in *The Struggle for Recognition in International Politics*, Thomas Lindemann and Erik Ringmar (Boulder: Paradigm, 2011), pp. 131–51. Also see Todd Hall, "We Will Not Swallow This Bitter Fruit: Theorizing a Diplomacy of Anger," *Security Studies* 20 (November 2011): 521–55.

52. Richard Nixon, "Address to the Nation on the Situation in Southeast Asia," quoted in Blema Steinberg, *Shame and Humiliation: Presidential*

Decision-Making on Vietnam: A Psychoanalytic Interpretation (Pittsburgh: University of Pittsburgh Press, 1996), pp. 201–4, 203.

53. John McNaughton, "Annex-Plan of Action for South Vietnam," *The Pentagon Papers: The Defense Department History of the United States Decisionmaking on Vietnam* (Boston: Beacon Press, 1971), vol. III, pp. 694–702, 695.

54. John Lewis Gaddis, *Strategies of Containment: A Critical Appraisal of American National Security Policy during the Cold War* (New York: Oxford University Press, 2005), pp. 89–90; also see Frank Ninkovich, *The Wilsonian Century: US Foreign Policy Since 1900* (Chicago: University of Chicago Press, 1999), p. 183; Robert McMahon, "Credibility and World Power: Explaining the Psychological Dimensions in Post–War American Diplomacy," *Diplomatic History* 15 (Fall 1991): 458–9.

55. For this identification of the national interest, see Robert Art, *Grand Strategy for America* (Ithaca: Cornell University Press, 2003), pp. 45–57.

56. On recalcitrant actors, see Yoav Gortzak, "How Great Powers Rule: Coercive and Positive Inducements in International Order Enforcement," *Security Studies* 14 (July 2005): 663–97; Robert Litwak, *Rogue States and US Foreign Policy: Containment after the Cold War* (Baltimore: Johns Hopkins University Press, 2000). On free-riding, see Mancur Olson and Richard Zeckhauser, "An Economic Theory of Alliances," *Review of Economics and Statistics* 48 (August 1966): pp. 266–79; Robert Keohane, *After Hegemony: Cooperation and Discord in World Political Economy* (Princeton: Princeton University Press, 1984). For related distinctions between "spoilers" and "shirkers," or "predators" and "parasites," see Randall Schweller and Xiaoyu Pu, "After Unipolarity: China's Visions of International Order in an Era of U.S. Decline," *International Security* 36 (Summer 2011): 41–72; Oded Löwenheim, *Predators and Parasites: Persistent Agents of Transnational Harm and Great Power Authority* (Ann Arbor: University of Michigan Press, 2007). However, by contrast to this book's argument, Schweller and Pu refer to spoilers mainly as agents who spite the United States on purpose, while Löwenheim refers to agents who inflict violent harm.

57. There is no legal criterion of inclusion in the category of recalcitrant polities, which is another label for rogue states, outlaw states, pariah states, or states of concern. Litwak argues that rogue states exhibit one or several traits: the development of unconventional weapons, support for international terrorism, or/and opposition to US foreign policy in key regions. In the post–Cold War, five states were seen by the United States as recalcitrant: Iraq, Iran, Libya, North Korea, and Cuba. Litwak, *Rogue States*, pp. 49–50, chap. 2.

58. Hedley Bull, *The Anarchical Society: A Study of Order in World Politics* (New York: Columbia University Press, 1977), p. 196; Levy, *Modern Great Power System*, p. 17.

59. Pitt-Rivers, "Honor and Social Status," p. 24.

60. Löwenheim and Heimann, "Revenge," pp. 694–8.
61. Henry Kissinger, *Years of Renewal* (New York: Simon & Schuster, 1999), pp. 551–3, 574–5.
62. Quoted in Arthur Schlessinger, *Robert Kennedy and His Times* (Boston: Houghton Mifflin, 1978), p. 705.
63. Jonathan Mercer, *Reputation and International Politics* (Ithaca: Cornell University Press, 1995), pp. 6–7; Glenn Snyder and Paul Diesing, *Conflict among Nations: Bargaining, Decision-Making and System Structure in International Crises* (Princeton: Princeton University Press, 1977), pp. 185, 432–3.
64. Thomas Schelling, *Arms and Influence* (New Haven: Yale University Press, 1966), pp. 124, 35–91; Morgenthau, *Politics among Nations*, pp. 69–70, 73, 75–78. Also see Paul Huth, "Reputations and Deterrence: A Theoretical and Empirical Assessment," *Security Studies* 7 (Autumn 1997): 72–99.
65. The point concerning the instrumental motivation behind prestige could also be extended to what may be termed assertiveness as a means to cooperation. This refers to those instances in which a state uses its image of a strong leader to elicit the cooperation of weaker polities, which would be cowed into agreeing to its terms. Charles Krauthammer, "The Unipolar Moment," *Foreign Affairs* 70 (1990–1991): 23–33; Charles Krauthammer, "The Unipolar Moment Revisited," *National Interest* 70 (Winter 2002/2003): 5–17; Charles Krauthammer, "A New Type of Realism," *National Interest* (January 2003), available at http://nationalinterest.org/article/a-new-type-of-realism-2238. See chapter five for an extended discussion.
66. Mercer, *Reputation*.
67. Snyder and Diesing, *Conflict among Nations*, pp. 185–9; Darryl Press, *Calculating Credibility: How Leaders Assess Military Threats* (Ithaca: Cornell University Press, 2005), pp. 73–5.
68. Gilpin, *War and Change*, p. 31; Barry O'Neill, "Nuclear Weapons and National Prestige," Cowles Foundation Discussion Paper no. 1560, February 2006, available at http: //www.cowles.econ.yale.edu/P/cd/d15b/d1560.pdf.
69. A closer investigation of such statements suggests that the invocation of tangible benefits constitutes a rationalization of action valued primarily because of its psychological payoffs. Thus, Löwenheim and Heimann have shown that even though Israeli decision-makers used the vocabulary of deterrence profusely to account for their 2006 intervention in Lebanon, they were unable to explain in a following parliamentary inquiry what they meant by it. Moreover, a series of interviews with US officials in the Department of State, the Pentagon, and congressmen in the defense committees, on their reasons to support a nuclear arms-building competition against the Soviet Union in the 1980s, concluded that many could not substantiate their statements that the policy was driven by the strategic manipulation of perceptions (reputation). Instead, the study found that

US defense policy-makers sought to stay ahead of the Kremlin due to considerations of prestige and public morale, and resorted to "developing complex *rationalizations* that explain how their emotionally gratifying behavior is objectively appropriate." Löwenheim and Heimann, "Revenge," pp. 705–6; Steven Kull, *Minds at War: Nuclear Reality and the Inner Conflicts of Defense Policymakers* (New York: Basic Books, 1988), chap. 10. The reason for such rationalizations is that psychological utility is assumed to be associated with an overall increased utility even in nonpsychological dimensions. To quote Jervis: "A person who believes that a policy is better than the alternatives on one value dimension is likely to believe that it is better on other important, although logically unrelated, dimensions as well." Jervis, "Rational Deterrence," p. 197.

70. Kenneth Waltz, *Theory of International Politics* (Reading: Addison Wesley, 1979), pp. 6–8.

71. Suboptimal strategic behavior can be contrasted with both optimal strategic behavior, which reduces costs and maximizes benefits and in which ends are appropriate to threats, and nonstrategic behavior in which the ends of the strategy are out of synch with the means by which they are pursued.

72. Mercer, *Reputation*; Shiping Tang, "Reputation, Cult of Reputation, and International Scholarship," *Security Studies* 14 (January/March 2005): 34–62.

73. This remains the case even if one assumes that the material costs of these policies were otherwise tolerable for the unipole.

74. For a similar point, see Löwenheim and Heimann, "Revenge," p. 705.

75. On the difference between compellence and deterrence, see Schelling, *Arms and Influence*, p. 69; Robert Art, "Introduction," in *The United States and Coercive Diplomacy*, ed. Robert Art and Patrick Cronin (Washington: United States Institute of Peace, 2005), p. 8.

76. Robert Art, "Coercive Diplomacy: What Do We Know?" in *The United States and Coercive Diplomacy*, ed. Art and Cronin, pp. 359–420, 378–83.

77. Antonio Damasio, *Descartes' Error: Emotion, Reason, and the Human Brain* (New York: G. P. Putnam's Sons, 1994); Jonathan Mercer, "Emotional Beliefs," *International Organization* 64 (Winter 2010): 1–31. Neurological research suggests that emotions play a key part in the unconscious information processing by the brain, which enables basic responses such as decision-making, imagining of things not present, memories, speaking grammatically, or making a judgment of value or comparison. Joseph LeDoux, *Emotional Brain: The Mysterious Underpinnings of Emotional Life* (New York: Phoenix Books, 1999).

78. Herbert Simon, "Motivational and Emotional Controls of Cognition," *Psychological Review* 74, no. 1 (1967): 29–39. On the functions of emotion in decision-making, also see Rose McDermott, *Political Psychology and International Relations* (Ann Arbor: University of Michigan Press, 2004), pp. 167–9.

79. Despite increasing theoretical recognition, emotions have not so far been employed in US foreign policy analysis. See Mercer, "Emotional Beliefs"; Neta Crawford, "The Passion of World Politics: Propositions on Emotion and Emotional Relationships," *International Security* 24 (Spring 2000): 116–56; Lebow, *Cultural Theory*; Rose McDermott, "The Feeling of Rationality: The Meaning of Neuroscientific Advances for Political Science," *Perspectives on Politics* 2 (December 2004): 691–706. Moreover, while emotions have been employed to analyze decision-making aspects such as wishful thinking, denial, and stress, they have not been mentioned (with the partial exception of Lebow) in connection with objectives such as status and prestige. See McDermott, *Political Psychology*, pp. 169–77.

80. A number of other schools may be added to this list, the most important being *innenpolitik*—comprising theories such as the influence of bureaucracies or of ethnic lobbies on US foreign policy. However, these theories were left out, because they only claim to explain isolated episodes in US foreign policy rather than provide accounts for its entire course. For instance, the theory of an Israel lobby is relevant to US involvement in the Middle East, but accounts for little for its foreign policy in the Balkans, or toward the ICC.

81. Jervis, "Unipolarity."

82. Arnold Wolfers, *Discord and Collaboration: Essays on International Politics* (Baltimore: Johns Hopkins University Press, 1962), p. 14.

83. Waltz, *Theory of International Politics*, p. 26; Gilpin, *War and Change*, pp. 10, 106–7.

84. Waltz, *Theory of International Politics*, pp. 26–7.

85. Ibid. p. 24.

86. John Mearsheimer, "The False Promise of International Institutions," *International Security* 19 (Winter 1994): pp. 5–49; John Mearsheimer, *Tragedy of Great Power Politics* (New York: W. W. Norton, 2001), pp. 29–42; Randall Schweller, *Unanswered Threats: Political Constraints on the Balance of Power* (Princeton: Princeton University Press, 2006), pp. 25–6.

87. Jervis, "Unipolarity."

88. Christopher Layne, *The Peace of Illusions: American Grand Strategy from 1940 to the Present* (Ithaca: Cornell University Press, 2006); Colin Dueck, *Reluctant Crusaders: Power, Culture, and Change in American Grand Strategy* (Princeton: Princeton University Press, 2006). Complex differences exist between offensive and defensive structuralism concerning the process resulting in assertiveness and the consequences of this policy. Jack Snyder, *Myths of Empire: Domestic Politics and International Ambitions* (Ithaca: Cornell University Press, 1991); Stephen Brooks, "Dueling Realisms," *International Organization* 51 (Summer 1997): 445–77; Jeffrey Taliaferro, "Security Seeking under Anarchy: Defensive Realism Revisited," *International Security* 25 (Winter 2000): 128–61; Schweller, *Unanswered Threats*.

89. Kenneth Waltz, "Structural Realism after the Cold War," *International Security* 25 (Summer 2000): 24–5; Kenneth Waltz, "The Emerging Structure of International Politics," *International Security* 18 (Fall 1993): 77.

90. Exceptionalism derives its name from Max Lerner's original argument that some analysts tend to see the US "as immune from the forces of history and the laws of life." Max Lerner, *America as Civilization: Life and Thought in the United States Today* (New York: Simon and Schuster, 1957), pp. 64–6. For a review, see Jonathan Monten, "The Roots of the Bush Doctrine: Power, Nationalism, and Democracy Promotion in US Grand Strategy," *International Security* 29 (Spring 2005): 112–56.

91. Anatol Lieven, *America Right or Wrong: An Anatomy of American Nationalism* (New York: Oxford University Press, 2004), p. 32.

92. Ibid. p. 46.

93. Loren Baritz, *City on a Hill: A History of Ideas and Myths in America* (New York: John Wiley, 1964), pp. 286–7; Joshua Muravchik, *Exporting Democracy: Fulfilling America's Destiny* (Washington: AEI Press, 1991), p. 222.

94. Muravchik, *Exporting Democracy*, pp. 6, 8.

95. Woodrow Wilson, "Address to Joint Chamber of Congress, April 2, 1917," quoted in Thomas Knock, *To End All Wars: Woodrow Wilson and the Quest for a New World Order* (New York: Oxford University Press, 1992), pp. 121–2.

96. For the distinction between a covenanted people versus a crusader approach, see Anthony Smith, *Chosen Peoples: Sacred Sources of National Identity* (Oxford: Oxford University Press, 2003), pp. 48–9; Walter McDougall, *Promised Land, Crusader State* (Boston: Houghton Mifflin, 1997); H. W. Brands, *What America Owes the World: The Struggle for the Soul of Foreign Policy* (Cambridge: Cambridge University Press, 1998); Dueck, *Reluctant Crusaders*. See also John Quincy Adams, "July 4, 1821 Address," reproduced in Walter LaFeber, ed., *John Quincy Adams and American Continental Empire: Letters, Papers and Speeches* (Chicago: Quadrangle Books, 1965), pp. 42–6.

97. Ninkovich, *Wilsonian Century*; Tony Smith, *America's Mission: The United States and the Worldwide Struggle for Democracy in the Twentieth Century* (Princeton: Princeton University Press, 1994). However, exceptionalists differ in their assessments of the desirability of democratic proselytism. For neoconservatives, as well as for liberal hawks, the promotion of democracy is both a moral duty and in the US national interest. However, for liberal doves and paleoconservatives, assertiveness may lead to disaster for America's democratic values.

98. For such a defensive interpretation of Wilsonianism, see Ninkovich, *Wilsonian Century*.

99. Williams, *Tragedy*, 55–7; LaFeber, *New American Empire*. As McCormick writes: "Instead of closed doors, open markets; instead of political dominance, economic hegemony; instead of large scale

colonialism, informal empire." McCormick, *China Market*, pp. 128, 131–6.

100. William Appleman Williams, *The Tragedy of American Diplomacy* (New York: W. W. Norton & Company, 1984), chap. 2, esp. pp. 54–7.

101. Ibid.; Richard Barnet, *Roots of War* (New York: Atheneum, 1972), pp. 5–8, 138–51, 155–63, 176–205, 266–7, 337–41.

102. Andrew Bacevich, *American Empire: The Realities and Consequences of US Diplomacy* (Cambridge: Harvard University Press, 2002), pp. 79, 85.

103. Ibid., pp. 34–43, 72–4, 79–88, 200–4, 214–23.

104. Ibid., pp. 122–8.

105. Ibid.; Chalmers Johnson, *Blowback: The Costs and Consequences of America's Empire* (New York: Henry Holt, 2000), pp. 93, 84–94; Chalmers Johnson, *The Sorrows of Empire: Militarism, Secrecy, and the End of the Republic* (New York: Henry Holt, 2004), p. 5.

3 THE US FAILED EXPERIMENT WITH RESTRAINT

1. "Excerpts from Bush's News Conference on Postwar Moves," *New York Times*, March 2, 1991.

2. William Hyland, "A Mediocre Record," *Foreign Policy* 101 (Winter 1995): 69–74; also see Hal Brands, *From Berlin to Baghdad: America's Search for Purpose in the Post–Cold War World* (Lexington: University Press of Kentucky, 2008), p. 195.

3. For a similar assessment of the post–Cold War, see Gideon Rachman, *Zero-Sum Future: America's Power in an Age of Anxiety* (New York: Simon & Schuster, 2011).

4. Joseph S. Nye, "What New World Order?" *Foreign Affairs* 71 (Spring 1992): 83–96.

5. Lake expressed the view that "backlash states" (basically recalcitrant challengers) had made a commitment "to remain on the wrong side of history." Anthony Lake, "Confronting Backlash States," *Foreign Affairs* 73 (March/April 1994): 55.

6. Francis Fukuyama, *The End of History and the Last Man* (New York: Free Press, 1992), pp. 211–2, 276–7.

7. Michael E. Brown, Sean Lynn-Jones, and Steven E. Miller, eds., *Debating the Democratic Peace* (Cambridge: MIT Press, 1996).

8. Anthony Lake, "From Containment to Engagement Speech at Johns Hopkins University, Washington DC, September 21, 1993," in *The Clinton Foreign Policy Reader: Presidential Speeches with Commentary*, ed. Alvin Rubinstein, Albina Shayevich, and Boris Zlotnikov (London: M. E. Sharpe, 2000), pp. 22–4.

9. Strobe Talbott, "Democracy and the National Interest," *Foreign Affairs* 75 (November/December 1996): 48–9, 63. In a footnote,

Talbott makes extensive reference to the literature on democratic peace theory. See notes 2 and 49.

10. White House, "A National Security Strategy of Engagement and Enlargement, February 1996," accessible at www. fas.org/spp/military /docops/national/1996stra.html.

11. Charles Krauthammer, "Unipolar Moment," *Foreign Affairs* 70 (1990/1991): 23–33, 24–5.

12. Nye, "What New World Order?" pp. 95–6.

13. Janne Nolan, "The Concept of Cooperative Security," in *Global Engagement: Cooperation and Security in the 21st Century*, ed. Janne Nolan (Washington: Brookings Institution, 1994), pp. 4–10; William Perry, "Military Action: When to Use It and How to Ensure its Effectiveness," in ibid. *Global Engagement*, ed. Nolan, pp. 235–41; Janne Nolan, "Cooperative Security in the United States," in *Global Engagement*, ed. Nolan, pp. 507–42, 512–7; Ashton Carter, William Perry, and John Steinbrunner, *A New Concept of Cooperative Security* (Washington: Brookings Institution, 1992), pp. 6–8, 24–5.

14. White House, "National Security Strategy of Engagement and Enlargement."

15. Thomas L. Friedman, *Lexus and Olive Tree* (New York: Farrar, Strauss and Giroux, 1999), pp. 195–8; Richard Rosecrance, *Rise of the Trading State: Commerce and Conquest in the Modern World* (New York: Basic Books, 1986).

16. Robert Keohane and Joseph S. Nye, *Power and Interdependence*, 2nd ed. (Glenview: Scott, Foresman, 1989), p. 18.

17. Eric Larson, David Orletsky, and Kristin Leuschner, *Defense Planning in a Decade of Change* (Santa Monica: Rand, 2001); Michael Klare, *Rogue States and Nuclear Outlaws: America's Search for a New Policy* (New York: Hill and Wang, 1995), pp. 108–19. Even so, the US military expenditures topped those of the next ten major powers combined. Both the Bush and Clinton administrations accepted the need for a large defense establishment as presented by the consecutive Pentagon plans: the Base Force plan (1991), the Bottom-Up Review (1993), and the Quadrennial Defense Review (1997).

18. Quoted in William Hyland, *Clinton's World: Remaking American Foreign Policy* (Westport: Praeger, 1999), p. 128.

19. Ibid.; Derek Chollet and James Goldgeier, *America between the Wars: From 11/9 to 9/11* (New York: Public Affairs, 2008), pp. 80–5.

20. The doctrine consisted of rules of intervention: conduct no interventions except in contexts vital to strategic interests, when deciding to do so use overwhelming force, have clearly defined objectives as well as an exit strategy, and amass sufficient domestic and international legitimacy to guarantee victory. Colin Powell, "US Forces: The Challenges Ahead," *Foreign Affairs* 71 (Winter 1992): 32–45; Colin Powell, *My American Journey* (New York: Random House, 1995), pp. 148–9, 576–7. The doctrine buttressed rather than contradicted restraint because it

was an all-or-nothing approach placing such demanding conditions on intervention that the United States often preferred not to act.

21. For the point that the Gulf War victory was more profoundly felt than the Cold War victory, see David Hendrickson and Robert Tucker, *Imperial Temptation: The New World Order and America's Purpose* (New York: Council of Foreign Relations Press, 1992), pp. 1–2.

22. George H. W. Bush and Brent Scowcroft, *A World Transformed* (New York: Knopf, 1998), p. 400; Christian Alfonsi, *Circle in the Sand: Why We Went Back to Iraq* (New York: Doubleday, 2006), pp. 109–10.

23. Chollet and Goldgeier, *America between the Wars*, p. 11; Brands, *From Berlin to Baghdad*, pp. 49–50.

24. Bush and Scowcroft, *World Transformed*, p. 400.

25. Lawrence Freedman and Ephraim Karsh, *The Gulf Conflict, 1990–1991: Diplomacy and War in the New World Order* (London: Faber and Faber, 1993), pp. 285–6, 408–9. The exact figure of Iraqi casualties varies, probably standing at around 35,000 killed and 60,000 wounded.

26. James Addison Baker, III, *Politics of Diplomacy: Revolution, War, and Peace* (New York: G. P. Putnam's Sons, 1995), pp. 414–5.

27. Basically, "Saddam was unfortunate to pick a unique period in international affairs. Had he invaded Kuwait a few years earlier, such wide-ranging collaboration would have been inconceivable." Freedman and Karsh, *Gulf Conflict*, p. 438.

28. Ibid. Chaps. 7, 9, 16; Brands, *From Berlin to Baghdad*, pp. 52–3; Baker, *Politics of Diplomacy*.

29. Chollet and Goldgeier, *America between the Wars*, p. 15; Bush and Scowcroft, *World Transformed*, pp. 487, 489–90; Alfonsi, *Circle in the Sand*, pp. 154–63.

30. Bush and Scowcroft, *World Transformed*, pp. 164–5, 353–, http://www.pbs.org/wgbh/pages/frontline/gulf/oral/scowcroft/1.html.

31. Alfonsi, *Circle in the Sand*, pp. 109–11.

32. Bush, "Address to the Joint Session of Congress, September 1990"; George H. W. Bush, "State of the Union Address, January 29, 1991," *New York Times*, January 30, 1991.

33. Similar provisos were added by Baker and by the Chairman of the Joint Chiefs of Staff Colin Powell. See Bush and Scowcroft, *World Transformed*, p. 355; Brands, *From Berlin to Baghdad*, pp. 85–7.

34. As Schroeder argues, "one could define the NWO [new world order] as an international system in which the United States and like-minded friends and allies act together, preferably under the aegis of the United Nations to preserve or establish peace by upholding international law and order against aggressors, law breakers, and oppressors." Paul Schroeder, "The New World Order: A Historical Perspective," *Washington Quarterly* 17 (Spring 1994): 26, 34–5.

35. Senior US commander quoted in Klare, *Rogue States*, p. 67.

36. For critiques of the new world order, see Lawrence Freedman, "Order and Disorder in the New World," *Foreign Affairs* 71 (Winter 1991):

20–37; Robin Wright, "World View: Old Ways Falling but 'New World Order' Is Still Murky," *Los Angeles Times*, June 25, 1991.

37. Zalmay Khalilzad, *From Containment to Global Leadership? America and the World after the Cold War* (Santa Monica: Rand, 1995), pp. 17–21, 41.

38. See "Excerpts from the Pentagon's Plan: 'Prevent the Reemergence of a New Rival,'" *New York Times*, March 8, 1992; Patrick Tyler, "US Strategy Plan Calls for Insuring No Rivals Develop," *New York Times*, March 8, 1992; Chollet and Goldgeier, *America between the Wars*, pp. 43–7; Eric Edelman, "The Strange Career of the 1992 Defense Planning Guidance," in *In Uncertain Times: American Foreign Policy after the Berlin Wall and 9/11*, ed. Melvyn Leffler and Jeffrey Legro (Ithaca: Cornell University Press, 2011), pp. 63–77.

39. Patrick Tyler, "Senior US Officials Assail Lone-Superpower Policy: Ammunition for Critics," *New York Times*, March 11, 1992.

40. Chollet and Goldgeier, *America between the Wars*, p.45.

41. Ibid. pp. 47–51.

42. Michael Mandelbaum, "Foreign Policy as Social Work," *Foreign Affairs* 75 (January/February 1996): 16–32. The recommendation was made by Thomas McLarty, the White House Chief of Staff, to Lake. Tom Matthews and Eleanor Clift, "Clinton's Growing Pains," *Newsweek*, May 3, 1993.

43. Barry Posen and Andrew Ross, "Competing Visions for US Grand Strategy," *International Security* 21 (Winter 1996/1997): 5–53; Brands, *From Berlin to Baghdad*; for the bumper sticker obsession, see Chollet and Goldgeier, *America between the Wars*, pp. 65–71; Douglas Brinkley, "Democratic Enlargement: The Clinton Doctrine," *Foreign Policy* 106 (Spring 1997): 110–27.

44. Mandelbaum, "Foreign Policy"; Schlessinger, "Quest for a Post–Cold War Foreign Policy," *Foreign Affairs* 72 (Winter 1993): 17–28; Paul Wolfowitz, "The Clinton Administration's First Year," *Foreign Affairs* 73 (January/February 1994): 1–25.

45. Steven Holmes, "Christopher Reaffirms Leading US Role," *New York Times*, May 28, 1993.

46. Quoted in William Hyland, *Clinton's World: Remaking American Foreign Policy* (Westport: Praeger, 1999), pp. 84–7; James Goldgeier and Michael McFaul, *Power and Purpose: US Policy toward Russia after the Cold War* (Washington: Brookings Institution, 2003), pp. 120–44; Strobe Talbott, *The Russia Hand: A Memoir of Presidential Decision-Making* (New York: Random House, 2002).

47. Goldgeier and McFaul, *Power and Purpose*, chaps. 6–7.

48. Robert Suettinger, *Beyond Tiananmen: The Politics of US-China Relations, 1989–2000* (Washington: Brookings Institution, 2003), pp. 79–83, 93–103, 107–22, 129–34.

49. James Mann, *About Face: A History of America's Curious Relationship with China from Nixon to Clinton* (New York: Knopf, 1999), pp. 276–81.

50. Barton Gellman, "US and China Nearly Came to Blows," *Washington Post*, June 21, 1996.
51. Mann, *About Face*, pp. 297–304.
52. Steven Burg and Paul Shoup, *The War in Bosnia-Herzegovina: Ethnic Conflict and International Intervention* (Armonk, New York: M. E. Sharpe, 1999), pp. 79–80, 100–1.
53. David Halberstam, *War in Time of Peace: Bush, Clinton, and the Generals* (New York: Touchstone, 2002), pp. 132–41; Burg and Shoup, *War in Bosnia*, pp. 201–2, 204, 210.
54. Burg and Shoup, *War in Bosnia*, pp. 84–5.
55. Ivo Daalder, *Getting to Dayton: The Making of America's Bosnia Policy* (Washington: Brookings Institution, 2000), pp. 8–11; Burg and Shoup, *War in Bosnia*, pp. 232–53.
56. Daalder, *Getting to Dayton*, chap. 1; Elizabeth Drew, *On the Edge: The Clinton Presidency* (New York: Simon & Schuster, 1994), pp.148–58.
57. Drew, *On the Edge*, pp. 161–2; Holmes, "Christopher Reaffirms."
58. Quoted in Brands, *From Berlin to Baghdad*, pp. 120–1.
59. Halberstam, *War in Time of Peace*, pp. 226–9; Drew, *On the Edge*, pp. 151–9; Daalder, *Getting to Dayton*, pp. 15–8.
60. Daalder, *Getting to Dayton*, p. 18; Warren Christopher, *In the Stream of History: Shaping Foreign Policy for a New Era* (Stanford: Stanford University Press, 1998), pp. 346–7. Hyland writes: "Obviously, Washington was determined not to act alone. Consistent with the administration's basic philosophy, it would act only within the safety and comfort of allied or international support." Hyland, *Clinton's World*, p. 38.
61. Daalder, *Getting to Dayton*, pp. 22–3. In April 1994, the UN Secretary General's representative Yasushi Akashi blocked strikes against the Serb troops attacking Goražde for fear of retaliation against the peacekeepers. Burg and Shoup, *War in Bosnia*, p. 150.
62. Burg and Shoup, *War in Bosnia*, pp. 157–8; Michael Gordon, Douglas Jehl, and Elaine Sciolino, "Colliding Missions—A Special Report: US and Bosnia: How a Policy Changed," *New York Times*, December 4, 1994; Daalder, *Getting to Dayton*, pp. 31–5.
63. Bob Woodward, *The Choice: How Clinton Won* (New York: Touchstone Books, 1996), p. 253.
64. Assistant Secretary of the State Robert Gallucci argued for intervention for public relations purposes in *either* Bosnia or Somalia. Jon Western, "Sources of Humanitarian Intervention: Beliefs, Information, and Advocacy in the US Decisions on Somalia and Bosnia," *International Security* 27 (August 1992): 117–30.
65. Quoted in Samantha Power, *'A Problem from Hell': America and the Age of Genocide* (New York: Basic Books, 2002), p. 293; also see Don Oberdorfer, "The Path to Intervention: A Massive Tragedy We Could Do Something About," *Washington Post*, December 6, 1992.

66. Ken Menkhaus and Louis Ortmayer, *Key Decisions in the Somalia Intervention* (Pittsburg: University of Pittsburg, 1995), pp. 5–6.
67. On the UN's considerably extended role in the post–Cold War, see Boutros Boutros-Ghali, "Empowering the United Nations," *Foreign Affairs* 71 (Winter 1992): 89–102; Boutros Boutros-Ghali, *An Agenda for Peace: Preventive Diplomacy, Peacemaking, and Peacekeeping* (New York: United Nations, 1992). On PRD 13, see Jeffrey Smith and Julia Preston, "United States Plans Wider Role in UN Peace Keeping," *Washington Post*, June 18, 1993; Barton Gellman, "Wider UN Police Role Supported," *Washington Post*, August 5, 1993.
68. William Durch, "Introduction to Anarchy: Humanitarian Intervention and 'State-Building' in Somalia," in *UN Peacekeeping, American Policy, and the Uncivil Wars of the 1990s*, ed. William Durch (New York: St. Martin's Press, 1996), pp. 311–65, 335–9; Drew, *On the Edge*, pp. 319, 327–8.
69. John Hirsch and Robert Oakley, *Somalia and Operation Restore Hope: Peacemaking and Peacekeeping* (Washington: United States Institute of Peace, 1995), pp. 103–11; Halberstam, *War in Time of Peace*, pp. 260–1.
70. Madeleine Albright, "Yes, There Is a Reason to Be in Somalia," *New York Times*, August 10, 1993.
71. Menkhaus and Ortmayer, *Key Decisions*, pp. 10–5.
72. Durch, "Introduction to Anarchy," pp. 339–48; Rick Atkinson, "The Raid That Went Wrong," *Washington Post*, January 30–31, 1994.
73. Burg and Shoup, *War in Bosnia*, pp. 148–9; Daalder, *Getting to Dayton*, pp. 18–9, 21–2, 187–8.
74. Hirsh and Oakley, *Somalia*, pp. 128–9; Menkhaus and Ortmayer, *Key Decisions*, pp. 20–2; Halberstam, *War in Time of Peace*, pp. 262–4.
75. George Stephanopoulos, *All Too Human: A Political Education* (Boston: Little, Brown, 1999), p. 214; Halberstam, *War in Time of Peace*, pp. 262–3; Hirsh and Oakley, *Somalia*, p. 129.
76. Stephanopoulos, *All Too Human*, pp. 217–9; Halberstam, *War in Time of Peace*, pp. 272–3. Clinton was repeating a position expressed by his political advisor David Gergen, who had favored intervention in the aftermath of the firefight in Mogadishu. Drew, *On the Edge*, p. 326.
77. Robert Pastor, "The Delicate Balance between Coercion and Diplomacy," in *The United States and Coercive Diplomacy*, ed. Robert Art and Patrick Cronin (Washington: United States Institute of Peace, 2005), pp. 119–95.
78. The deal resulted in an amnesty for the junta leaders, which also allowed them to depart Haiti with all their assets. Philippe Girard, *Clinton in Haiti: The 1994 US Invasion of Haiti* (New York: Palgrave Macmillan, 2004), chaps. 5–7, p. 120.
79. Michael Gordon and Thomas Friedman, "Details of US Raid in Somalia," *New York Times*, October 25, 1993.

NOTES 193

80. "Presidential Decision Directive/NSC-25, May 3, 1994," at http://www.fas.org/irp/offdocs/pdd/pdd-25.pdf.
81. Power, *Problem from Hell*, pp. 358–64; Gerard Prunier, *Rwanda Crisis: History of a Genocide* (New York: Columbia University Press, 1997).
82. Bill Clinton, *My Life* (New York: Knopf, 2004), p. 594.
83. William Drennan, "Nuclear Weapons and North Korea: Who's Coercing Whom?" in *The United States and Coercive Diplomacy*, ed. Art and Cronin, pp. 157–223.
84. Ashton Carter and William Perry, *Preventive Defense: A New Security Strategy for America* (Washington: Brookings Institution, 1999), pp. 123–4.
85. Robert Gallucci, Joel Wit, and Daniel Poneman, *Going Critical: The First North Korean Nuclear Crisis* (Washington: Brookings Institution, 2004), chaps. 10–11; Don Oberdorfer, *The Two Koreas: A Contemporary History* (New York: Basic Books, 2001), chaps. 12–13; Leon Sigal, *Disarming Strangers: Nuclear Diplomacy with North Korea* (Princeton: Princeton University Press, 1998); Victor Cha, *The Impossible State: North Korea, Past and Future* (New York: Ecco, 2012), pp. 251–5.
86. Alfonsi, *Circle in the Sand*, pp. 235–6.
87. Graham Sarah Brown, *Sanctioning Saddam: The Politics of Intervention in Iraq* (London: I. B. Tauris, 1999); Andrew Cockburn and Patrick Cockburn, *Out of the Ashes: The Resurrection of Saddam Hussein* (New York: Harper, 2000).
88. Clinton made this point explicit: "The Iraqi attack against President Bush was an attack against our country and against all Americans. We could not and have not let such action against our Nation go unanswered. From the first days of our Revolution, America's security has depended on the clarity of this message: Don't tread on us." Bill Clinton, "Address to the Nation on the Strike on Iraqi Intelligence Headquarters, June 26, 1993," available at http://www.presidency.ucsb.edu/ws/index.php?pid=46758#axzz1sn2M8Y00.
89. Daalder, *Getting to Dayton*, pp. 64–8.
90. Burg and Shoup, *War in Bosnia*, pp. 323–7; Richard Holbrooke, *To End a War* (New York: Random House, 1998), pp. 65–8; Woodward, *Choice*, pp. 253–7; Daalder, *Getting to Dayton*, pp. 40–61, 64–73, 163–6.
91. Daalder, *Getting to Dayton*, pp. 91–10; Woodward, *Choice*, pp. 260–3.
92. Woodward, *Choice*, p. 267; Burg and Shoup, *War in Bosnia*, pp. 342–6.
93. Burg and Shoup, *War in Bosnia*, pp. 167–8, 347–67.
94. Chollet and Goldgeier, *America between the Wars*, pp. 130–1; Daalder, *Getting to Dayton*, pp. 179, 182–7.
95. Christopher, *In the Stream of History*, pp. 358–9.
96. Holbrooke, *To End a War*, pp. 358–9.

97. James Goldgeier, *Not Whether, but When: The US Decision to Enlarge NATO* (Washington: Brookings Institution, 1999); Suettinger, *Beyond Tiananmen.*
98. Krauthammer, "Unipolar Moment," pp. 24–5.

4 PRESTIGE AND ASSERTIVENESS IN KOSOVO

1. Stephen Budianski, "Missions Implausible," *US News & World Report* 111 (October 14, 1991), pp. 24–31.
2. Kosovo represents a stronger case for unilateralism than for multilateralism because, while the United States acted with others, it restricted at the same time the universe of cooperation by giving up on securing the approval of non-NATO partners represented in the Security Council (Russia and China). This was a serious threshold to cross, because, later on in the case of the invasion of Iraq, the United States could and in fact did shrink even further the number of states it cooperated with when deciding to use force. It is true that in a recent endeavor Sarah Kreps describes Kosovo as a multilateral operation because of the level of involvement by other parties and because of the approval by a regional organization (NATO). But this assessment is possible only because Sarah Kreps does not take into consideration the evolution over time of a state policy in the direction of either unilateralism or multilateralism. Thus, she does not discuss the previous instance of the United States doing away with Security Council approval in the bombing of Iraq in December 1998. Sarah Kreps, *Coalitions of Convenience: United States Military Interventions after the Cold War* (New York: Oxford University Press, 2011), pp. 20–1; also see Marc Weller, "The US, Iraq, and the Use of Force in a Unipolar World," *Survival* 41 (Winter 1999): 81–100.
3. Ivo Daalder and Michael O'Hanlon, *Winning Ugly: NATO's War to Save Kosovo* (Washington: Brookings Institution, 2000), p. 117.
4. For a similar interpretation, see Jeffrey Taliaferro, "Neoclassical Realism: The Psychology of Great Power Intervention," in *Making Sense of International Relations Theory*, ed. Jennifer Sterling-Folker (Boulder: Lynne Rienner, 2006), pp. 38–54. However, Taliaferro considers prestige as the equivalent of reputation. Also see Sean Kay, "After Kosovo: NATO's Credibility Dilemma," *Security Dialogue* 31, no. 1 (2000): 71–84.
5. Daalder and O'Hanlon, *Winning Ugly*, pp. 91–2; Elaine Sciolino and Ethan Bronner, "How a President, Distracted by Scandal, Entered a Balkan War," *New York Times*, April 18, 1999.
6. Barry Posen, "The War for Kosovo," *International Security* 24 (Spring 2000): 39–84, fn. 24; International Strategic Studies Institute, *The Military Balance, 1999–2000* (Oxford: Oxford University Press, 1999); Daalder and O'Hanlon, *Winning Ugly*, pp. 103, 140.
7. Quoted in John Norris, *Collision Course: Russia, NATO, and Kosovo* (Westport: Praeger, 2005), p. 32; Wesley Clark, *Waging Modern War:*

Bosnia, Kosovo, and the Future of Combat (New York: Public Affairs, 2002), pp. 376–400.

8. Moreover, of the 300,000 internally displaced persons in Yugoslavia, only 180,000 were Kosovars, the rest representing Serbs displaced from Kosovo. US Committee for Refugees, *World Refugee Survey, 1999* (New York: US Committee for Refugees, 1998); Daalder and O'Hanlon, *Winning Ugly*, p. 280, fn. 24.
9. Bill Clinton, "Remarks on the United States Foreign Policy, San Francisco, February 26, 1999," available at http://www.mtholyoke.edu/acad/intrel/clintfps.htm.
10. Daalder interview with PBS Frontline, "War in Europe," February 22, 2000, www.pbs.org/wgbh/pages/frontline/shows/Kosovo/interviews. Gelbard branded the KLA as a terrorist group in a press conference on February 23. Steven Burg, "Coercive Diplomacy in the Balkans," in *The United States and Coercive Diplomacy*, ed. Robert Art and Patrick Cronin (Washington: United States Institute of Peace, 2005), pp. 75–6.
11. Madeline Albright, *Madam Secretary* (New York: Miramax Books, 2003), p. 383; Sciolino and Bronner, "How a President." Berger went on to accuse the State Department personnel who had come up with the "irresponsible" proposal of acting like "lunatics." As Halberstam writes: "To know what Clinton felt, you only needed to know what Berger felt, and if Berger was not ready to take a position on a complicated and pressing issue like Kosovo, it meant that the President wasn't either." David Halberstam, *War in Time of Peace: Bush, Clinton, and the Generals* (New York: Touchstone, 2002), pp. 404–9.
12. Tim Judah, *Kosovo: War and Revenge* (New Haven: Yale University Press, 2000); Sciolino and Bronner, "How a President."
13. Berger interview with PBS *Frontline*, "War in Europe," February 22, 2000, www.pbs.org/wgbh/pages/frontline/shows/Kosovo/interviews. Also see on the same site the interviews of Madeleine Albright, Wesley Clark, William Cohen, Richard Holbrooke, and Ivo Daalder.
14. Albright, *Madam Secretary*, pp. 391–2.
15. Richard Holbrooke, *To End a War* (New York: Random House, 1998), pp. 305–9.
16. Madeleine Albright, "Remarks at the United States Institute for Peace, February 4, 1999," available at http://secretary.state.gov/www/statements/1999/990204.html; Albright, *Madam Secretary*, pp. 381–4, 388–9; Albright interview with PBS *Frontline*; Daalder interview with PBS *Frontline*.
17. "In the President's Words," *New York Times*, March 25, 1999.
18. Albright, *Madam Secretary*, pp. 500–1.
19. Roger Cohen, "Who Really Brought Down Milosevic?" *New York Times Magazine*, November 26, 2000; Michael Dobbs, "US Advice Guided Milosevic Opposition," *Washington Post*, December 11, 2001; Adam LeBor, *Milosevic: A Biography* (New Haven: Yale University Press, 2004), pp. 298–308; Louis Sell, *Slobodan Milosevic and the Destruction of Yugoslavia* (Durham: Duke University Press, 2002), pp. 340–2.

Dobbs places the total US aid to Serb opposition at $41 million, while LeBor argues for a $70 million figure and Sell for a $77 million figure.

20. Derek Chollet and James Goldgeier, *America between the Wars: From 11/9 to 9/11* (New York: Public Affairs, 2008), pp.179–204.
21. Steven Erlanger, "NATO Was Closer to Ground War in Kosovo Than It Is Widely Realized," *New York Times*, November 7, 1999.
22. Jane Perlez, "NATO Confronts a New Role: Regional Policeman," *New York Times*, April 22, 1999.
23. Newshour with Jim Lehrer, transcript Online Focus, Assessing the Situation, April 2, 1999, accessible at www.pbs.org/newshour/bb /europe/jan-june99/assessment_4-2.html; Henry Kissinger, *Does America Need A Foreign Policy? Toward a Diplomacy for the Twenty First Century* (New York: Simon & Schuster, 2001), p. 263.
24. Daalder interview with PBS *Frontline*. Daalder is much more supportive of prestige and credibility as the chief reasons to intervene over Kosovo than in his coauthored book, in which he and O'Hanlon make the case for humanitarian intervention.
25. In Daalder's words: "Since the beginning of the Clinton administration Secretary (sic) Albright has been perhaps the most forceful advocate for the strong forceful opposition to the kind of policies Milošević was conducting in Croatia, then in Bosnia, and by February 1998, inside Kosovo." Daalder interview with PBS *Frontline*.
26. Albright interview with PBS *Frontline*; Barton Gellman, "The Path to Crisis: How the United States and Its Allies Went to War," *Washington Post*, April 18, 1999.
27. Michael Dobbs, "Annals of Diplomacy: Double Identity," *New Yorker*, March 29, 1999, pp. 50–5; Albright interview with PBS *Frontline*; Daalder interview with PBS *Frontline*.
28. Albright, "Remarks."
29. Judah, *Kosovo*, pp. 137–45. The Contact Group had been established in the spring of 1994 and comprised the United States, Russia, Britain, France, and Spain.
30. Daalder and O'Hanlon, *Winning Ugly*, pp. 24–8; Walter Isaacson, "Madeleine's War," *Time*, May 17, 1999, pp. 26–7.
31. Judah, *Kosovo*, pp. 159–69; Cohen interview with PBS *Frontline*.
32. Quoted in Judah, *Kosovo*, pp. 184–5, 169–89.
33. Ibid. pp. 185–6; Gellman, "Path to Crisis."
34. Daalder interview with PBS *Frontline*; Cohen interview with PBS *Frontline*; Berger interview with PBS *Frontline*.
35. Gellman, "Path to Crisis"; Albright, *Madam Secretary*, pp. 392–7; Judah, *Kosovo*, pp. 192–6.
36. Cohen interview with PBS *Frontline*; Berger interview with PBS *Frontline*.
37. Gellman, "Path to Crisis"; Albright interview with PBS *Frontline*.
38. Gellman, "Path to Crisis."

39. Daalder interview with PBS *Frontline*.
40. Gellman, "Path to Crisis."
41. "Statement by the North Atlantic Council on Kosovo, January 30, 1999," available at http://www.nato.int/docu/pr/1999/p99–012e .htm.
42. The United States hoped to get Russia on board, but failure to do so no longer represented a veto to action against Belgrade. The United States already had acted unilaterally in the summer of 1998 in response to al Qaeda's bombings in Africa, and had dispensed with Security Council authorization in the December 1998 Operation Desert Fox against Iraq. Norris, *Collision Course*; James Goldgeier and Michael McFaul, *Power and Purpose: US Policy toward Russia after the Cold War* (Washington: Brookings Institution, 2003), chap. 10.
43. Daalder and O'Hanlon, *Winning Ugly*, p. 89; Isaacson, "Madeleine's War."
44. Daalder and O'Hanlon, *Winning Ugly*, pp. 77–84; Judah, *Kosovo*, pp. 201–28.
45. James Rubin, "Press Briefing on the Kosovo Peace Talks, Rambouillet, France, 21 February 1999," in *The Crisis in Kosovo 1989–1999*, ed. Marc Weller (Cambridge: Documents & Analysis Publishing, 2001), p. 451.
46. The letter to the Albanian delegation stated that it concerned the future of the province article in the agreement and that "we will regard this proposal or any other formulation, of that Article that may be agreed at Rambouillet, as confirming a right for the people of Kosovo to hold a referendum of the final status of Kosovo after three years." Marc Weller, "The Rambouillet Conference on Kosovo," *International Affairs* 75 (April 1999): 211–5, 232–4. Getting the Kosovars to sign was a hard-fought victory for Albright—some calling Rambouillet the "most difficult moment of her secretaryship." Judah, *Kosovo*, pp. 214–5.
47. "Rambouillet Agreement: Interim Agreement for Peace and Self-Government of Kosovo," accessible at http://www. gov/www/regions /eur/ksvo_rambouillet_text.html.
48. "In the President's Words," *New York Times*, March 25, 1999. The first draft of Clinton's message announced that the United States had no plans to send ground troops to Kosovo. It was Daalder who argued that the speech be changed to announce a lack of intentions, since, in his opinion, either the United States did not have the plans and appeared incompetent, or, it had them, and was hence appearing to be lying. Daalder interview with PBS *Frontline*.
49. Daalder and O'Hanlon, *Winning Ugly*, pp.108–9.
50. Eric Schmitt and Michael Gordon, "British Pressing Partner to Deploy Ground Troops," *New York Times*, May 18, 1999; "Before Winter Arrives in Kosovo," *New York Times*, May 20, 1999; Eric Schmitt and Michael Gordon, "Time Running Out for NATO to Plan a Kosovo Invasion," *New York Times*, May 23, 1999.

51. Daalder interview with PBS *Frontline*. Also see the response by Strobe Talbott to the question how do you define success in Kosovo: "Very simple. They're going home." Gellman, "Path to Crisis."

52. "NATO Statement Setting Forth Demands on Kosovo," in Daalder and O'Hanlon, *Winning Ugly*, pp. 262–4. No mention of the previous goal of signing Rambouillet was made in the demands.

53. Erlanger, "NATO Closer to Ground War."

54. Daalder and O'Hanlon, *Winning Ugly*, pp. 158–60. As Daalder argues, the message was essentially "we were going to win, no matter what it took." Daalder interview with PBS *Frontline*.

55. Berger interview with PBS *Frontline*.

56. This interpretation receives further support from Clinton's aide Sidney Blumenthal who describes a meeting with the president before Berger's announcement. Both Clinton and Blumenthal were in agreement that victory in Kosovo was imperative so that the United States would avoid appearing ineffective on the world stage. Daalder and O'Hanlon, *Winning Ugly*, p. 159; Sidney Blumenthal, *The Clinton Wars* (New York: Farrar, Straus and Giroux, 2003), p. 648.

57. Eric Schmitt, "Germany's Leader Pledges to Block Combat on Ground," *New York Times*, May 20, 1999. Schröder is quoted as saying, "This is first and foremost a German position. That position is also the present position of NATO and the strategy of an alliance can only be changed if all the parties involved agree to it. I am against any change of NATO strategy." Privately though, the German foreign minister Joschka Fischer signaled that Germany might have given its blessing to a smaller coalition of the willing, even if it declined participation. Blumenthal, *Clinton Wars*, pp. 646–7.

58. Erlanger, "NATO Was Closer to Ground War."

59. "In the President's Words."

60. Ethan Bronner, "Historians Note Flaws in President's Speech," *New York Times*, March 26, 1999.

61. The NATO allies were considerably more nervous about Russia's reaction as seen in the refusal of British General Mike Jackson to obey the order of Clark to stop the Russian troops from reaching the airport: "I'm not going to start World War Three for you." Clark, *Waging Modern War*, pp. 389–96; Norris, *Collision Course*, pp. 250–1.

62. Francis Clines, "Strike Goes On As Serbs Step Up Campaign," *New York Times*, March 27, 1999.

63. James Kurth, "First War of the Global Era," in *War over Kosovo: Politics and Strategy in a New Age*, ed. Andrew Bacevich and Eliot Cohen (New York: Columbia University Press, 2001), pp. 63–96, 77.

64. Samantha Power, *A "Problem From Hell": America and the Age of Genocide* (New York: Basic Books, 2002), pp. 288, 446; David Binder, "Bush Warns Serbs Not to Widen War," *New York Times*, December 28, 1992; Stephen Engelberg, "Weighing Strikes in Bosnia, US Warns of Wider War," *New York Times*, April 25, 1993.

65. Sell describes the Christmas warning as an effort by the United States to signal that it should not have been judged by its lack of reaction in Bosnia. Sell, *Milosevic*, pp. 265–6.

66. Elisabeth Barker, "The Origins of the Macedonian Question," in *The New Macedonia Question*, ed. James Pettifer (Basingstoke: Macmillan, 1999), pp. 3–14; James Pettifer, "The New Macedonian Question," in *New Macedonia Question*, Pettifer, ed., pp. 15–27; Evangelos Kofos, "Greek Policy Considerations over FYROM Independence and Recognition," in *New Macedonia Question*, Pettifer, ed., pp. 226–62.

67. Jens Reuter, "Policy and Economy in Macedonia," in *New Macedonia Question*, Pettifer, ed., pp. 43–5. By the 2000s, most states employed the name Macedonia, although no satisfactory compromise was ever reached with Greece.

68. Kofos, "Greek Policy Considerations," pp. 234–6, 254–6.

69. Reuter, "Policy and Economy in Macedonia," p. 42.

70. Elez Biberaj, *Albania in Transition: The Rocky Road to Democracy* (Boulder: Westview Press, 1998), p. 11.

71. Pettifer, *New Macedonia Question*, pp. 16–7; James Pettifer, "The Albanians in Western Macedonia after FYROM Independence," in *New Macedonia Question*, Pettifer, ed., pp. 137–47; Biberaj, *Albania in Transition*, pp. 13–5. The figures of a census in 1994, which the Albanians contest, put the total number of Albanians in Macedonia at 442,000 or 23 percent of the population. At the time, it was suspected that the real number was somewhere between 30 and 40 percent. However, a new census in 2002 under international auspices confirmed that the percentage of Albanians in FYROM was 25.7 percent. See John Philips, *Macedonia: Warlords and Rebels in the Balkans* (New Haven: Yale University Press, 2004), pp. 80–1.

72. Albright, "Remarks." The prospect of conflict in Macedonia was not just theoretical. This was proven by events in 2001, when a civil conflict that killed more than 200 people erupted between Slavs and Albanians in FYROM. James Pettifer and Miranda Vickers, *The Albanian Question: Reshaping the Balkans* (London: I. B. Tauris, 2009), pp. 243–53; Philips, *Macedonia*.

73. Pettifer and Vickers, *Albanian Question*, p. 243.

74. "NATO Bombing Tears at Greek Opinion: Reawaken Anti-Americanism," *New York Times*, April 25, 1999. This level of dissent was the highest in NATO. Daalder and O'Hanlon, *Winning Ugly*, p. 161.

75. Pettifer, "Albanians in Western Macedonia," p. 143.

76. Sciolino and Bronner, "How a President"; Gellman, "Path to Crisis"; Daalder and O'Hanlon, *Winning Ugly*, pp. 53–5, 71.

77. Biberaj, *Albania in Transition*, pp. 316–27; Pettifer and Vickers, *Albanian Question*.

78. The only international reaction was the Italian-led limited intervention known as Operation Alba, whose goal was to stop the influx of Albanian refugees. Pettifer and Vickers, *Albanian Question*, pp. 67–74.

79. At the time a Kalashnikov rifle could be bought for $5 in Albania. Judah, *Kosovo*, pp. 126–9.
80. Daalder interview with PBS *Frontline*.
81. Daalder and O'Hanlon, *Winning Ugly*, fn. 21, p. 283; Philip Shennon, "US Says It Might Consider Attacking Serbs," *New York Times*, March 13, 1998; Gellman, "Path to Crisis."
82. Christopher Layne and Benjamin Schwartz, "For the Record: Kosovo II," *National Interest* 57 (Fall 1999): 9–15; Michael McGwire, "Why Did We Bomb Belgrade?" *International Affairs* 76 (January 2000): 1–23.
83. If there was a dominant theme to US policy toward the region, this was finding a way to exit Bosnia, where the United States had stationed thousands of troops. Hal Brands, *From Berlin to Baghdad: America's Search for Purpose in the Post–Cold War World* (Lexington: University Press of Kentucky, 2008), pp. 204–7.
84. Daalder and O'Hanlon, *Winning Ugly*, pp. 108–9.
85. Ibid. pp. 11–2, 194–6; Joseph S. Nye, "Redefining the National Interest," *Foreign Affairs* 78 (July/August 1999): 22–44; Michael Ignatieff, *Virtual War: Kosovo and Beyond* (Toronto: Viking, 2000); Tony Judt, "The Reason Why," *New York Review of Books*, May 20, 1999.
86. For critical views, see Isaacson, "*Madeleine's War*"; Kissinger, *Does America Need a Foreign Policy*, pp. 255–64; Michael Mandelbaum, "A Perfect Failure," *Foreign Affairs* 78 (September/October 1999): 2–8.
87. Cohen interview with PBS *Frontline*; Berger interview with PBS *Frontline*.
88. Ivo Daalder and Michael O'Hanlon, "Unlearning the Lessons of Kosovo," *Foreign Policy* 116 (Autumn 1999): 128–40, 129, 139.
89. Daalder and O'Hanlon, *Winning Ugly*, p. 116.
90. Craig Whitney and Eric Schmitt, "NATO Had Signs Its Strategy Would Fail in Kosovo," *New York Times*, April 1, 1999; Craig Whitney, "For NATO, Doubts Nag," *New York Times*, March 31, 1999.
91. Daalder and O' Hanlon, *Winning Ugly*, pp. 106–7.
92. Jeffrey Smith and William Drozdiak, "The Anatomy of a Purge," *Washington Post*, April 11, 1999; Sciolino and Bronner, "How a President"; Johana McGeary, "The Road to Hell Was Paved with Good Intentions," but Muddled Planning," *Time*, April 12, 1999. However, see Judah's argument against the existence of a Serb master plan to oust the Kosovars from the province. Judah, *Kosovo*, pp. 240–6.
93. Berger admitted that no more than 350,000 refugees were anticipated. Sciolino and Bronner, "How a President."
94. Clark, *Waging Modern War*, pp. 170–1.
95. Ibid. p. 183.
96. On NATO's tactics, see Daalder and O'Hanlon, *Winning Ugly*, pp. 122–3; on airpower, see Benjamin Lambeth, *NATO's War for Kosovo: A Strategic and Operational Assessment* (Santa Monica: Rand, 2001).

97. Daalder and O'Hanlon, *Winning Ugly*, pp. 33–4, 96–9; Sciolino and Bronner, "How a President," p. 13.

98. Clark, *Waging Modern War*, pp. 246–88; Dana Priest, "Risks and Restraints: Why the Apaches Never Flew in Kosovo," *Washington Post*, December 29, 1999.

99. Roger Cohen, "Already Burdened, Western Europe Is Reluctant to Take in Kosovo's Outcasts," *New York Times*, April 2, 1999.

100. Philip Shenon, "US Grapples with Issue of Finding Refugees Homes," *New York Times*, April 3, 1999; Joanne Van Selm, ed., *Kosovo Refugees in the EU* (London: Pinter, 2000).

101. The Guantanamo initiative cannot be attributed to the decisions of a separate government agency, as it was announced by the White House spokesman Joe Lockhart. Philip Shenon, "US Chooses Guantanamo Bay Base in Cuba for Refugee Site," *New York Times*, April 7, 1999; Katharine Seelye, "Gore Says US Will Open Door to 20,000 Kosovars," *New York Times*, April 22, 1999.

102. Andrew Bacevich, *American Empire: The Realities and Consequences of US Diplomacy* (Cambridge: Harvard University Press, 2002), pp. 182–97.

103. Chalmers Johnson, *Blowback: The Costs and Consequences of America's Empire* (New York: Henry Holt, 2000), pp. 93–4.

104. Halberstam, *War in Time of Peace*, pp. 441–56, 468–9; Clark, *Waging Modern War*, pp. 253–62, 409.

105. Fareed Zakaria, *The Future of Freedom: Illiberal Democracies at Home and Abroad* (New York: W. W. Norton, 2004); Thomas L. Friedman, *The Lexus and the Olive Tree* (New York: Farrar, Strauss and Giroux, 1999), p. 195.

5 THE INDISPENSABLE NATION AND US UNILATERALISM

1. Ivo Daalder and James Lindsay, *America Unbound: The Bush Revolution in Foreign Policy* (Washington: Brookings Institution, 2003), pp. 13–4, 40–1; Charles Krauthammer, "The Bush Doctrine: In American Foreign Policy, a New Motto: Don't Ask, Tell," *Time*, March 5, 2001, p. 42.

2. For analyses stressing the continuity between Clinton and George W. Bush, see James Mann, *Rise of the Vulcans: The History of Bush's War Cabinet* (New York: Viking Books, 2004), pp. 214, 286–8; Timothy Lynch and Robert Singh, *After Bush: The Case for Continuity in American Foreign Policy* (New York: Cambridge University Press, 2008).

3. Comprehensive lists should also include peacekeeping, relations with the UN, chemical weapons, the Landmine Treaty, the ban on nuclear

tests, human rights, global warming, and international trade relations. Steward Patrick and Shepard Forman, eds., *Multilateralism and US Foreign Policy: Ambivalent Engagement* (Boulder: Lynne Rienner, 2002); David Malone and Yuen Foong Khong, eds., *Unilateralism and US Foreign Policy: International Perspectives* (Boulder: Lynne Rienner, 2003).

4. Elizabeth Pond, *Friendly Fire: The Near-Death of the Transatlantic Alliance* (Pittsburgh: European Union Studies Association, 2004), p. 34.

5. Robert Kagan, *Of Paradise and Power: America and Europe in the New World Order* (New York: Knopf, 2003), pp. 144–5, 147; Niall Ferguson, *Colossus: The Price of America's Empire* (New York: Penguin Press, 2004), p. 133, chap. 4.

6. John Gerard Ruggie, "Multilateralism: The Anatomy of an Institution," in *Multilateralism Matters: The Theory and Praxis of an Institutional Form*, ed. Ruggie (New York: Columbia University Press, 1993).

7. Stephen Brooks and William Wohlforth, "International Relations Theory and the Case against Unilateralism," *Perspectives on Politics* 3 (September 2005): 509–24, esp. 509–10; also see David Malone and Yuen Foong Khong, "Unilateralism and US Foreign Policy: International Perspectives," in *Unilateralism*, ed. Malone and Khong, p. 3; Sarah Kreps, *Coalitions of Convenience: United States Military Interventions after the Cold War* (New York: Oxford University Press, 2011), pp. 15–20.

8. Stephen Brooks and William Wohlforth, *World Out of Balance: International Relations and the Challenge of American Primacy* (Princeton: Princeton University Press, 2008), p. 149.

9. Charles Krauthammer, "A New Type of Realism," *National Interest* (January 2003), available at http://nationalinterest.org/article/a-new-type-of-realism-2238. As Krauthammer writes: "Countries will cooperate with us, first, out of their own self-interest and second, out of the need and desire to cultivate good relations with the world's superpower. Warm and fuzzy feelings are a distant third."

10. The very historical evidence used by Krauthammer to support his argument, derived from the Gulf War, is tenuous, because no country joined the coalition solely because the United States made it clear that the invasion of Kuwait would not stand. Considerable diplomatic finesse and tact were used to secure and maintain the help of the coalition partners (especially in the cases of Saudi Arabia, Israel, and the Soviet Union). James Addison Baker, III, *The Politics of Diplomacy: Revolution, War, and Peace* (New York: G. P. Putnam's Sons, 1995); Lawrence Freedman and Ephraim Karsh, *Gulf Conflict, 1990–1991: Diplomacy and War in the New World Order* (London: Faber and Faber, 1993).

11. Voeten argues convincingly that a credible outside option, i.e. taking matters in one's own hands, actually strengthens the bargaining position of the United States vis-à-vis other states. But Voeten's model

differs substantially from Krauthammer's assertiveness as a means to cooperation argument. In the latter, assertiveness is not practiced occasionally, but regularly so as to force other states to comply with US wishes. In the former, the US decision-makers employ (but do not necessarily use and certainly not permanently) the threat of resorting to unilateralism. Accordingly, shrewd US decision-makers resort to a strategic oscillation between unilateralism (assertiveness) and multilateralism, rather than employing rigid unilateralism so as to solicit the cooperation of other parties. Voeten, "Outside Options."

12. Malone and Khong, *Unilateralism and US Foreign Policy*, pp. 86–90, 93, 97.

13. Ibid. p. 88; Thom Shanker, "White House Says the US Is Not a Loner, Just Choosy," *Washington Post*, July 31, 2001.

14. Derek Chollet and James Goldgeier, *America between the Wars: From 11/9 to 9/11* (New York: Public Affairs, 2008), pp. 146–7; Sidney Blumenthal, *The Clinton Wars* (New York: Farrar, Straus and Giroux, 2003), pp. 155–6; "Transcript of President Bill Clinton Second Inaugural Speech to the Nation," *New York Times*, January 21, 1997.

15. Madeleine Albright, "Prepared Statement, Senate Foreign Relations Committee Confirmation Hearings, January 8, 1997," at http://www.fas.org/man/nato/congress/1997/s970108a.htm.

16. "Transcript, Madeleine's Albright Interview on NBC TV, February 19, 1998," at http://www. fas.org/news/iraq/1998/02/19/98021907_tpo.html.

17. Madeleine Albright, *Madam Secretary* (New York: Miramax Books, 2003), p. 506.

18. Blumenthal, *Clinton Wars*, pp. 146–7, 157.

19. Ibid. p. 155.

20. Robert Jervis, *American Foreign Policy in a New Era* (New York: Routledge, 2005), pp. 79–80.

21. George W. Bush, "State of the Union Address, January 28, 2003," available at http://www.cnn.com/2003/ALLPOLITICS/01/28/sotu/transcript/.

22. George W. Bush, "State of the Union Address, January 29, 2002," available at http:// www.cnn.com/2002/ALLPOLITICS/01/29/bush.speech.txt/.

23. Bob Woodward, *Bush at War* (New York: Simon & Schuster, 2002), pp. 65–6.

24. Charles Krauthammer, "The Bush Doctrine: 'New Unilateralism,'" *Chronicle*, June 8, 2001.

25. "Secretary Rumsfeld's Media Stakeout in Washington, September 14, 2001," available at http://www.defense.gov/transcripts/transcript.aspx?transcriptid=1926.

26. Ruth Wedgewood, "Fiddling in Rome," *Foreign Affairs* 77 (November 1998): 20–4.

27. *Rome Statute of the International Criminal Court*, in Roy S. Lee, ed., in *The International Criminal Court: The Making of the Rome Statute: Issues, Negotiations, Results* (The Hague: Kluwer Law International, 1999), pp. 479–572; Philippe Kirsch and John T. Holmes, "The Rome Conference on the International Criminal Court: The Negotiation Process," *American Journal of International Law* 93 (January 1999): 2–12; Cherif Bassiouni, "Negotiating the Treaty of Rome on the Establishment of the International Criminal Court," *Cornell Journal of International Law and Public Policy* 32, no. 3 (1999): 443–70.

28. Philipp Meißner, *The International Criminal Court Controversy: An Analysis of the United States' Major Objections against the Rome Statute* (Münster: Lit Verlag, 2005), 33–56.

29. Kirsch and Holmes, "Rome Conference"; Lawrence Weschler, "Exceptional Cases in Rome: The United States and the Struggle for an ICC," in *The United States and the International Criminal Court: National Security and International Law*, ed. Sarah Sewall and Carl Kaysen (Lanham: Rowman & Littlefield, 2000).

30. Bassiouni, "Negotiating the Treaty of Rome," p. 457; Weschler, *United States and ICC*, p. 105.

31. David Scheffer, "The United States and the International Criminal Court," *American Journal of International Law* 93 (January 1999): 18–9.

32. Quoted in Barbara Crosette, "World Criminal Court Having a Painful Birth," *New York Times*, August 13, 1998.

33. Weschler, "Exceptional Cases," pp. 102–3.

34. David Frum, "The International Criminal Court Must Die," *Weekly Standard*, August 10, 1999, p. 27; also see John Bolton, "The Risks and Weaknesses of the International Criminal Court from America's Perspective," *Law and Contemporary Problems* 64 (Winter 2001): 167–80.

35. Benjamin Schiff, *Building the International Criminal Court* (New York: Cambridge University Press, 2008), pp. 172–9. The president has the right to waver annually such requirements, so that major allies are exempt.

36. *Treaty between the United States of America and the Union of Soviet Socialist Republics on the Limitation of Anti-Ballistic Missile Systems*, signed at Moscow, May 26, 1972, reproduced in James Lindsay and Michael O'Hanlon, *Defending America: The Case for Limited National Missile Defense* (Washington: Brookings Institution, 2001), pp. 169–74.

37. Bill Clinton News Conference, March 5, 1999, at www.presidency.ucsb.edu/ws/index.php?pid=57203.

38. Derek Smith, *Deterring America: Rogue States and the Proliferation of Weapons of Mass Destruction* (New York: Cambridge University Press, 2006), pp. 36–40.

39. Bradley Graham, *Hit to Kill: The New Battle over Shielding America from Missile Attack* (New York: Public Affairs, 2003), p. 92.
40. Ibid. pp. 163–4; Walter Slocombe, "The Administration's Approach," *Washington Quarterly* 23 (Summer 2000): 79–85; Walter Slocombe, "Remarks at the Center for Strategic and International Studies," November 5, 1999, at www.defenselink.mil/speeches/speech.aspx? speechid=550.
41. John Holum, "Presentation at the Conference on International Reactions to US National and Theater Missile Defense Deployments," Stanford University, March 3, 2000, at.www.fas.org/nuke/control /abmt/news/030300holum.htm.
42. Reproduced in Anthony Cordesman, *Strategic Threats and National Missile Defenses: Defending the US Homeland* (Westport: Praeger, 2002), p. 21.
43. George W. Bush, "Speech at National Defense University, May 1, 2000," accessible at http://www.fas.org/nuke/control/abmt/news /010501bush.html. Also see for this point White House, *National Security Strategy of the United States*, September 2002, at www .whitehouse.gov/nsc/nss.pdf.
44. Lindsay and O'Hanlon, *Defending America*, pp. 18–9, 71–2.
45. Victor Cha, *The Impossible State: North Korea, Past and Future* (New York: Ecco, 2012), p. 237.
46. Ibid.; Mike Chinoy, *Meltdown: The Inside Story of the North Korean Nuclear Crisis* (New York: St. Martin's Press, 2008). On Kuwait, see Freedman and Karsh, *Gulf Conflict*. On the European opposition to NMD see Graham, *Hit to Kill*, pp. 153–6.
47. This assessment was accurate. Although in 2006, 2009, and 2012, North Korea tested the Taepodong II model, which has a range of 2,420–2,670 miles (about 4,000 kilometers) and allows the missile to reach the continental United States, all tests have resulted in failures, with the missile falling apart within a minute of its launch. Cha, *Impossible State*, pp. 227, 273; Choe Sang Hun and Rick Gladstone, "North Korean Rocket Fails Moments after Liftoff," *New York Times*, April 12, 2012.
48. The Taepodong I missile could not have reached the United States, since it had a range of 2,000 miles. Graham, *Hit to Kill*, pp. 57–65; chap. 2, pp. 38–9, 47–8. The quote should not be understood as a form of extreme risk aversion on the part of the administration, since it reflected the views of the commission criticizing it. In fact, members of the Clinton team as seen in the earlier quotes in this chapter were much less worried about a missile attack by a rogue state against the US.
49. Richard Garwin, "A Defense That Will Not Defend," *Washington Quarterly* 23 (Summer 2000): 109–26; George Lewis, Lisbeth Gronlund, and David Wright, "National Missile Defense: An Indefensible System,"

Foreign Policy 117 (Winter 1999): 120–39; Lindsay and O'Hanlon, *Defending America*, chaps. 2, 4; Richard Dean Burns, *The Missile Defense Systems of George W. Bush: A Critical Assessment* (Denver: Praeger, 2010), p. 149.

50. Ibid. pp. 67, 79–84; Graham, *Hit to Kill*, pp. 211–4, 315.
51. Bush, "Speech at National Defense University."
52. Graham, *Hit to Kill*, p. 344.
53. Anthony Cordesman, *Iraq and the War of Sanctions: Conventional Threats and Weapons of Mass Destruction* (Westport: Praeger, 1999), p. 178; Graham Sarah Brown, *Sanctioning Saddam: The Politics of Intervention in Iraq* (London: I. B. Tauris, 1999), p. 57; Andrew Cockburn and Patrick Cockburn, *Out of the Ashes: The Resurrection of Saddam Hussein* (New York: Harper, 2000).
54. On these efforts, see Andrew Cockburn and Patrick Cockburn, *Saddam Hussein: An American Obsession* (London: Verso, 2002); Robert Baer, *See No Evil: The True Story of a Ground Soldier in the CIA's War on Terrorism* (New York: Crown Publishers, 2002).
55. Brown, *Sanctioning Saddam*, pp. 58–60, 78–9; Phoebe Marr, "Symposium on Dual Containment," *Middle East Policy* 3, no. 1 (1994): 1–26.
56. Brown, *Sanctioning Saddam*, p. 80.
57. Ibid. pp. 84–5.
58. Cordesman, *Iraq and the War of Sanctions*; Richard Butler, *Saddam Defiant: The Threat of Weapons of Mass Destruction and the Crisis of Global Security* (London: Weidenfeld & Nicolson, 1999), pp. 96–119, 137–63, 192–5, 219–35; Dilip Hiro, *Iraq: In the Eye of the Storm* (New York: Nation Books, 2002).
59. Cordesman, *Iraq and the War of Sanctions*, pp. 242–63, 223–9, 330–65; Hiro, *Iraq*, pp. 107–31.
60. Cordesman, *Iraq and the War of Sanctions*, pp. 225–42; Bob Woodward, *Shadow: Five Presidents and the Legacy of Watergate* (New York: Simon & Schuster, 1999), p. 492.
61. Butler, *Saddam Defiant*, pp. 212, 225; Brown, *Sanctioning Saddam*, p. 86.
62. Woodward, *Shadow*, pp. 493–4.
63. "We Are Delivering a Powerful Message to Saddam," *New York Times*, December 17, 1998.
64. Marc Weller, "The US, Iraq, and the Use of Force in a Unipolar World," *Survival* 41 (Winter 1999): 81–100.
65. James Goldgeier and Michael McFaul, *Power and Purpose: US Policy toward Russia after the Cold War* (Washington: Brookings Institution, 2003), pp. 249–50.
66. Paul Heinbecker, "Kosovo," in *The UN Security Council: From the Cold War to the 21st Century* (Boulder: Lynne Rienner, 2004), ed. David Malone, pp. 545–8.

67. Wesley Clark, *Waging Modern War: Bosnia, Kosovo, and the Future of Combat* (New York: Public Affairs, 2002).
68. Mann, *Rise of the Vulcans*, pp. 304–5.
69. Suzanne Daley, "NATO Says It Has Proof against Bin Laden's Group: Alliance Says It Will Fight If Asked," *New York Times*, October 2, 2001.
70. R. W. Apple, "Piece-by-Piece Coalition: Rumsfeld Visits Region with Delicate Job of Rallying Countries to Anti-terrorism Cause," *New York Times*, October 4, 2001.
71. Philip Gordon and Jeremy Shapiro, *Allies at War: America, Europe, and the Crisis over Iraq* (New York: McGraw-Hill, 2004), pp. 77–80, 121–2, 146–7.
72. Dick Cheney, "Speech to the Veterans of Foreign Wars," August 26, 2002, at www.cnn.com/ALLPOLITICS/08/26/cheney/iraq.
73. "President Bush's Address to the United Nations, September 12, 2002," accessible at http://www.transcripts/cnn.com/2002/US/09/12/bush.transcript/.
74. Cheney interview, accessible at http://www.mtholyoke.edu/acad/intrel/bush/ cheneymeetthepress.htm; Hans Blix, *Disarming Iraq* (New York: Pantheon Books, 2004), pp. 86–7.
75. Blix, *Disarming Iraq*, pp. 7–12, 249–53.
76. The Bush administration also took as a personal affront the comment by the German justice minister Herta Daübler-Gmelin that it was using diversionary tactics similar to Hitler's. Although Chancellor Schröder sent an apologetic letter to Bush, promising not to name her in his new cabinet, this gesture was not deemed a contrite enough effort by the United States because it did not entail the immediate dismissal of the offending minister. Gordon and Shapiro, *Allies at War*, pp. 100–1.
77. "Old Europe" was contrasted with new Europe, the eight Western European and the so-called "Vilnius ten" Eastern European signatories of letters supporting the US position on Iraq. Ibid. pp. 128–36.
78. Ibid. pp. 100–4, 119–20, 123–4, 137–8, 171–2.
79. Kenneth Waltz, *Theory of International Politics* (Reading: Addison Wesley, 1979), pp. 159, 105–7, 129–59.
80. John Mearsheimer, "The False Promise, of International Institutions," *International Security* 19 (Winter 1994): 5–49, esp. fn. 13. Mearsheimer's critique is all the more poignant since he identifies institutions with multilateralism: "The term 'multilateralism' is also virtually synonymous with institutions."
81. Max Boot, "Doctrine of the 'Big Enchilada,'" *Washington Post*, October 14, 2002.
82. Kagan, *Of Paradise and Power*, pp. 10–11, 31–4, 37–9.
83. For a recent argument that power does not necessarily lead to unilateralism, see Kreps, *Coalitions of Convenience*. Kreps also argues that US decisions in favor of multilateralism depend on how pressing the threat is and on how resource-intensive the intervention will be, which,

while a different argument from my own, does not necessarily represent a contradiction.

84. See for a similar argument that the United States cannot promote, but can only prohibit policies, Samuel Huntington, "The Lonely Superpower," *Foreign Affairs* 78 (March/April 1999): 35–50.

85. Charles Krauthammer, "The Unipolar Moment Revisited," *National Interest* 70 (Winter 2002/2003): 5–17.

86. The original preference of the United States was for a negotiated settlement, so unilateralism was not the optimal way to realize political preferences, because in this case it would have been implemented from the start, instead of as a reaction to the failure of multilateralism.

87. The alleged threat was made against Germany by Secretary of Defense Cohen and involved Germany giving up its lobbying in favor of universal jurisdiction. Cohen appears to have threatened Germany with a possible withdrawal of American forces from Europe, an allegation that the Pentagon denied, but for which proof documents were available. Alessandra Stanley, "US Presses Allies to Rein In Proposed War Crimes Court," *New York Times*, July 15, 1998.

88. Bassiouni, "Negotiating the Treaty of Rome," pp. 459–60.

89. Lindsay and O'Hanlon, *Defending America*, pp. 156–8; Cordesman, *Strategic Threats*, pp. 66–77, 80–1; Ivo Daalder and James Goldgeier, "Russia," in *Rocket's Red Glare: Missile Defenses and the Future of World Politics*, ed. James Wirtz and Jeffrey Larsen (Boulder: Westview, 2001), pp. 219–20.

90. Graham, *Hit to Kill*, pp. 153–62.

91. Goldgeier and McFaul, *Power and Purpose*, pp. 287–97, 357–8; Lindsay and O'Hanlon, *Defending America*, pp. 118–21.

92. Anthony Cordesman, *Iraq and the War of Sanctions: Conventional Threats and Weapons of Mass Destruction* (Westport: Praeger, 1999), pp. 261–3, 273; Weller, "The US, Iraq, and the Use of Force," pp. 84–6; Heinbecker, "Kosovo"; Gordon and Shapiro, *Allies at War*, pp. 122–4, 146–9.

93. Gordon and Shapiro, *Allies at War*, pp. 115–7, 146–54.

94. Walter McDougall, *Promised Land, Crusader State* (Boston: Houghton Mifflin, 1997), pp. 39–51; Bradford Perkins, The *Creation of a Republican Empire, Cambridge History of American Foreign Relations, Vol. 1* (New York: Cambridge University Press, 1993), pp. 22–4; Manfred Jonas, *Isolationism in America, 1935-1941* (Ithaca: Cornell University Press, 1966), pp. 5–15.

95. Arthur Schlesinger, Jr., "Unilateralism in Historical Perspective," in *Understanding Unilateralism in American Foreign Relations*, ed. Gwyn Prins (London: Royal Institute of International Affairs, 2000), pp. 20–9, 20, 24; Lieven, *America Right or Wrong*; Lynch and Singh, *After Bush*, pp. 37–8; Leffler, "Bush's Foreign Policy"; Gaddis, *Surprise, Security and the American Experience*.

96. Mead contends in a similar argument that Bush stands for Jacksonianism, a US strategic culture emphasizing not only unilateralism, but also

vindication of insults to the nation's honor. Walter Russell Mead, *Special Providence*, pp. 244–5, 261–2, 297–300.

97. Brands, *What America Owes the World*.

98. Chollet and Goldgeier, *America Between the Wars*.

99. Congress also had its share of victories—the most significant being the vote against the ratification of the Comprehensive Test Ban Treaty in the fall of 1998.

100. Heilbrunn, *They Knew They Were Right*, pp. 212–8; Kagan and Kristol, "Towards a Neo-Reaganite Foreign Policy."

101. George Washington, "Farewell Address," in Gilbert, *To the Farewell Address*, pp. 144–7.

102. Ibid., p. 145.

103. Bacevich, *American Empire*, pp. 215–23.

104. Bartram Brown, "Unilateralism, Multilateralism, and the International Criminal Court," in Patrick and Forman, eds., *Multilateralism*, pp. 324–5.

105. Graham, *Hit to Kill*, pp. 114–5, 118–20; Goldgeier and McFaul, *Power and Purpose*, pp. 292–3.

6 THE UNITED STATES SUPREME: THE INVASION OF IRAQ

1. On neoconservatives in the administration, see Stefan Halper and Jonathan Clarke, *America Alone: The Neo-Conservatives and the Global Order* (New York: Cambridge University Press, 2004), p. 14. On the central role of Rumsfeld and Cheney, see James Mann, *Rise of the Vulcans: The History of Bush's War Cabinet* (New York: Viking Books, 2004); Michael Gordon and Bernard Trainor, *Cobra II: The Inside Story of the Invasion and the Occupation of Iraq* (New York: Pantheon Books, 2006).

2. Harvey correctly denounces the error of "neoconism"—tracing the invasion of Iraq solely to the influence of neoconservatives. Harvey also makes the important counterfactual point that had Al Gore been elected president in 2000, his administration would have still invaded Iraq. However, this argument is dependent on the debatable assumptions that a Gore presidency would have faced the exact same sequence of events as the Bush administration, and, as a result, that its election would not have affected in any way events such as September 11, the intervention of Afghanistan, the siege of Tora Bora, relations with allies, and the decision to conduct a ground invasion of Iraq. Frank Harvey, *Explaining the Iraq War: Counterfactual Theory, Logic, and Evidence* (New York: Cambridge University Press, 2012).

3. The neoconservatives were actually critical of Bush's initial foreign policy of containment toward Iraq. Reuel Marc Gerecht, "Liberate Iraq," *Weekly Standard*, May 14, 2001; Reuel Marc Gerecht, "A Cowering Superpower," *Weekly Standard*, July 30, 2001. On the secondary

importance of neoconservatives in the administration, see Max Boot, "Myths About Neoconservatism," in *The Neocon Reader*, ed. Irwin Stelzer (New York: Grove Press, 2004), pp. 45–52; on the enclave plan see Robert Kagan, "A Way to Oust Saddam," *Weekly Standard*, September 28, 1998; on Chalabi, see Jane Mayer, "The Manipulator," *New Yorker*, June 7, 2004.

4. Gary Dorrien, *Imperial Designs: The Neocons and the New Pax Americana* (New York: Routledge, 2004), pp. 135–7; also see Condoleezza Rice, "Promoting the National Interest," *Foreign Affairs* 79 (January/ February 2000): 45–62.
5. While neoconservatives downplay their ability to influence Bush's foreign policy, they admit that the administration employed their arguments. Boot, "Myths," pp. 45–6; David Brooks, "The Neocon Cabal and Other Fantasies," in *The Neocon Reader*, ed. Stezler, pp. 39–42, 41–2; Joshua Muravchik, "Neoconservative Cabal," in *The Neocon Reader*, ed. Stezler, pp. 255–6.
6. Robert Kagan and William Kristol, "Towards a Neo-Reaganite Policy," *Foreign Affairs* 75 (July/August 1996): 20, 23.
7. Robert Kagan and William Kristol, "Burden of Power Is Having to Wield It," *Washington Post*, March 19, 2000.
8. Robert Kagan and William Kristol, "Introduction: National Interest and Global Responsibility," in *Present Dangers: Crisis and Opportunity in American Foreign Policy*, ed. Kagan and Kristol (San Francisco: Encounter Books, 2000), pp. 3, 4, 12.
9. Lawrence Kaplan and William Kristol, *The War over Iraq: Saddam's Tyranny and America's Mission* (San Francisco: Encounter Books, 2003), p. 118.
10. Paul Wolfowitz, "Remembering the Future," *National Interest* 59 (Spring 2000): 44.
11. Kagan and Kristol, "Towards a Neo-Reaganite Policy," pp. 20, 23, 32.
12. Ibid. p. 26; Project for the New American Century, *Rebuilding America's Defenses: Strategy, Forces, and Resources for a New Century* (Washington: Project for the New American Century, 2000), pp. iv–v, 22–49.
13. Kagan and Kristol, "Towards a Neo-Reaganite Policy," pp. 26–7, 31.
14. Kaplan and Kristol, *War over Iraq*, pp. 117–8, 120–1.
15. Ibid. pp. 120–1, 124; Kagan and Kristol, "Burden."
16. Project for New American Century, "Statement of Principles," June 3, 1997, accessible at www. newamericancentury.org/statementofprinciples .htm; Halper and Clarke, *America Alone*, pp. 98–110.
17. Robert Kagan, "Saddam Wins Again," *Weekly Standard*, January 4, 1999; Richard Perle, "Saddam Unbound," in *Present Dangers*, ed. Kagan and Kristol, pp. 99–110, 105; Robert Kagan and William Kristol, "A Great Victory for Iraq," *Washington Post*, February 26, 1998; "How to Attack Iraq," *Weekly Standard*, November 16, 1998; Kaplan and Kristol, *War over Iraq*, pp. 50–62.

18. Project for New American Century, "Open Letter to President Clinton," January 26, at www.newamericancentury/org.iraqclintonletter.htm; Kaplan and Kristol, *War over Iraq*, p. 92; Robert Kagan and William Kristol, "Saddam Must Go," *Weekly Standard*, November 1997.
19. Zalmay Khalilzad and Paul Wolfowitz, "Overthrow Him," *Weekly Standard*, December 1, 1997.
20. David Von Drehle, "World War, Cold War Won. Now the Gray War," *Washington Post*, September 12, 2001; also see George W. Bush, "Address to the Joint Session of Congress," September 20, 2001, available at http:// www.cnn.com/2001/US/ 09/20/gen. bush. transcript/.
21. R. W. Apple, "Awaiting the Aftershocks," *New York Times*, September 12, 2001.
22. Trauma represents "exposure to an event so shocking that our everyday expectations of how the world works are severely disrupted." Jenny Edkins, "Forget Trauma? Responses to September 11," *International Relations* 16, no. 2 (2002): 245–6.
23. Apple, "Awaiting the Aftershocks"; David Singer, "Bin Laden Is Wanted 'Dead or Alive,'" *New York Times*, September 18, 2001; Bush, "Address to Joint Session of Congress."
24. For a different view of 9/11 and humiliation, see Paul Saurette, "You Dissin Me? Humiliation and Post 9/11 Global Politics," *Review of International Studies* 32 (2006): 495–522.
25. Daniel Benjamin and Steven Simon, *The Age of Sacred Terror* (New York: Random House, 2002), pp. 156–7.
26. "Statement by the President in His Address to the Nation," available at http://georgewbush-whitehouse.archives.gov/news/releases /2001/09/20010911-16.html. "Excerpts from President's Remarks on Investigation into Attacks," *New York Times*, September 14, 2001; Robert McFadden, "Bush Leads Prayer," *New York Times*, September 15, 2001; Bush, "Address to Joint Session of Congress."
27. "Statement by the President in His Address to the Nation."
28. "Remarks by the President Upon Arrival at Barksdale Air Force Base," available at http://georgewbushwhitehouse.archives.gov/news /releases/2001/09/20010911-1.html.
29. Dick Cheney on NBC Meet the Press, available at http://www .fromthewilderness.com/timeline/2001/meetthepress091601.html.
30. "Remarks at Barksdale"; McFadden, "Bush Leads Prayer"; Singer, "Bin Laden Wanted"; Todd Purdum, "Bush Warns of a Wrathful, Shadowy, and Inventive War," *New York Times*, September 16, 2001; Cheney on NBC Meet the Press; "Almost 90% Want US to Retaliate," *Washington Post*, September 12, 2001; for the public's reaction, also see Harden Blaine, "For Many, Sorrow Turns to Anger and Talk of Vengeance," *New York Times*, September 14, 2001.
31. Bush, "Address to Joint Session of Congress." Also see Condoleezza Rice, *No Higher Honor: A Memoir of My Years in Washington* (New York: Crown, 2011), p. 79.

32. Frank Bruni, "For President a Mission and a Role in History," *New York Times*, September 22, 2001; Condoleeza Rice, "Speech at Johns Hopkins University," April 29, 2002 ,at merln.ndu.edu./archivepdf /iran/WH/20020429–9.pdf; Dick Cheney, "Remarks to the Council of Foreign Relations," February 16, 2002, at http://www.mtholyoke .edu/acad/intrel/bush/cheneyiraq.htm; Mann, *Rise of the Vulcans*, pp. 297–9, 315–7; Ivo Daalder and James Lindsay, *America Unbound: The Bush Revolution in Foreign Policy* (Washington: Brookings Institution, 2003), pp. 78–80, 82–3.

33. For a discussion of Iraq in terms of concerns for prestige that stresses the significance of the individual psychology of Bush decision-makers, see Richard Ned Lebow, *A Cultural Theory of International Relations* (Cambridge: Cambridge University Press, 2008), pp. 459–80.

34. Gary Schmitt and Thomas Donnelly, "A War with a Purpose," *Weekly Standard*, September 17, 2001; Project for the New American Century, "Open Letter to President Bush," September 19, 2001, at www .neawamericancentury.org/Bushletter.htm.

35. Richard Perle, "Next Stop Iraq," November 30, 2001, accessible at http://www.fpri.org/enotes/americawar.20011130.perle.nextstopiraq .html.

36. David Frum and Richard Perle, *An End to Evil: How to Win the War on Terror* (New York: Random House, 2003), pp. 28–9.

37. Robert Kagan and William Kristol, "The Wrong Strategy," *Washington Post*, October 30, 2001; Robert Kagan and William Kristol, "Getting Serious," *Weekly Standard*, November 19, 2001; Robert Kagan and William Kristol, "The Right War," *Weekly Standard*, October 1, 2001.

38. Donald Rumsfeld, *Known and Unknown: A Memoir* (New York: Sentinel, 2011), pp. 203, 210–2, 282, 312–4.

39. Ibid. pp. 286, 342–3.

40. Dan Balz and Bob Woodward, "Secretary Rumsfeld Interview," *Washington Post*, January 9, 2002; James Carney and John Dickerson, "Inside the War Room," *Time*, December 31, 2001; Thom Shanker, "For Rumsfeld, A Reputation and a Role Are Transformed," *New York Times*, October 13, 2001.

41. Balz and Woodward, "Secretary Rumsfeld Interview"; Rumsfeld, *Known and Unknown*, pp. 283, 342–3.

42. Kagan and Kristol, "Introduction," p. 14.

43. Bob Woodward, *Bush at War* (New York: Simon & Schuster, 2002), pp. 83–5; Gordon and Trainor, *Cobra II*, pp. 15–9. Rumsfeld's immediate reaction to 9/11 was to ask for information so as to "judge whether good enough hit SH [Saddam Hussein] at same time, not only UBL [Usama Bin Laden]…go massive, sweep it all up, things related and not." Bob Woodward, *Plan of Attack* (New York: Simon & Schuster, 2004), p. 25.

44. Gordon and Trainor, *Cobra II*, pp. 3–4.

45. Barton Gellman, *Angler: The Cheney Vice-Presidency* (New York: Penguin Press, 2008), pp. 231–2, 226–36. Also see Gordon and Trainor, *Cobra II*, pp. 38–9.
46. Bob Woodward, *State of Denial* (New York: Simon & Schuster, 2006), pp. 84–5.
47. Elisabeth Bumiller and Jane Perlez, "Bush Top Aides Proclaim Policy of Ending States That Support Terror," *New York Times*, September 14, 2001; Donald Rumsfeld, "A New Kind of War," *New York Times*, September 27, 2001.
48. Possible targets for regime change in a third or fourth phase were Iran, Syria, Hezbollah, and the Palestinian Authority. Max Boot, "What Next? The Foreign Policy Agenda Beyond Iraq," *Weekly Standard*, May 5, 2003; Frum and Perle, *An End to Evil*, p. 114; Thomas Powers, "Tomorrow the World," *New York Review of Books*, March 11, 2004.
49. Woodward, *State of Denial*, p. 85.
50. Gellman, *Angler*, pp. 227–30, 232.
51. Woodward, *Bush at War*, pp. 83–5.
52. Wesley Clark, *Winning Modern Wars: Iraq, Terrorism, and the American Empire* (New York: Public Affairs, 2003), pp. 119–20; Rumsfeld, *Known and Unknown*, p. 346.
53. Clark, *Winning Modern Wars*, pp. 119–20.
54. Andrew Cockburn and Patrick Cockburn, *Saddam Hussein: An American Obsession* (London: Verso, 2002).
55. Richard Clarke, *Against All Enemies: Inside America's War on Terror* (New York: Free Press, 2004), p. 32; Gordon and Trainor, *Cobra II*, pp. 16–7; Rice, *No Higher Honor*, pp. 170–1.
56. The label WMD obscures the fact that these weapons vary considerably in their capacity for deployment, ease of acquisition, and destructiveness. Joseph Cirincione, Jessica Matthews, and George Perkovich, *WMD in Iraq: Evidence and Implications* (Washington: Carnegie Endowment for International Peace, 2004), pp. 52–4.
57. Rumsfeld, *Known and Unknown*, pp. 435–6, also see pp. 345, 418, 422–3.
58. Rice, *No Higher Honor*, pp. 195–8.
59. Ibid. p.198. For similar arguments that Saddam, not the WMD, was the real threat, see Robert Kagan and William Kristol, "The Right War for the Right Reasons," *Weekly Standard*, February 23, 2004; Charles Krauthammer, "Why Did Bush Go to War," *Washington Post*, July 18, 2003.
60. Paul Wolfowitz, "The United States and Iraq," in *Future of Iraq*, ed. John Calabrese(Washington: The American Enterprise Institute, 1997), pp. 107–13, 110.
61. "Bush Links End of Trading Ban to Hussein Exit," *New York Times*, May 21, 1991; Christian Alfonsi, *Circle in the Sand: Why We Went Back to Iraq* (New York: Doubleday, 2006), pp. 235–6.

62. Madeleine Albright, "Remarks at Georgetown University," March 26, 1997, in *Future of Iraq*, ed. Calabrese, pp. 122–6.
63. George W. Bush, "Address to the UN General Assembly," September 12, 2002, at http://www/trasncripts.cnn.com/2002/US/09/12/bush.transcript/; George W. Bush, "Address to the Nation on War with Iraq," March 17, 2003, at http://www.cnn.com/2003/WORLD/meast/03/17/sprj.irq.bush.transcript/; George W. Bush, "Address on Iraq," October 7, 2002, at http://www.archives.cnn com/2002/ALLPOLITICS/10/07/bush.transcript/
64. Woodward, *Plan of Attack*, p. 234.
65. George Packer, *The Assassins' Gate: America in Iraq* (New York: Farar, Straus and Giroux, 2005), p. 46.
66. The most extensive overview is by Kenneth Pollack, *The Threatening Storm: The Case for Invading Iraq* (New York: Random House, 2002), chaps. 5, 7, 11.
67. Bush, "Address on Iraq." .
68. George W. Bush, "State of the Union Address," January 30, 2003, at http://www. cnn.com/2003/ALLPOLITICS/01/28/sotu.transcript/.
69. Bush, "Address to the Nation on War with Iraq."
70. Colin Powell, "Address to the UN Security Council," February 5, 2003, at http://www.cnn.com/2003/US/02/05/sprj.irq.powell.transcript/.
71. Maria Ryan, "Inventing the Axis of Evil: The Myth and Reality of US Intelligence and Policy-Making After 9/11," *Intelligence and National Security* 17, no. 4 (December 2002): 55–76, 55. Lawrence Freedman writes that "the prominence of intelligence assessments in justifying a war against Iraq was really without precedence." Lawrence Freedman and Ephraim Karsh, "War in Iraq: Selling the Threat," *Survival* 46 (Summer 2004): 8.
72. "Kay: No Evidence Iraq Stockpiled WMDs," January 26, 2004, at http://www/cnn.com/2004/WORLD/meast/01/25/sprj.nirq.kay/.
73. Jervis argues that the intelligence failure on Saddam's weapons was general, not limited only to the US intelligence community. But as he admits, proving intelligence has failed owing to misperception does not mean that the decision to invade Iraq was caused by the intelligence failure. Robert Jervis, *Why Intelligence Fails: Lessons from the Iranian Revolution and the Iraq War* (Ithaca: Cornell University Press, 2010), chap. 5, esp. pp. 124–6, 134.
74. Woodward, *Plan of Attack*, p. 27.
75. Jonathan Renshon, *Why Leaders Choose War: The Psychology of Prevention* (Westport: Praeger, 2006), chap. 6; Robert Jervis, *American Foreign Policy in a New Era* (New York: Routledge, 2005), pp. 115–6, chaps. 3–4; Jack Levy, "Preventive War and the Bush Doctrine: Theoretical Logic and Historical Roots," in *The Bush Doctrine: Psychology and Strategy in an Age of Terrorism*, ed. Stanley Renshon and Peter Suedfeld (London: Routledge, 2007), pp. 175–200.

76. Renshon, *Why Leaders Choose War*, pp. 126–7; White House, "National Security Strategy of the United States," September 17, 2002, preamble, 16, 13–7, available at http://www. nytimes.com/2002/09/20 /politics/20STEXT_FULL.html.

77. Paul Pillar, "Intelligence, Policy, and the War in Iraq," *Foreign Affairs* 85 (March/April 2006): 15–27; Greg Thielmann interview on PBS *Frontline*, "Iraq, Truth, War, and Consequences," October 9, 2003, at http:// www/pbs.org/frontline/shows/truth/interviews/thielmann.html. On cognitive consistency and dissonance, see Robert Jervis, *Perception and Misperception in International Politics* (Princeton: Princeton University Press, 1976), chaps. 4 and 11; Jervis, *Why Intelligence Fails*, pp. 126–9.

78. Jervis, *American Foreign Policy*, pp. 117–8.

79. Robert Jervis, "Reports, Politics, and Intelligence Failures: The Case of Iraq," *Journal of Strategic Studies* 29 (February 2006): 20–1; Irving Janis, *Groupthink: Psychological Studies of Political Decisions and Fiascoes* (Boston: Houghton Mifflin, 1983). Jervis contests this was an instance of groupthink for the intelligence community, since groupthink only takes place in small groups, not in organizations, but groupthink is still possible among the principal decision-makers. Jervis, *Why Intelligence Fails*, pp. 129–30.

80. Frank Rich, *The Greatest Story Ever Sold: The Decline and Fall of Truth in Bush's America* (New York: Penguin Books, 2007), pp. 191–2. On denial, see Jervis, "Reports," pp. 7–8; John Prados, *Hoodwinked: The Documents That Reveal How Bush Sold Us a War* (New York: New Press, 2004), pp. 308–15, 320–1, 344–6; Kenneth Pollack, "Saddam's Bombs: We'll Find Them," *New York Times*, June 20, 2003.

81. Prados, *Hoodwinked*, pp. 32–49; Spencer Ackerman and John Judis, "The First Casualty: The Selling of the Iraq War," *New Republic*, June 30, 2003.

82. For a similar point, see Paul Pillar, *Intelligence and US Foreign Policy: Iraq, 9/11, and Misguided Reform* (New York: Columbia University Press, 2011), pp. 35–6.

83. Paul O'Neill, the former secretary of Treasury, as well as the antiterrorism czar Richard Clarke intimated that the decision was taken in January 2001, but, even though Iraq was discussed, prior to September 11, Bush continued the policy of keeping Saddam in the box. Ron Suskind, *The Price of Loyalty: George W. Bush, the White House, and the Education of Paul O'Neill* (New York: Simon & Schuster, 2004), pp. 70–6, 81–6; Clarke, *Against All Enemies*, pp. 264–6.

84. Woodward, *Bush at War*, pp. 48–50, 83–5; Patrick Tyler and Elaine Sciolino, "Bush Advisors Split on Scope of Retaliation," *New York Times*, September 20, 2001; Patrick Tyler and Elaine Sciolino, "Some Pentagon Officials and Advisors Seek to Oust Iraq's Leader in War's Next Phase," *New York Times*, October 12, 2001.

85. Rumsfeld, *Known and Unknown*, pp. 425–7; Gordon and Trainor, *Cobra II*, pp. 3–4, 19; Bryan Burrough, Evgenia Peretz, David Rose,

and David Wise, "The Path to War," *Vanity Fair* 516 (May 2004): 228–32.

86. David Frum, *The Right Man: The Surprise Presidency of George W. Bush* (New York: Random House, 2003), pp. 224–5, 231–9; George W. Bush, "State of the Union Address," January 29, 2002, at http://www .cnn.com/2002/ALLPOLITICS/01/29/bush.speech.txt/.

87. Pillar, "Intelligence, Policy, and War," p. 134. Decision makers deny any such formal meeting had taken place: according to Powell there was no "moment when we all made our recommendations" and Rice argues that "there's no decision meeting." Rumsfeld writes that he was first informed of a decision to use force against Iraq by Cheney in January 2003. Glenn Kessler, "US Decision on Iraq Has Puzzling Past," *Washington Post*, January 12, 2003; Mann, *Rise of the Vulcans*, pp. 333–4; Rumsfeld, *Known and Unknown*, p. 450.

88. Daniel Eisenberg, "We're Taking Him Out," *Time*, May 5, 2002; Burrough, "Path to War"; Michael Eliott, "First Stop Iraq," *Time*, March 31, 2003.

89. Nicholas Lemann, "How It Came to War," *New Yorker*, March 31, 2003.

90. "Rycroft Memo: Minutes of British Cabinet Meeting on the Subject of Iraq, 23 July 2002," *London Sunday Times*, May 1, 2005; Mark Danner, "The Secret Way to War," *New York Review of Books*, June 9, 2005.

91. Seymour Hersh, "Selective Intelligence," *New Yorker*, May 12, 2003; Pillar, "Intelligence, Policy, and War"; Chaim Kaufmann, "Threat Inflation and the Failure of the Market of Ideas," *International Security* 29 (2004): 1–48.

92. For such sophisticated interpretations, see Jervis, "Reports"; Jervis, *Why Intelligence Fails.* For Jervis, misperception was not a straight process of missing the contradicting evidence, and was not produced by political pressure, but rather was caused by the cognitive biases and organizational practices of the US intelligence community that could not imagine that Saddam did not have weapons and interpreted the available evidence in light of this assessment.

93. Pillar, "Intelligence, Policy, and War."

94. Dick Cheney, "Speech to the Veterans of Foreign Wars," August 26, 2002, at http:/www. cnn.com/ALLPOLITICS/08/26/cheney.iraq/; Barton Gellman and Walter Pincus, "Depiction of Threat Outgrew Supporting Evidence," *Washington Post*, August 10, 2003.

95. Bush, "Address on Iraq."

96. Powell, "Address to the UN Security Council."

97. Richard Betts, "Suicide from Fear of Death?" *Foreign Affairs* 82 (January/February 2003): 34–43.

98. Mann, *Rise of the Vulcans*, pp. 345–6; Bush, "Address on Iraq."

99. Bush, "Address on Iraq." The mushroom cloud metaphor had been employed before by Rice. See "Top Bush Officials Push the Case against Saddam," available at http://articles.cnn.com/2002-09-08/politics

/iraq.debate_1_nuclear-weapons-top-nuclear-scientists-aluminum
-tubes?_s=PM:ALLPOLITICS.

100. Ole Holsti, "Public Opinion and Foreign Policy," in *Eagle Rules? Foreign Policy and American Primacy in the Twenty-First Century*, ed. Robert Lieber (Upper Saddle River: Prentice Hall, 2002), pp. 22–4.

101. David Albright, "Iraq's Aluminum Tubes: Separating Fact from Fiction," http://www/isis-online.org/publications/iraq/IraqAluminum Tubes12–05–03.pdf; Ackerman and Judis, "First Casualty"; Prados, *Hoodwinked*, pp. 94–102.

102. Quoted in Ackerman and Judis, "First Casualty." The tubes were longer, narrower, thicker, had twice the diameter of those used in centrifuges, and had anodized coating, which had to be removed. Albright, "Iraq's Aluminum Tubes."

103. Mohammed ElBaradei, "The Status of Nuclear Inspections in Iraq: An Update," March 7, 2003, http://www.iaea.org/NewsCenter /Statements/2003/ebsp2003n006.shtml; Hans Blix, *Disarming Iraq* (New York: Pantheon Books, 2004), pp. 208–11.

104. Albright, "Iraq's Aluminum Tubes"; Prados, *Hoodwinked*, pp. 98–9. Jervis argues that the intelligence community over-relied on the opinion of a single lead CIA analyst. But this still does not explain why decision-makers did not mention at all the dissenting views of other parties on the tubes. Jervis, *Why Intelligence Fails*, pp. 143–4.

105. Powell, "Address to the UN"; Bush, "State of the Union Address, 2003."

106. Joseph Wilson, "What I Didn't Find in Africa," *New York Times*, July 6, 2003; Prados, *Hoodwinked*, pp. 186–93; Ackerman and Judis, "First Casualty." For instance, the documents on the alleged transaction referred to the 1965 constitution of Niger, while a new constitution had come into place in August 1999; the foreign minister of Niger whose signature was on the documents dated 2000 had been in office in 1988 but not afterward; and the government of Niger did not operate the mines.

107. Wilson, "What I Didn't Find in Africa."

108. Prados, *Hoodwinked*, pp. 124–6. Jervis argues that the intelligence community discounted the evidence of the Niger deal so much that it did not bother to tell Cheney about the result of Wilson's trip. But this did not mean that their objections were unknown to decision-makers, as shown by the repeated CIA objections to using this example in the Cincinnati speech. Jervis, *Why Intelligence Fails*, pp. 144–5.

109. Barton Gellman and Dafna Linzer, "A Concerted Effort to Discredit Bush Critic," *Washington Post*, April 9, 2006.

110. Bush, "State of the Union Address, 2003."

111. Condoleezza Rice, "Why We Know Iraq Is Lying," *New York Times*, January 23, 2003.

112. Rich, *Greatest Story Ever Sold*, pp. 97–9.

113. Nicholas Kristof, "White House in Denial," *New York Times*, June 13, 2003; Ackerman and Judis, "First Casualty"; Seymour Hersh, "The Stovepipe," *New Yorker*, October 27, 2003.

114. Prados, *Hoodwinked*, pp. 193–5; Ackerman and Judis, "First Casualty." Harvey contests the validity of the aluminum tubes and of the Niger documents for selling the war to Congress. However, his analysis overlooks that besides Congress, the administration was concerned with domestic and international public opinion; that most members of the Congress did not even bother to consult the intelligence, since they did not want to repeat the 1990 mistake of opposing a war with Iraq; and that forged evidence shows intentionality, and, as such, is not compatible with misperception. Harvey, *Explaining Iraq*; Thomas Ricks, *Fiasco: The American Military Adventure in Iraq* (New York: Penguin Books, 2006), pp. 61–4; Pillar, "Intelligence, Policy, and War," pp. 33, 69–75.

115. Samuel Tannenhaus, "Bush's Brain Trust," *Vanity Fair* (July 2003); Woodward, *Plan of Attack*, p. 220.

116. Kaufmann, "Threat Inflation," pp. 36–43.

117. Mike Chinoy, *Meltdown: The Inside Story of the North Korean Nuclear Crisis* (New York: St. Martin's Press, 2008), pp. 82–3, 85–91, 118–24, 127–31.

118. Thomas L. Friedman, "The Long Bomb," *New York Times*, March 2, 2003; Packer, *Assassins' Gate*, pp. 57–64; Dorrien, *Imperial Designs*, chaps. 5 and 6.

119. George W. Bush, "Remarks at the 20th Anniversary of the National Endowment for Democracy," November 6, 2003, at http://www.ned.org/events/anniversary/20thAniv-Bush.html.

120. George W. Bush, "State of the Union Address," January 31, 2006, www.cnn.com/2006/POLITICS/01/31/sotu.transcript/.

121. George Packer, "Dreaming of Democracy," *New York Time Magazine*, March 2, 2003; "Bush's Domino Theory," *Christian Science Monitor*, January 28, 2003; Nicholas Lemann, "After Iraq: The Plan to Remake the Middle East," *New Yorker*, February 17, 2003; Michael McFaul, "The Liberty Doctrine," *Policy Review* 112 (April/May 2002): 3–24; Thomas Carothers, "Promoting Democracy and Fighting Terror," *Foreign Affairs* 82 (January/February 2003): 84–97; Michael Ignatieff, "The Burden," *New York Times Magazine*, January 5, 2003.

122. Tannenhaus, "Bush's Brain Trust"; Woodward, *Plan of Attack*, p. 220. While the prevention of proliferation scored the support of around 82 percent of the public, democracy promotion scored support only in the upper 20 percent. Holsti, "Public Opinion and Foreign Policy," p. 23.

123. Rice, *No Higher Honor*, p.187.

124. Lawrence Freedman, *A Choice of Enemies: America Confronts the Middle East* (New York: Public Affairs, 2008), pp. 423–4.

125. James Fallows, "Blind into Baghdad," *Atlantic Monthly*, 293 (January/February 2004).

126. Ibid.; Packer, *Assassins' Gate*, pp. 124–6; David Rieff, "Blueprint for a Mess," *New York Times Magazine*, November 2, 2003.

127. Rieff, "Blueprint for a Mess"; Packer, *The Assassins' Gate*, pp. 110–48; Larry Diamond, *Squandered Victory: The American Occupation and the Bungled Effort to Bring Democracy to Iraq* (New York: Times Books, 2005), pp. 27–52; Gordon and Trainor, *Cobra II*, pp. 160–1, 475–9.

128. Gordon and Trainor, *Cobra II*, pp. 103, 151–2, 463.

129. Noah Chomsky, *Imperial Ambitions: Conversations in the Post 9/11 World* (New York: Metropolitan Books, 2005); Stephen Pelletiere, *America's Oil Wars* (Westport: Praeger, 2004); Michael Klare, "Deciphering the Bush Administration's Motives," in *The Iraq War Reader: History, Documents, Opinions*, ed. Michah Sifry and Christopher Cerf (New York: Simon & Schuster, 2003), pp. 392–402.

130. Present revised figures show Iraq in fifth place, after Saudi Arabia, Venezuela, Canada, and Iran. For the 2011 figures, see https://www.cia.gov/library/publications/the-world-factbook/rankorder/2178rank.html.

131. Peter Grier, "Is It All About Oil?" *Christian Science Monitor*, October 16, 2002; Craig Unger, *House of Bush, House of Saud: The Secret Relationship between the World's Two Most Powerful Dynasties* (New York: Scribner, 2004), pp. 222–6.

132. Grier, "Is It All About Oil?"

133. John Judis, "Why Iraq?" *American Prospect*, March 2003; also see for this point Lebow, *Cultural Theory*, pp. 464–5.

134. Freedman and Karsh, "War on Iraq," pp. 23–4.

135. Pollack, *Threatening Storm*, pp. 397–8; Packer, *Assassins' Gate*, pp. 115–6.

136. Andrew Bacevich, *The Limits of Power: The End of American Exceptionalism* (New York: Metropolitan Books, 2008), pp. 53–65; Andrew Bacevich, *American Empire: The Realities and Consequences of US Diplomacy* (Cambridge: Harvard University Press, 2002).

137. Klare, "Deciphering Motives"; Unger, *House of Bush, House of Saud*, p. 279.

138. Chalmers Johnson, *The Sorrows of Empire: Militarism, Secrecy, and the End of the Republic* (New York: Henry Holt, 2004).

139. Alfonsi, *Circle in the Sand*, pp. 239–245; Pelletiere, *America's Oil Wars*, pp. 122–6.

140. Benjamin and Simon, *Age of Sacred Terror*, pp. 106–9, 140–2, 147–50, 224–5, 301–2.

141. Don van Natta, "Last American Combat Troop Quit Saudi Arabia," *New York Times*, September 22, 2003.

142. Michael Gordon, "U.S. Is Preparing Base in Gulf State to Run Iraq War," *New York Times*, December 1, 2002; Michael Gordon and Eric Schmitt, "US Will Move Air Operations to Qatar Base," *New York Times*, April 28, 2003. Far from being coerced into accepting US bases, Qatar induced the United States to open a base on its territory

in order to strengthen its own security vis-à-vis Tehran and Riyadh. Steven Wright, "Foreign Policies with an International Reach: The Case of Qatar," in *Transformation of the Gulf: Politics, Economics, and the Global Order*, ed. David Held and Kristian Ulriksen (London: Routledge, 2011).

7 The Future of US Foreign Policy: Reset Game

1. Philip Gordon, "The End of the Bush Revolution," *Foreign Affairs* 85 (July/August 2006): 75–86; G. John Ikenberry, "The End of the Neo-Conservatism Movement," *Survival* (Spring 2004): 7–22. On the occupation of Iraq, see Bob Woodward, *State of Denial* (New York: Simon & Schuster, 2006); Michael Gordon and Bernard Trainor, *Cobra II: The Inside Story of the Invasion and the Occupation of Iraq* (New York: Pantheon Books, 2006); Thomas Ricks, *Fiasco: The American Military Adventure in Iraq* (New York: Penguin Books, 2006); Thomas Ricks, *The Gamble: General Petraeus and the American Military Adventure in Iraq* (New York: Penguin Books, 2009).

2. Christopher Layne, "America's Middle East Strategy after Iraq," *Review of International Studies* 35 (January 2009): 5–25.

3. Reproduced in Alan Cullson, "Inside Al Qaeda's Hard Drive," *Atlantic Monthly* 294, no. 2 (September 2004).

4. Kary Lydersen, "War Costing $720 Million Each Day, Group Says," *Washington Post*, September 22, 2007; Joseph Stiglitz and Linda Bilmes, *The Three Trillion Dollar War: The True Cost of the Iraq War* (New York: Norton, 2008).

5. Several commentators noticed the inability of the Obama administration to articulate a grand strategy to replace the Bush revolution. Walter Russell Mead, "The Carter Syndrome," *Foreign Policy* 89 (January/February 2010): 58–64; Daniel Drezner, "Does Obama Have a Grand Strategy?" *Foreign Affairs* 90 (July/August 2011): 57–68; Leslie Gelb, "The Elusive Obama Doctrine," *National Interest* (September 2012), available at http://nationalinterest.org/article/the-elusive-obama-doctrine-7340.

6. James Mann, *The Obamians: The Struggle Inside the White House to Redefine American Power* (New York: Viking, 2012), pp. 11, 164–7; David Brooks, "Obama Admires Bush," *New York Times*, May 16, 2008; Ryan Lizza, "The Consequentialist: How the Arab Spring Remade Obama's Foreign Policy," *New Yorker*, May 2, 2011.

7. Mann, *Obamians*, p. 17.

8. "President Barack Obama's Inaugural Address, January 21, 2009," available at http://www.whitehouse.gov/blog/inaugural-address.

9. David Sanger, *Confront and Conceal: Obama's Secret War and Surprising Use of American Power* (New York: Crown, 2012), p. 156; Helen

NOTES 221

Cooper and David Sanger, "Obama's Message to Iran Is Opening Bid in Diplomatic Drive," *New York Times*, March 20, 2009.

10. Sanger, *Confront and Conceal*, pp. 383–6; Victor Cha, *The Impossible State: North Korea, Past and Future* (New York: Ecco, 2012), pp. 295–6.

11. "Obama's Nobel Remarks," *New York Times*, December 10, 2009.

12. White House, "National Security Strategy," available at http://www.whitehouse.gov/sites/default/files/rss_viewer/national_security_strategy.pdf.

13. "Remarks by Vice President Biden at 45th Munich Conference on Security Policy," http://www.whitehouse.gov/the-press-office/remarks-vice-president-biden-45th-munich-conference-security-policy.

14. American Non-Governmental Organizations Coalition for the International Criminal Court (AMICC), "Administration Update," accessible at http://www.amicc.org/usicc/administration/; Peter Baker, "White House Scraps Bush's Approach to Missile Defense," *New York Times*, September 17, 2009; Nicholas Kulish and Ellen Barry, "Romanians Accept Plan for Basing of Missiles," *New York Times*, February 4, 2010.

15. Also, unlike Clinton, Obama was willing to contemplate the use of force as in the deployments in Afghanistan, in the drone assassinations and the bin Laden raid in Pakistan, and in the air strikes in Libya. Mann, *Obamians*, pp. xiv, 299; Jane Mayer, "The Predator War," *New Yorker*, October 26, 2009.

16. Ann Scott Tyson, "Pentagon Critical of NATO Allies," *Washington Post*, December 12, 2007.

17. Ahmed Rashid, *Pakistan on the Brink: The Future of America, Pakistan, and Afghanistan* (New York: Viking Books, 2012), pp. 73–4.

18. The insurgents active in Afghanistan are the so-called Afghan Taliban, comprising the Quetta Shura headed by Mullah Omar, and located in the province of Baluchistan in Pakistan; the Haqqani network, which pledges allegiance to Mullah Omar, but acts independently and is located in Pakistan's Federal Administered Tribal Areas (FATA); and the Islamic militant group Hezb e Islami Gulbuddin led by warlord Gulbuddin Hekmatyar and located in Northern Pakistan. Ibid; Ahmed Rashid, *Descent into Chaos: The US and the Disaster in Pakistan, Afghanistan, and Central Asia* (New York: Penguin Books, 2009); Seth Jones, *In the Graveyard of Empires: America's War in Afghanistan* (New York: W. W. Norton, 2010), esp. chaps. 10–11.

19. Jones, *Graveyard of Empires*; Rashid, *Pakistan on the Brink*, p. 75; Rashid, *Descent into Chaos*, pp. 351–72.

20. "Commander's Initial Assessment, August 30, 2009," available at http://media.washingtonpost.com/wp-srv/politics/documents/Assessment_Redacted_092109.pdf?hpid=topnews.

21. "Text of President Obama's Speech on Afghanistan," *New York Times*, June 22, 2011.

22. Bob Woodward, *Obama's Wars* (New York: Simon & Schuster, 2010), pp. 186–7, 126–7.
23. Ibid. pp. 219–20, 258–60, 269–70, 290–2, 332–3.
24. Ibid. pp. 385–90, 385–6.
25. Successful extrication from Afghanistan remains conditional on developments on the ground, and could be reverted should the government in Kabul seem in danger of being overthrown or overtaken by the insurgents. The United States will maintain after the troops depart in 2014 a 15,000-strong contingent in Afghanistan and has signed in May 2012 an Enduring Strategic Partnership Agreement, which de facto commits Washington to the defense of what is now its official ally. John Cushman, "In Speech, Obama Says U.S. Will Stand by Afghans After Troop Withdrawal," *New York Times*, May 1, 2012.
26. Sanger, *Confront and Conceal*, pp. 338–44.
27. Ibid. pp. 345, 349–50; "Remarks by the President in Address to the Nation on Libya, March 28, 2011," available at http://www.whitehouse.gov/the-press-office/2011/03/28/remarks-president-address-nation-libya.
28. The Obama team rebuked the notion perpetrated by the media that it was "leading from behind." Ryan Lizza, "Leading from Behind," *New Yorker*, April 27, 2011; Roger Cohen, "Leading from Behind," *New York Times*, October 31, 2012.
29. A possible objection is the comparative US lack of reaction to the ongoing Damascus repression of anti-Assad rebels. Yet, it should not be ruled out that the United States may still become involved in the future. The United States has moved toward assertiveness by pressing for sanctions at the UN Security Council on three occasions, the latest such endeavor taking place in July 2012, and by warning Syria of military action in case it moved or used its chemical arsenal against the insurgents. Rick Gladstone, "Friction at the UN as Russia and China Veto Another Resolution on Syria Sanctions," *New York Times*, July 19, 2012; Mark Landler, "US Threatens Force against Syria," *New York Times*, August 20, 2012.
30. North Korea has conducted two nuclear tests so far in 2006 and 2009 and is enriching uranium, in addition to its earlier plutonium-based program that has yielded material for eight to ten nuclear weapons. Meanwhile, Iran is on the verge of nuclear capability. Mann, *Obamians*, pp. 195–205; "Panetta: Iran Will Not Be Allowed Nukes," http://www.cbsnews.com/8301-18563_162-57345322/panetta-iran-will-not-be-allowed-nukes/.
31. Charles Blair and Mark Jansson, "Sanctions, Military Strikes, and Other Potential Actions Against Iran," Federation of American Scientists Special Report, November 2012, available at http://www.fas.org/_docs/2012_Iran_and_Global_Economy.pdf.
32. Cha, *Impossible State*, pp. 219–21.
33. On Iran, see Sanger, *Confront and Conceal*, pp. 149–87; Lynn Davis, Jeffrey Martini, Alireza Nader, Dalia Dassa Kaye, James Quinlivan, and

Paul Steinberg, *Iran's Nuclear Future: Critical US Policy Choices* (Santa Monica: Rand, 2011); Dana Allin and Steven Simon, *Sixth Crisis: Iran, Israel, America, and Rumors of War* (New York: Oxford University Press, 2010). On North Korea, see Cha, *Impossible State*, pp. 263–314; Jonathan Pollack, *No Exit: North Korea, Nuclear Weapons and International Security* (New York: Routledge, 2011).

34. Yet several scholars have downplayed the security risks posed by a nuclear-armed Iran. Kenneth Waltz, "Why Iran Should Get the Bomb," *Foreign Affairs* 91 (July 2012): 2–5; Barry Posen, "A Nuclear Armed Iran: A Difficult, but Not Impossible Policy Problem," available at http://tcf.org/publications/pdfs/pb596/posen_nuclear-armed.pdf.

35. Posen, "A Nuclear Armed Iran."

36. North Korea challenges were especially brazen, since the 2009 and 2013 nuclear tests were conducted in response of international condemnation on days of particular significance to the United States: on Memorial Day and on the day of State of the Union Address, respectively.

37. Anthony Cordesman, Alexander Wilner, and Sam Khazai, "US and Iranian Strategic Competition: The Sanctions Game: Energy, Arms Control, and Regime Change," available at http://csis.org/files/publication/120221_Iran_Gulf_MilBal_ConvAsym.pdf.

38. David Sanger and Thom Shanker, "Gates Says US Lacks a Policy to Thwart Iran," *New York Times*, April 17, 2010; Sanger, *Confront and Conceal*, pp. 238–40.

39. "Remarks by the President at AIPAC Policy Conference," available at http://www.whitehouse.gov/the-press-office/2012/03/04/remarks-president-aipac-policy-conference-0; Sanger, *Confront and Conceal*, pp. 228, 231–2.

40. China has been reluctant to condemn North Korea except in the aftermath of nuclear tests (2006, 2009, and 2013).

41. Cha, *Impossible State*, pp. 237, 272–4.

42. Moreover, even these efforts were listless, as al Qaeda resurfaced in the FATA in 2005, and its leader Osama bin Laden was killed in May 2011 by US Special Forces in Abbottabad, barely a mile away from Pakistan's Kakul Military Academy.

43. Rashid, *Descent into Chaos*, esp. chap. 12, also see pp. 38–42, 110–24; Rashid, *Pakistan on the Brink*, pp. 24–8, 49–52; Jones, *In the Graveyard of Empires*, chap. 4.

44. Rashid, *Pakistan on the Brink*, pp. 140–4.

45. Rashid, *Descent into Chaos*, pp. 381–3. The Pakistani government had engaged in sporadic fighting with the militants. However, in 2004, 2006, 2007, and 2008, these efforts resulted in cease-fire accords, which left the militants in de facto control of the seven agencies making up FATA and allowed them to push into Northern Pakistan. Ibid, pp. 270–1, 274–7, 383–4, 404–10.

46. Agents of the ISI were accused of having trained the members of the Lashkar-e-Taiba group who conducted in November a coordinate major

attack in Mumbai killing 164 people. Rashid, *Pakistan on the Brink*, pp. 57, 66–7, 156. Furthermore, in September 2011, the Chairman of the Joint Chiefs of Staff, Admiral Mike Mullen stated that the Haqqani network, responsible for a flurry of attacks in Afghanistan, including against the US Embassy in Kabul, "acts as a veritable arm of Pakistan's Inter-Services Intelligence agency." Elizabeth Bumiller and Jane Perlez, "Pakistan's Spy Agency Is Tied to Attack on US Embassy," *New York Times*, September 22, 2011.

47. Khan has never been charged for smuggling, to which he confessed to in 2004. Job Warrick, "Nuclear Scientist Is Freed from House Arrest," *Washington Post*, February 7, 2009. On the network and connections with the Pakistani military and intelligence establishment, see Gordon Corera, *Shopping for Bombs: Nuclear Proliferation, Global Insecurity, and the Fall of the A. Q. Khan Network* (New York: Oxford University Press, 2006); Rashid, *Descent into Chaos*, pp. 287–9; Rashid, *Pakistan on the Brink*, pp. 63–4.

48. Rashid, *Pakistan on the Brink*. p. 58; Mann, *Obamians*, pp. 234–5.

49. Bruce Riedel, *Deadly Embrace: Pakistan, America, and the Future of Global Jihad* (Washington: Brookings Institution, 2011), p. 125.

50. "Drone Attacks in Pakistan," available at http://www.satp.org/satporgtp /countries/pakistan/database/Droneattack.htm; Peter Bergen and Katherine Tiedmann, "Year of the Drone: An Analysis of Drone Strikes in Pakistan, 2004–2010," available at http://counterterrorism.newamerica .net/sites/newamerica.net/files/policydocs/bergentiedemann2.pdf.

51. Rashid, *Pakistan on the Brink*, pp. 8–10, 54–6. Drone strikes are unpopular in Pakistan, because of claims they infringe sovereignty and because they cause a high number of civilian victims, about 32 percent of the total number of strike casualties. Bergen and Tiedmann, "Year of the Drone."

52. Eric Schmitt and Jane Perlez, "US Is Deferring Millions in Pakistani Military Aid," *New York Times*, July 9, 2011.

53. For the G2 argument, see Robert Zoellick and Justin Yifu Lin, "Recovery: A Job for China and the US," *Washington Post*, March 6, 2009; Fred Bergsten, "A Partnership of Equals: How Washington Should Respond to China's Economic Challenge," *Foreign Affairs* 87 (July/August 2008): 57–69; for Chimerica, see Niall Ferguson, "What Chimerica Hath Wrought," *American Interest* (January/February 2009); Aaron Friedberg, *A Contest for Supremacy: China, America, and the Struggle for Mastery in East Asia* (New York: W. W. Norton, 2011), pp. 46, 112–3, 256–7. For the G2 rebuke, see "Clinton's Speech on US-China Relations in the 21st Century, January 14, 2011," accessible at http://www.cfr.org/china/clintons-speech-us-china-relations-21st -century-january-2011/p23813.

54. Robert Zoellick, "Whither China: From Membership to Responsibility? September 21, 2005," accessible at http://www.kas.de/wf/doc /kas_7358-544-1-30.pdf.

55. Kenneth Lieberthal and Wang Jisi, "Addressing US-China Strategic Distrust," at http://www.brookings.edu/~/media/research/files/papers/2012/3/30%20us%20china%20lieberthal/0330_china_lieberthal.pdf; Michael Swaine, *America's Challenge: Engage a Rising China in the Twenty First Century* (Washington: Carnegie Endowment for International Peace, 2011); Mann, *Obamians*, pp. 205–6, 242–5.

56. Lieberthal and Wang, "Addressing US-China Distrust."

57. Mann, *Obamians*, pp. 179–183; John Broder, "Many Goals Remain Unmet in 5 Nations' Climate Deal," *New York Times*, December 18, 2009; Joseph Nye, "The US, Japan, and China: Focus on the Long Term, Pacific Forum CSIS Lecture, February 23, 2010," pp. 2–3, accessible at http://csis.org/files/publication/issuesinsights_v10n14.pdf.

58. Swaine, *America's Challenge*, pp. 160–1.

59. "Remarks at Press Availability, National Convention Center Hanoi, Vietnam, July 23, 2010," available at http://www.state.gov/secretary/rm/2010/07/145095.htm; Center for Strategic and International Studies, "CSIS Bob Schieffer School of Journalism Dialogue: South China Sea: A Key Indicator for Asian Security Cooperation in the 21st Century," available at http://csis.org/files/attachments/100928_schieffer_transcript.pdf.

60. "Remarks by President Obama to the Australian Parliament, November 17, 2011," available at http://www.whitehouse.gov/the-press-office/2011/11/17/remarks-president-obama-australian-parliament; Mark Manyin, Stephen Daggett, Ben Dolven, Susan Lawrence, Michael Martin, Ronald O'Rourke, and Bruce Vaughn, "Pivot to the Pacific: The Obama Administration's 'Rebalancing' Toward Asia," available at http://www.fas.org/sgp/crs/natsec/R42448.pdf.

61. Center for Strategic and International Studies, "CSIS Dialogue"; Mann, *Obamians*, p. 247.

8   CONCLUSION

1. For convenient access to every State of the Union Addresses from 1790 up to 2007, see http://www.infoplease.com/t/hist/state-of-the-union/. The 2007–2012 interval is covered by publications such as *The New York Times*. For instance, for the Obama quotes see "President Obama's Address to Congress," *New York Times*, February 24, 2009; "President Obama's State of the Union Address," *New York Times*, January 24, 2012.

2. Liah Greenfeld, *Nationalism: Five Roads to Modernity* (Cambridge: Harvard University Press, 1992).

3. Benjamin Valentino, "Survey on Foreign Policy and American Overseas Commitment," available at http://www.dartmouth.edu/~benv/files/poll%20responses%20by%20party%20ID.pdf; Raymond Aron, *Peace and War: A Theory of International Relations* (Garden City: Doubleday, 1966), p. 74, fn. 8.

4. James Woolsey, "Hearing Before the Select Committee on Intelligence of the United State Senate, February 2, 1993," available at http://intelligence.senate.gov/pdfs103rd/103296.pdf, p. 76.
5. Bob Woodward, *The Choice: How Clinton Won* (New York: Touchstone Books, 1996), pp. 253–7.
6. Ken Adelman, "Cakewalk in Iraq," *Washington Post*, February 13, 2002; Robert Kagan and William Kristol, "Burden of Power Is Having to Wield It," *Washington Post*, March 19, 2000.
7. As prospect theory argues, losses are resented to a stronger degree than gains, and lead to more risk-acceptant behavior. Daniel Kahneman and Amos Tversky, "Prospect Theory: An Analysis of Decision under Risk," *Econometrica* 47 (March 1979): 263–92; for the application of prospect theory to prestige, see Richard Ned Lebow, *A Cultural Theory of International Relations* (Cambridge: Cambridge University Press, 2008), pp. 31, 537–9.
8. William Wohlforth, "Unipolarity, Status Competition, and Great Power War," *World Politics* 61 (January 2009): 28–57.
9. Ibid.
10. For this structuralist argument, see Nuno Monteiro, "Unrest Assured: Why Unipolarity Is Not Peaceful," *International Security* 36 (Winter 2011): 9–40. Monteiro explains dominant-recalcitrant conflict by reference to the strategy of the dominant state, itself determined by structural (security) considerations. If, giving in to the temptation of capitalizing on its greater relative power, the dominant state opts for offensive dominance it will change the system to fit its own interests, provoking conflict with states that resist such efforts. If, conversely, the dominant state is defensively minded it will still resist the efforts of revision of the status quo by recalcitrant states. However, this manuscript has not found evidence of a physical security motivation for US foreign policy in the interval. Moreover, the outcome that Monteiro seeks to explain does not follow from his structuralist logic. Since only major powers are able to produce a change in the status quo in the sense of a revision of the global distribution of power, the challenges of minor states should be seen by the dominant state as negligible and should not elicit a response.
11. For alternative accounts of US strategic suboptimal behavior, see inter alia Stephen Walt, *Taming American Power: The Global Response to US Primacy* (New York: W. W. Norton & Company, 2005); John Mearsheimer and Stephen Walt, *The Israel Lobby and US Foreign Policy* (New York: Farrar, Strauss and Giroux, 2007); Christopher Layne, *The Peace of Illusions: American Grand Strategy from 1940 to the Present* (Ithaca: Cornell University Press, 2006); Colin Dueck, *Reluctant Crusaders: Power, Culture, and Change in American Grand Strategy* (Princeton: Princeton University Press, 2006); Richard Betts, *American Force: Dangers, Delusions, and Dilemmas in National Security* (New York: Columbia University Press, 2012); Jeffrey Taliaferro,

Balancing Risks: Great Power Intervention in the Periphery (Ithaca: Cornell University Press, 2004).

12. Stanley Hoffmann, "Sheriff and Missionary," in *The Imperial Tense: Prospects and Problems of the American Empire*, ed. Andrew Bacevich (Chicago: Ivan Dee, 2003), pp. 176–81; Peter Katzenstein and Robert Keohane, eds., "Varieties of Anti-Americanism: A Framework for Analysis," in *Anti-Americanisms in World Politics*, ed. Katzenstein and Keohane (Ithaca: Cornell University Press, 2007); Christopher Prebble, *The Power Problem: How American Military Dominance Makes Us Less Safe, Less Prosperous, and Less Free* (Ithaca: Cornell University Press, 2009).

13. However, the costs might not necessarily be catastrophic, and the fear of decline may be exaggerated. Joseph S. Nye, "The Future of American Power," *Foreign Affairs* 89 (November/December 2010): 2–12; Timothy Lynch and Robert Singh, *After Bush: The Case for Continuity in American Foreign Policy* (New York: Cambridge University Press, 2008); Niall Ferguson, *Colossus: The Price of America's Empire* (New York: Penguin Press, 2004).

14. Amy Belasco, "The Cost of Iraq, Afghanistan, and Other Global War on Terror Operations since 9/11, March 29, 2011," accessible at http://www.fas.org/sgp/crs/natsec/RL33110.pdf; Joseph Stiglitz and Linda Bilmes, *The Three Trillion Dollar War: The True Cost of the Iraq War* (New York: Norton, 2008); http://costsofwar.org/article/economic-cost-summary. The three-trillion-dollar estimate comprises not only the costs of operations, but also the veteran benefits, the assistance extended to foreign partners, the costs of homeland security, and the interest on the war debt, and is adjusted for inflation.

15. https://www.cia.gov/library/publications/the-world-factbook/geos/us.html.

16. Andrew Kohut and Bruce Stokes, *America against the World: How We Are Different and Why We Are Disliked* (New York: Times Books, 2006), pp. 25–8. The figures improved with the advent in office of Obama, although by 2012 they had declined in the case of Muslim and Chinese publics, and remained low among Russian and Indian publics. Global Attitudes Project, "Global Opinion of Obama Slips, International Policies Faulted, June 13, 2012," accessible at http://www.pewglobal.org/files/2012/06/Pew-Global-Attitudes-U.S.-Image-Report-FINAL-June-13-2012.pdf.

17. Ewen MacAskill, "US Seen as a Bigger Threat to Peace than Iran, Worldwide Poll Suggests," *The Guardian*, June 15, 2006.

18. Aristotle, "Nicomachean Ethics," in *Complete Works of Aristotle. The Revised Oxford Translation*, transl. W. D. Ross (Princeton: Princeton University Press, 1984), p. 1777.

19. Jonathan Mercer, *Reputation and International Politics* (Ithaca: Cornell University Press, 1995), p. 1; Shiping Tang, "Reputation, Cult of Reputation, and International Scholarship," *Security Studies* 14 (January/March 2005): 46; Daryll Press, *Calculating Credibility:*

How Leaders Assess Military Threats (Ithaca: Cornell University Press, 2005).

20. Henry Kissinger, *White House Years* (Boston: Little Brown, 1979), p. 228.

21. Stephen Brooks, G. John Ikenberry, and William Wohlforth, "Don't Come Home America: The Case Against Retrenchment," *International Security* 37 (Winter 2012): 7–51; Stephen Brooks and William Wohlforth, *World Out of Balance: International Relations and the Challenge of American Primacy* (Princeton: Princeton University Press, 2008); Ferguson, *Colossus*; Michael Mandelbaum, *The Case for Goliath: How America Acts as the World Government in the Twenty-First Century.* New York: Public Affairs, 2005.

SELECTIVE BIBLIOGRAPHY

Albright, Madeleine. *Madam Secretary.* New York: Miramax Books, 2003.

Alfonsi, Christian. *Circle in the Sand: Why We Went Back to Iraq.* New York: Doubleday, 2006.

Allin, Dana, and Steven Simon. *Sixth Crisis: Iran, Israel, America, and Rumors of War.* New York: Oxford University Press, 2010.

Aristotle. "Nicomachean Ethics." In *Complete Works of Aristotle. The Revised Oxford Translation,* translated by W. D. Ross. Princeton: Princeton University Press, 1984.

———. "Rhetoric." In *Complete Works of Aristotle: The Revised Oxford Translation,* translated W. Rhys Roberts. Princeton: Princeton University Press, 1984.

Art, Robert. *A Grand Strategy for America.* Ithaca: Cornell University Press, 2003.

Art, Robert, and Patrick Cronin, eds. *The United States and Coercive Diplomacy.* Washington: United States Institute of Peace, 2005.

Bacevich, Andrew. *American Empire: The Realities and Consequences of US Diplomacy.* Cambridge: Harvard University Press, 2002.

Bacevich, Andrew, ed. *The Imperial Tense: Prospects and Problems of the American Empire.* Chicago: Ivan Dee, 2003.

Bacevich, Andrew. *The Limits of Power: The End of American Exceptionalism.* New York: Metropolitan Books, 2008.

Bacevich, Andrew, and Eliot Cohen, eds. *War over Kosovo: Politics and Strategy in a New Age.* New York: Columbia University Press, 2001.

Bacevich, Andrew. *Washington Rules: America's Path to Permanent War.* New York: Metropolitan Books, 2010.

Baer, Robert. *See No Evil: The True Story of a Ground Soldier in the CIA's War on Terrorism.* New York: Crown, 2002.

Baker, James Addison, III. *The Politics of Diplomacy: Revolution, War, and Peace.* New York: G. P. Putnam's Sons, 1995.

Baldwin, David, ed. *Neorealism and Neoliberalism: The Contemporary Debate.* New York: Columbia University Press, 1993.

———. *Paradoxes of Power.* New York: Basil Blackwell, 1989.

Baritz, Loren. *City on a Hill: A History of Ideas and Myths in America.* New York: John Wiley, 1964.

Barnett, Richard. *Roots of War.* New York: Atheneum, 1972.

Barrett, Matthew. "Ratify or Reject: Examining the United States' Opposition to the International Criminal Court." *Georgia Journal of International and Comparative Law* 28 (Fall 1999): 83–110.

Bassiouni, Cherif. "Negotiating the Treaty of Rome on the Establishment of the International Criminal Court." *Cornell Journal of International Law and Public Policy* 32, no. 3 (1999): 443–70.

Benjamin, Daniel, and Steven Simon. *The Age of Sacred Terror.* New York: Random House, 2002.

Bergsten, Fred. "A Partnership of Equals: How Washington Should Respond to China's Economic Challenge." *Foreign Affairs* 87 (July/August 2008): 57–69.

Beschloss, Michael, and Strobe Talbott. *At the Highest Levels: The Inside Story of the End of the Cold War.* Boston: Little, Brown, 1993.

Betts, Richard. *American Force: Dangers, Delusions, and Dilemmas in National Security.* New York: Columbia University Press, 2012.

———. "The Delusion of Impartial Intervention." *Foreign Affairs* 73 (November 1994).

———. "Suicide from Fear of Death?" *Foreign Affairs* 82 (January/February 2003): 34–43.

Biberaj, Elez. *Albania in Transition: The Rocky Road to Democracy.* Boulder: Westview Press, 1998.

Blix, Hans. *Disarming Iraq.* New York: Pantheon Books, 2004.

Blumenthal, Sidney. *The Clinton Wars.* New York: Farrar, Straus and Giroux, 2003.

Bolton, John. "Courting Danger: What's Wrong with the International Criminal Court." *National Interest* 54 (Winter 1998): 60–72.

———. "The Risks and Weaknesses of the International Criminal Court from America's Perspective." *Law and Contemporary Problems* 64 (Winter 2001): 167–80.

Boot, Max. "Neither New nor Nefarious: The American Empire Strikes Back." *Current History* 102 (November 2003): 361–6.

Booth, Alan, Greg Shelley, Allan Mazur, Gerry Tharp, and Roger Kittok. "Testosterone, and Winning and Losing in Human Competition." *Hormones and Behavior* 23 (1989): 556–71.

Boutros-Ghali, Boutros. *An Agenda for Peace: Preventive Diplomacy, Peacemaking, and Peacekeeping.* New York: United Nations, 1992.

———. "Empowering the United Nations." *Foreign Affairs* 71 (Winter 1992): 89–102.

———. *Unvanquished: A US-UN Saga.* London: I. B. Tauris, 1999.

Bowden, Mark. *Black Hawk Down: A Story of Modern War.* New York: Atlantic Monthly Books, 1999.

Brands, Hal. *From Berlin to Baghdad: America's Search for Purpose in the Post–Cold War World.* Lexington: University Press of Kentucky, 2008.

Brands, H. W. *What America Owes the World: The Struggle for the Soul of Foreign Policy.* Cambridge: Cambridge University Press, 1998.

Brinkley, Douglas. "Democratic Enlargement: The Clinton Doctrine." *Foreign Policy* 106 (Spring 1997): 110–27.

Brooks, Stephen. "Dueling Realisms." *International Organization* 51 (Summer 1997): 445–77.

Brooks, Stephen, and William Wohlforth. "International Relations Theory and the Case against Unilateralism." *Perspectives on Politics* 3 (September 2005): 509–24.

———. *World Out of Balance: International Relations and the Challenge of American Primacy.* Princeton: Princeton University Press, 2008.

Brown, Graham Sarah. *Sanctioning Saddam: The Politics of Intervention in Iraq.* London: I. B. Tauris, 1999.

Brown, Michael, Sean Lynn-Jones, and Steven E. Miller, eds. *Debating the Democratic Peace.* Cambridge: MIT Press, 1996.

Burg, Steven, and Paul Shoup. *The War in Bosnia-Herzegovina: Ethnic Conflict and International Intervention.* Armonk, New York: M. E. Sharpe, 1999.

Burckhardt, Jacob. *The Civilization of the Renaissance in Italy.* London: Penguin Books, 1990.

Burns, Edward McNall. *The American Idea of Mission: Concepts of National Purpose and Destiny.* New Brunswick: Rutgers University Press, 1957.

Burns, Richard Dean. *The Missile Defense Systems of George W. Bush: A Critical Assessment.* Denver: Praeger, 2010.

Bush, George H. W., and Brent Scowcroft. *A World Transformed.* New York: Knopf, 1998.

Bush, George W. *Decision Points.* New York: Crown, 2010.

Butler, Richard. *Saddam Defiant: The Threat of Weapons of Mass Destruction and the Crisis of Global Security.* London: Weidenfeld & Nicolson, 1999.

Buzan, Barry. *The United States and the Great Powers: World Politics in the 21st Century.* Cambridge: Polity Press, 2004.

Byman, Daniel, and Matthew Waxman. *Confronting Iraq: US Policy and the Use of Force since the Gulf War.* Santa Monica: Rand, 2000.

Calabrese, John, ed. *The Future of Iraq.* Washington: The American Enterprise Institute, 1997.

Carothers, Thomas. *Aiding Democracy Abroad: The Learning Curve.* Washington: Carnegie Endowment for International Peace, 1999.

———. "Promoting Democracy and Fighting Terror." *Foreign Affairs* 82 (January/February 2003): 84–97.

Carpenter, Ted Galen. *NATO's Empty Victory: A Postmortem on the Balkan War.* Washington: CATO Institute, 2000.

Carr, E. H. *The Twenty Years' Crisis, 1919–1939: An Introduction to the Study of International Relations.* New York: Palgrave, 2001.

Carter, Ashton, and William Perry. *Preventive Defense: A New Security Strategy for America.* Washington: Brookings Institution, 1999.

Carter, Ashton, William Perry, and John Steinbrunner. *A New Concept of Cooperative Security.* Washington: Brookings Institution, 1992.

Cha, Victor. *The Impossible State: North Korea, Past and Future.* New York: Ecco, 2012.

Chinoy, Mike. *Meltdown: The Inside Story of the North Korean Nuclear Crisis.* New York: St. Martin's Press, 2008.

Chollet, Derek, and James Goldgeier. *America between the Wars: From 11/9 to 9/11.* New York: Public Affairs, 2008.

Chomsky, Noah. *Imperial Ambitions: Conversations in the Post 9/11 World.* New York: Metropolitan Books, 2005.

Christopher, Warren. *In the Stream of History: Shaping Foreign Policy for a New Era.* Stanford: Stanford University Press, 1998.

Chua, Amy. *Day of Empire: Why Hyperpowers Rise to Global Dominance— and Why They Fall.* New York: Doubleday, 2007.

Cialdini, Robert, Richard J. Borden, Avril Thorne, Marcus Randall Walker, Stephen Freeman, and Lloyd Reynolds Sloan. "Basking in Reflected Glory: Three (Football) Field Studies." *Journal of Personality and Social Psychology* 34, no. 3 (1976): 366–75.

Cialdini, Robert, and K. Richardson, "Two Indirect Tactics of Image Management: Basking and Blasting." *Journal of Personality and Social Psychology* 57 (1980): 626–31.

Cirincione, Joseph, Jessica Matthews, and George Perkovich. *WMD in Iraq: Evidence and Implications.* Washington: Carnegie Endowment for International Peace, 2004.

Clark, Wesley. *Waging Modern War: Bosnia, Kosovo, and the Future of Combat.* New York: Public Affairs, 2002.

———. *Winning Modern Wars: Iraq, Terrorism, and the American Empire.* New York: Public Affairs, 2003.

Clarke, Richard. *Against All Enemies: Inside America's War on Terror.* New York: Free Press, 2004.

Clarke, Walter, and Jeffrey Herbst, eds. *Learning from Somalia: The Lessons of Armed Humanitarian Intervention.* Boulder: Westview Press, 1997.

Clinton, Bill. *My Life.* New York: Knopf, 2004.

Cockburn, Andrew. *Rumsfeld: His Rise, Fall, and Catastrophic Legacy.* New York: Scribner, 2007.

Cockburn, Andrew, and Patrick Cockburn. *Out of the Ashes: The Resurrection of Saddam Hussein.* New York: Harper, 2000.

———. *Saddam Hussein: An American Obsession.* London: Verso, 2002.

Cohen, Eliot. "History and the Hyperpower." *Foreign Affairs* 83 (July/August 2004): 49–63.

———. "A Revolution in Warfare." *Foreign Affairs* 75 (March/April 1996): 37–54.

Conley, Thomas. *Toward a Rhetoric of Insult.* Chicago: University of Chicago Press, 2010.

Cordesman, Anthony. *Iraq and the War of Sanctions: Conventional Threats and Weapons of Mass Destruction.* Westport: Praeger, 1999.

————. *Strategic Threats and National Missile Defenses: Defending the US Homeland.* Westport: Praeger, 2002.

Corera, Gordon. *Shopping for Bombs: Nuclear Proliferation, Global Insecurity, and the Fall of the A. Q. Khan Network.* New York: Oxford University Press, 2006.

Crawford, Neta. "The Passion of World Politics: Propositions on Emotion and Emotional Relationships." *International Security* 24 (Spring 2000): 116–56.

Daalder, Ivo. *Getting to Dayton: The Making of America's Bosnia Policy.* Washington: Brookings Institution, 2000.

Daalder, Ivo, and James Goldgeier. "Russia." In *Rocket's Red Glare: Missile Defenses and the Future of World Politics,* edited by James Wirtz and Jeffrey Larsen, 213–33. Boulder: Westview, 2001.

Daalder, Ivo, and James Lindsay. *America Unbound: The Bush Revolution in Foreign Policy.* Washington: Brookings Institution, 2003.

Daalder, Ivo, and Michael O'Hanlon. *Winning Ugly: NATO's War to Save Kosovo.* Washington: Brookings Institution, 2000.

Damasio, Antonio. *Descartes' Error: Emotion, Reason, and the Human Brain.* New York: G. P. Putnam's Sons, 1994.

Davis, Lynn, Jeffrey Martini, Alireza Nader, Dalia Dassa Kaye, James Quinlivan, and Paul Steinberg. *Iran's Nuclear Future: Critical US Policy Choices.* Santa Monica: Rand, 2011.

Deschesne, Mark, Jeff Greenberg, Jamie Arndt, and Jeff Schimel. "Terror Management and the Vicissitudes of Sports Fan Affiliation." *European Journal of Social Psychology* 30 (2000): 813–35.

Diamond, Larry. *Squandered Victory: The American Occupation and the Bungled Effort to Bring Democracy to Iraq.* New York: Times Books, 2005.

Dorrien, Gary. *Imperial Designs: The Neocons and the New Pax Americana.* New York: Routledge, 2004.

Drew, Elizabeth. *On the Edge: The Clinton Presidency.* New York: Simon & Schuster, 1994.

Drezner, Daniel. "Does Obama Need a Grand Strategy?" *Foreign Affairs* 90 (July/August 2011): 57–68.

Druckman, Daniel. "Nationalism, Patriotism, and Group Loyalty: A Social Psychological Perspective." *Mershon International Studies Review* 38 (1994): 43–68.

Dueck, Colin. *Reluctant Crusaders: Power, Culture, and Change in American Grand Strategy.* Princeton: Princeton University Press, 2006.

Durch, William, ed. *UN Peacekeeping, American Policy, and the Uncivil Wars of the 1990s.* New York: St. Martin's Press, 1996.

Edkins, Jenny. "Forget Trauma? Responses to September 11." *International Relations* 16, no. 2 (2002): 243–56.

Fearon, James. "Counterfactuals and Hypothesis Testing in Political Science." *World Politics* 43 (January 1991): 169–95.

Ferguson, Niall. *Colossus: The Price of America's Empire*. New York: Penguin Press, 2004.

Festinger, Leon. *A Theory of Cognitive Dissonance*. Stanford: Stanford University Press, 1957.

Fliessbach, K., B. Weber, P. Trautner, T. Dohmen, U. Sunde, C. E. Elger, and A. Falk. "Social Comparison Affects Reward-Related Brain Activity in the Human Ventral Striatum." *Science* 318, no. 23 (November 2007): 1305–8.

Flynn, Charles. *Insult and Society: Patterns of Comparative Interaction*. London: Kennikat Press, 1977.

Folker-Sterling, Jennifer, ed. *Making Sense of International Relations Theory*. Boulder: Lynne Rienner, 2006.

Frank, Robert. *Choosing the Right Pond: Human Behavior and the Quest for Status*. New York: Oxford University Press, 1985.

———. *Luxury Fever: Why Money Fails to Satisfy in an Era of Excess*. New York: Free Press, 1999.

Freedman, Lawrence. *A Choice of Enemies: America Confronts the Middle East*. New York: Public Affairs, 2008.

———. "Order and Disorder in the New World." *Foreign Affairs* 71 (Winter 1991): 20–37.

Freedman, Lawrence, and Ephraim Karsh. *The Gulf Conflict, 1990–1991: Diplomacy and War in the New World Order*. London: Faber and Faber, 1993.

———. "War in Iraq: Selling the Threat." *Survival* 46 (Summer 2004): 7–50.

Friedberg, Aaron. *A Contest for Supremacy: China, America, and the Struggle for Mastery in East Asia*. New York: W. W. Norton, 2011.

———. "The Future of US China Relations: Is Conflict Inevitable?" *International Security* 30 (Fall 2005): 7–45.

Friedman, Thomas L. *The Lexus and the Olive Tree*. New York: Farrar, Strauss and Giroux, 1999.

Frum, David. *The Right Man: The Surprise Presidency of George W. Bush*. New York: Random House, 2003.

Frum, David, and Richard Perle. *An End to Evil: How to Win the War on Terror*. New York: Random House, 2003.

Fukuyama, Francis. "The End of History?" *National Interest* 16 (Summer 1989): 3–18.

———. *The End of History and the Last Man*. New York: Free Press, 1992.

Gaddis, John Lewis. *Strategies of Containment: A Critical Appraisal of American National Security Policy during the Cold War*. New York: Oxford University Press, 2005.

———. *Surprise, Security, and the American Experience*. Cambridge: Harvard University Press, 2004.

Gallucci, Robert, Joel Wit, and Daniel Poneman. *Going Critical: The First North Korean Nuclear Crisis*. Washington: Brookings Institution, 2004.

Garwin, Richard. "A Defense That Will Not Defend." *Washington Quarterly* 23 (Summer 2000): 109–26.

Gellman, Barton. *Angler: The Cheney Vice-Presidency.* New York: Penguin Press, 2008.

George, Alexander, and Andrew Bennett. *Case Studies and Theory Development in Social Sciences.* Cambridge: MIT Press, 2005.

Gerth, H. H., and C. Wright Mills, eds. *From Max Weber: Essays in Sociology.* New York: Oxford University Press, 1946.

Gholz, Eugene, Darryl Press, and Harvey Sapolsky. "Come Home America: The Strategy of Restraint in the Face of Temptation." *International Security* 21 (Spring 1997): 5–48.

Gilbert, Felix. *To the Farewell Address: Ideas of Early American Foreign Policy.* Princeton: Princeton University Press, 1961.

Gilpin, Robert. *War and Change in World Politics.* Cambridge: Cambridge University Press, 1981.

Girard, Philippe. *Clinton in Haiti: The 1994 US Invasion of Haiti.* New York: Palgrave Macmillan, 2004.

Goffman, Erving. *Interaction Ritual: Essays in Face-to-Face Behavior.* Chicago: Aldine, 1967.

Goldgeier, James. *Not Whether, but When: The US Decision to Enlarge NATO.* Washington: Brookings Institution, 1999.

Goldgeier, James, and Michael McFaul. *Power and Purpose: US Policy toward Russia after the Cold War.* Washington: Brookings Institution, 2003.

Gordon, Michael, and Bernard Trainor. *Cobra II: The Inside Story of the Invasion and the Occupation of Iraq.* New York: Pantheon Books, 2006.

Gordon, Philip. "The End of the Bush Revolution." *Foreign Affairs* 85 (July/August 2006): 75–86.

Gordon, Philip, and Jeremy Shapiro. *Allies at War: America, Europe, and the Crisis over Iraq.* New York: McGraw-Hill, 2004.

Gortzak, Yoav. "How Great Powers Rule: Coercive and Positive Inducements in International Order Enforcement." *Security Studies* 14 (July 2005): 663–97.

Gould, Roger. *Collision of Wills: How Ambiguity about Social Rank Breeds Conflict.* Chicago: University of Chicago Press, 2003.

Gourevitch, Philip. *We Wish to Inform You That Tomorrow We Will Be Killed with Our Families: Stories from Rwanda.* New York: Farrar, Straus and Giroux, 1998.

Graham, Bradley. *Hit to Kill: The New Battle over Shielding America from Missile Attack.* New York: Public Affairs, 2003.

Greenberg, Jeff, Sheldon Solomon, Mitchell Veeder, Tom Pyszczynski, Abram Rosenblatt, and Shari Kirkland. "Evidence for Terror Management Theory II: The Effects of Mortality Salience on Reactions to Those Who Threaten or Bolster the Cultural Worldview." *Journal of Personality and Social Psychology* 58 (1990): 308–18.

Greenfeld, Liah. *Nationalism: Five Roads to Modernity.* Cambridge: Harvard University Press, 1992.

Haass, Richard. *The Reluctant Sheriff: The United States after the Cold War.* New York: Council of Foreign Relations, 1997.

Hachigian, Nina, and Mona Sutphen. *The Next American Century: How the U.S. Can Thrive as Other Powers Rise.* New York: Simon & Schuster, 2008.

Halberstam, David. *War in Time of Peace: Bush, Clinton, and the Generals.* New York: Touchstone, 2002.

Hall, Todd. "We Will Not Swallow This Bitter Fruit: Theorizing a Diplomacy of Anger." *Security Studies* 20 (November 2011): 521–55.

Halper, Stefan, and Jonathan Clarke. *America Alone: The Neo-Conservatives and the Global Order.* New York: Cambridge University Press, 2004.

Hartz, Louis. *The Liberal Tradition in America: An Interpretation of American Political Thought since the Revolution.* New York: Harcourt, Brace and World, 1955.

Heilbrunn, Jacob. *They Knew They Were Right: The Rise of the Neocons.* New York: Doubleday, 2008.

Held, David, and Kristian Ulriksen, eds. *The Transformation of the Gulf: Politics, Economics, and the Global Order.* London: Routledge, 2011.

Hendrickson, David, and Robert Tucker. *The Imperial Temptation: The New World Order and America's Purpose.* New York: Council of Foreign Relations Press, 1992.

Hersh, Seymour. *Chain of Command: From 9/11 to Abu Ghraib.* New York: Harper Collins, 2004.

Hiro, Dilip. *Iraq: In the Eye of the Storm.* New York: Nation Books, 2002.

Hirsch, Fred. *Social Limits to Growth.* Cambridge: Harvard University Press, 1978.

Hirsh, John, and Robert Oakley. *Somalia and Operation Restore Hope: Peacemaking and Peacekeeping.* Washington: United States Institute of Peace, 1995.

Ho, David Yan Fai. "The Concept of Face." *American Journal of Sociology* 81 (January 1976): 867–84.

Hogg, Michael, and Dominic Abrams. *Social Identifications: A Social Psychology of Intergroup Relations and Group Processes.* London: Routledge, 1988.

Holbrooke, Richard. *To End a War.* New York: Random House, 1998.

Holsti, Ole. "Public Opinion and Foreign Policy." In *Eagle Rules? Foreign Policy and American Primacy in the Twenty-First Century*, edited by Robert Lieber. Upper Saddle River: Prentice Hall, 2002.

Horowitz, Donald. *Ethnic Groups in Conflict.* Berkeley: University of California Press, 1985.

Huizinga, Johan. *Homo Ludens: A Study of the Play Element in Culture.* New York: Roy, 1950.

Hunt, Michael. *The American Ascendancy: How the United States Gained and Wielded Global Dominance.* Chapel Hill: University of North Carolina Press, 2007.

Huntington, Samuel. "The Lonely Superpower." *Foreign Affairs* 78 (March/April 1999): 35–50.

―――. *The Third Wave: Democratization in the Late Twentieth* Century. Norman: University of Oklahoma Press, 1991.

Hu, Hsien Chin. "The Chinese Concepts of Face." *American Anthropologist* 46 (January 1944): 45–64.

Huth, Paul. *Extended Deterrence and the Prevention of War*. New Haven: Yale University Press, 1988.

―――. "Reputations and Deterrence: A Theoretical and Empirical Assessment." *Security Studies* 7 (Autumn 1997): 72–99.

Hyland, William. *Clinton's World: Remaking American Foreign Policy*. Westport: Praeger, 1999.

Ignatieff, Michael. *Empire Lite: Nation-Building in Bosnia, Kosovo, and Afghanistan*. Toronto: Penguin Canada, 2003.

―――. *Virtual War: Kosovo and Beyond*. Toronto: Viking, 2000.

Ikenberry, John G. *After Victory: Institutions, Strategic Restraint, and the Rebuilding of Order after Major Wars*. Princeton: Princeton University Press, 2001.

Ikenberry, John G., ed. *America Unrivalled: The Future of the Balance of Power*. Ithaca: Cornell University Press, 2002.

Ikenberry, John G. "Is American Multilateralism in Decline?" *Perspectives on Politics* 1 (September 2003): 533–50.

Ikenberry, John G. "The End of the Neo-Conservatism Movement." *Survival* (Spring 2004): 7–22.

Ikenberry, John G., Michael Mastanduno, and William Wohlforth. "Unipolarity, State Behavior, and System Consequences." *World Politics* 61 (January 2009): 1–27.

Isikoff, Michael, and David Corn. *Hubris: The Inside Story of Spin, Scandal, and the Selling of the Iraq War*. New York: Crown, 2006.

Jervis, Robert. *American Foreign Policy in a New Era*. New York: Routledge, 2005.

―――. "The Compulsive Empire." *Foreign Policy* 137 (July 2003): 82–7.

―――. *The Logic of Images in International Relations*. Princeton: Princeton University Press, 1970.

―――. *The Meaning of Nuclear Revolution: Statecraft and the Prospect of Armageddon*. Ithaca: Cornell University Press, 1989.

―――. *Perception and Misperception in International Politics*. Princeton: Princeton University Press, 1976.

―――. "Rational Deterrence: Theory and Evidence." *World Politics* 41 (January 1989): 183–207.

―――. "The Remaking of a Unipolar World." *Washington Quarterly* 29 (Summer 2006): 7–19.

―――. "Reports, Politics, and Intelligence Failures: The Case of Iraq." *Journal of Strategic Studies* 29 (February 2006): 3–52.

―――. "Unipolarity: A Structural Perspective." *World Politics* 61 (January 2009): 188–213.

―――. *Why Intelligence Fails: Lessons from the Iranian Revolution and the Iraq War*. Ithaca: Cornell University Press, 2010.

Joffe, Josef. "Bismarck or Britain? Toward an American Grand Strategy after Bipolarity." *International Security* 19 (Spring 1995): 94–117.

———. "Who's Afraid of Mr. Big?" *National Interest* 69 (Summer 2001): 43–52.

Johnson, Chalmers. *Blowback: The Costs and Consequences of America's Empire.* New York: Henry Holt, 2000.

———. *Nemesis: The Last Days of the American Republic.* New York: Metropolitan Books, 2006.

———. *The Sorrows of Empire: Militarism, Secrecy, and the End of the Republic.* New York: Henry Holt, 2004.

Johnston, Alastair Iain. "Is China a Status Quo Power?" *International Security* 27 (Spring 2003): 5–56.

———. *Social States: China in International Institutions.* Princeton: Princeton University Press, 2008.

Judah, Tim. *Kosovo: War and Revenge.* New Haven: Yale University Press, 2000.

Kagan, Robert. *Of Paradise and Power: America and Europe in the New World Order.* New York: Knopf, 2003.

Kagan, Robert, and William Kristol, eds. *Present Dangers: Crisis and Opportunity in American Foreign Policy.* San Francisco: Encounter Books, 2000.

———. "Towards a Neo-Reaganite Foreign Policy." *Foreign Affairs* 75 (July/August 1996): 18–32.

Kahneman, Daniel, and Amos Tversky. "Prospect Theory: An Analysis of Decision under Risk." *Econometrica* 47 (March 1979): 263–92.

Kampfner, John. *Blair's Wars.* London: Free Press, 2004.

Kaplan, Lawrence, and William Kristol, *The War over Iraq: Saddam's Tyranny and America's Mission.* San Francisco: Encounter Books, 2003.

Katzenstein, Peter, and Robert Keohane, eds. *Anti-Americanisms in World Politics.* Ithaca: Cornell University Press, 2007.

Kaufmann, Chaim. "Threat Inflation and the Failure of the Market of Ideas." *International Security* 29 (2004): 1–48.

Kay, Sean. "After Kosovo: NATO's Credibility Dilemma." *Security Dialogue* 31, no. 1 (2000): 71–84.

Kemp, Geoffrey, and Janis Gross Stein, eds. *Powder Keg in the Middle East: The Struggle for Gulf Security.* London: Rowman & Littlefield, 1995.

Kennedy, Paul. "The Eagle Has Landed." *Financial Times,* February 2, 2002.

———. *The Rise and Fall of Great Powers: Economic Change and Military Conflict From 1500–2000.* New York: Random House, 1987.

Keohane, Robert. *After Hegemony: Cooperation and Discord in World Political Economy.* Princeton: Princeton University Press, 1984.

Keohane, Robert, and Joseph S. Nye. *Power and Interdependence,* 2nd ed. Glenview: Scott, Foresman, 1989.

Khalilzad, Zalmay. *From Containment to Global Leadership? America and the World after the Cold War.* Santa Monica: Rand, 1995.

Kirsch, Philippe, and Holmes, John T. "The Rome Conference on the International Criminal Court: The Negotiation Process." *American Journal of International Law* 93 (January 1999): 2–12.

Kissinger, Henry. *Does America Need a Foreign Policy? Toward a Diplomacy for the Twenty First Century.* New York: Simon & Schuster, 2001.

———. *Years of Renewal.* New York: Simon & Schuster, 1999.

Klare, Michael. *Rogue States and Nuclear Outlaws: America's Search for a New Policy.* New York: Hill and Wang, 1995.

Knock, Thomas. *To End All Wars: Woodrow Wilson and the Quest for a New World Order.* New York: Oxford University Press, 1992.

Kohut, Andrew, and Bruce Stokes. *America against the World: How We Are Different and Why We Are Disliked.* New York: Times Books, 2006.

Krauthammer, Charles. "A New Type of Realism." *National Interest* (January 2003), available at http://nationalinterest.org/article/a-new-type-of-realism-2238.

———. "The Unipolar Moment." *Foreign Affairs* 70 (1990/1991): 23–33.

———. "The Unipolar Moment Revisited." *National Interest* 70 (Winter 2002/2003): 5–17.

Kreps, Sarah. *Coalitions of Convenience: United States Military Interventions after the Cold War.* New York: Oxford University Press, 2011.

Kull, Steven. *Minds at War: Nuclear Reality and the Inner Conflicts of Defense Policymakers.* New York: Basic Books, 1988.

LaFeber, Walter, ed. *John Quincy Adams and American Continental Empire: Letters, Papers and Speeches.* Chicago: Quadrangle Books, 1965.

———. *The New Empire: An Interpretation of American Expansion, 1860–1898.* Ithaca: Cornell University Press, 1963.

Lake, Anthony. "Confronting Backlash States." *Foreign Affairs* 73 (March/April 1994): 45–55.

———. "From Containment to Enlargement Speech at Johns Hopkins University, Washington DC, September 21, 1993." In *The Clinton Foreign Policy Reader: Presidential Speeches with Commentary,* edited by Alvin Rubinstein, Albina Shayevich, and Boris Zlotnikov. London: M. E. Sharpe, 2000.

Lambeth, Benjamin. *NATO's Air War for Kosovo: A Strategic and Operational Assessment.* Santa Monica: Rand, 2001.

Larson, Deborah, and Alexander Shevchenko. "Shortcut to Greatness: The New Thinking and the Revolution in Soviet Foreign Policy." *International Organization* 57 (Winter 2003): 77–109.

———. "Status Seekers: Chinese and Russian Responses to US Primacy." *International Security* 34 (Spring 2010): 63–95.

Larson, Eric, David Orletsky, and Kristin Leuschner. *Defense Planning in a Decade of Change.* Santa Monica: Rand, 2001.

Layne, Christopher. "America's Middle East Strategy after Iraq." *Review of International Studies* 35 (January 2009): 5–25.

———. "From Preponderance to Offshore Balancing: America's Future Grand Strategy." *International Security* 22 (Summer 1997): 86–124.

Layne, Christopher. *The Peace of Illusions: American Grand Strategy from 1940 to the Present*. Ithaca: Cornell University Press, 2006.

———. "The Unipolar Illusion: Why Great Powers Will Rise." *International Security* 17 (Spring 1993): 5–51.

———. "The Unipolar Illusion Revisited: The Coming End of the United States' Unipolar Moment." *International Security* 31 (Fall 2006): 7–41.

Lebor, Adam. *Milosevic: A Biography*. New Haven: Yale University Press, 2004.

Lebow, Richard Ned. *A Cultural Theory of International Relations*. Cambridge: Cambridge University Press, 2008.

———. *The Tragic Vision of World Politics: Ethics, Interests and Orders*. Cambridge: Cambridge University Press, 2003.

———. *Why Nations Fight: Past and Future Motives for War*. New York: Cambridge University Press, 2010.

LeDoux, Joseph. *The Emotional Brain: The Mysterious Underpinnings of Emotional Life*. New York: Phoenix Books, 1999.

Leffler, Melvyn. "9/11 and American Foreign Policy." *Diplomatic History* 29 (June 2005): 395–413.

———. "Bush's Foreign Policy." *Foreign Policy* 144 (September 2004): 22–8.

Leffler, Melvyn, and Jeffrey Legro, eds. *To Lead the World: American Strategy after the Bush Doctrine*. Oxford: Oxford University Press, 2008.

Levy, Jack. "Preventive War and the Bush Doctrine: Theoretical Logic and Historical Roots." In *The Bush Doctrine: Psychology and Strategy in an Age of Terrorism*, edited by Stanley Renshon and Peter Suedfeld, 175–200. London: Routledge, 2007.

———. *War in the Modern Great Power System, 1495–1975*. Lexington: University Press of Kentucky, 1983.

Lewis, George, Lisbeth Gronlund, and David Wright. "National Missile Defense: An Indefensible System." *Foreign Policy* 117 (Winter 1999): 120–39.

Lieven, Anatol. *America Right or Wrong: An Anatomy of American Nationalism*. New York: Oxford University Press, 2004.

Lindemann, Thomas, and Erik Ringmar, eds. *The Struggle for Recognition in International Politics*. Boulder: Paradigm, 2011.

Lindner, Evelyn. *Making Enemies: Humiliation and International Conflict*. Westport: Praeger, 2006.

Lindsay, James, and Michael O'Hanlon. *Defending America: The Case for Limited National Missile Defense*. Washington: Brookings Institution, 2001.

Lipset, Seymour Martin. *American Exceptionalism: A Double-Edged Sword*. New York: W. W. Norton & Company, 1996.

Litwak, Robert. *Rogue States and US Foreign Policy: Containment after the Cold War*. Baltimore: Johns Hopkins University Press, 2000.

Löwenheim, Oded. *Predators and Parasites: Persistent Agents of Transnational Harm and Great Power Authority*. Ann Arbor: University of Michigan Press, 2007.

Löwenheim, Oded, and Gadi Heimann. "Revenge in International Politics." *Security Studies* 17 (2008): 685–724.

Lynch, Timothy, and Robert Singh. *After Bush: The Case for Continuity in American Foreign Policy.* New York: Cambridge University Press, 2008.

Malone, David, and Yuen Foong Khong, eds. *Unilateralism and US Foreign Policy: International Perspectives.* Boulder: Lynne Rienner, 2003.

Mandelbaum, Michael. *The Case for Goliath: How America Acts as the World Government in the Twenty-First Century.* New York: Public Affairs, 2005.

———. "Foreign Policy as Social Work." *Foreign Affairs* 75 (January/February 1996): 16–32.

———. "A Perfect Failure." *Foreign Affairs* 78 (September/October 1999): 2–8.

Mann, James. *About Face: A History of America's Curious Relationship with China from Nixon to Clinton.* New York: Knopf, 1999.

———. *The Obamians: The Struggle Inside the White House to Redefine American Power.* New York: Viking, 2012.

———. *Rise of the Vulcans: The History of Bush's War Cabinet.* New York: Viking Books, 2004.

Markey, Daniel. "Prestige and the Origins of War: Returning to Realism's Roots." *Security Studies* 8 (Summer 1999): 126–73.

Markey, Daniel. "The Prestige Motive in International Relations." Unpublished doctoral dissertation, Princeton University Department of Politics, November 2000.

Marr, Phoebe. "Symposium on Dual Containment." *Middle East Policy* 3, no. 1 (1994): 1–26.

McCormick, Thomas. *China Market: America's Quest for Informal Empire.* Chicago: Quadrangle Books, 1967.

McDermott, Rose. "The Feeling of Rationality: The Meaning of Neuroscientific Advances for Political Science." *Perspectives on Politics* 2 (December 2004): 691–706.

———. *Political Psychology and International Relations.* Ann Arbor: University of Michigan Press, 2004.

McDougall, Walter. *Promised Land, Crusader State.* Boston: Houghton Mifflin, 1997.

McFaul, Michael. "The Liberty Doctrine." *Policy Review* 112 (April/May 2002): 3–24.

McGinn, Robert. "About Face." *Social Theory and Practice* 1 (Spring 1971): 87–96.

———."Prestige and the Logic of Political Argument." *The Monist* 56 (January 1972): 100–16.

McMahon, Robert. "Credibility and World Power: Explaining the Psychological Dimensions in Post-War American Diplomacy." *Diplomatic History* 15 (Fall 1991): 455–71.

Mead, Walter Russell. "The Carter Syndrome." *Foreign Policy* 89 (January/February 2010): 58–64.

Mead, Walter Russell. *Special Providence: American Foreign Policy and How It Changed the World*. New York: Knopf, 2001.

Mearsheimer, John. "Back to the Future: Instability in Europe after the Cold War." *International Security* 15 (Summer 1990): 5–56.

———. "China's Unpeaceful Rise." *Current History* 150 (April 2006): 160–3.

———. "The False Promise of International Institutions." *International Security* 19 (Winter 1994): 5–49.

———. *Tragedy of Great Power Politics*. New York: W. W. Norton, 2001.

Mercer, Jonathan. "Emotional Beliefs." *International Organization* 64 (Winter 2010): 1–31.

———. *Reputation and International Politics*. Ithaca: Cornell University Press, 1995.

Menkhaus, Ken, and Louis Ortmayer. *Key Decisions in the Somalia Intervention*. Pittsburg: University of Pittsburg, 1995.

Midlarsky, Manus. *On War: Political Violence in the International System*. New York: Free Press, 1975.

Miller, William Ian. *Humiliation and Other Essays on Honor, Social Discomfort, and Violence*. Ithaca: Cornell University Press, 1993.

Mishan, E. J. *What Political Economy Is All About?* Cambridge: Cambridge University Press, 1982.

Mitzen, Jennifer. "Ontological Security in World Politics." *European Journal of International Relations* 12, no. 3 (2006): 341–70.

Monteiro, Nuno. "Unrest Assured: Why Unipolarity Is Not Peaceful." *International Security* 36 (Winter 2011): 9–40.

Monten, Jonathan. "The Roots of the Bush Doctrine: Power, Nationalism, and Democracy Promotion in US Grand Strategy." *International Security* 29 (Spring 2005): 112–56.

Morgenthau, Hans. *Politics among Nations: The Struggle for Power and Peace*. New York: Knopf, 1967.

Neu, Jerome. *Sticks and Stones: The Philosophy of Insults*. New York: Oxford University Press, 2008.

Nicolson, Harold. *The Meaning of Prestige*. London: Weidenfeld and Nicolson, 1937.

Ninkovich, Frank. *The Wilsonian Century: US Foreign Policy Since 1900*. Chicago: University of Chicago Press, 1999.

Nolan, Janne, ed. *Global Engagement: Cooperation and Security in the 21st Century*. Washington: Brookings Institution, 1994.

Norris, John. *Collision Course: Russia, NATO, and Kosovo*. Westport: Praeger, 2005.

Nye, Joseph S. "The Future of American Power." *Foreign Affairs* 89 (November/December 2010): 2–12.

———. *The Paradox of American Power: Why the World's Only Superpower Can't Go It Alone*. New York: Oxford University Press, 2002.

———. "Redefining the National Interest." *Foreign Affairs* 78 (July/August 1999): 22–44.

———. "What New World Order?" *Foreign Affairs* 71 (Spring 1992): 83–96.

Oberdorfer, Don. *The Two Koreas: A Contemporary History.* New York: Basic Books, 2001.

Olson, Mancur, and Richard Zeckhauser. "An Economic Theory of Alliances." *Review of Economics and Statistics* 48 (August 1966): 266–79.

O'Neill, Barry. *Honor, Symbols and War.* Ann Arbor: Michigan University Press, 1999.

Packer, George. *The Assassins' Gate: America in Iraq.* New York: Farar, Straus and Giroux, 2005.

Patrick, Stewart, and Shepard Forman, eds. *Multilateralism and US Foreign Policy: Ambivalent Engagement.* Boulder: Lynne Rienner, 2002.

Patrick, Stewart. "America's Retreat from Multilateral Engagement." *Current History* 99 (December 2000): 430–9.

Pelletiere, Stephen. *America's Oil Wars.* Westport: Praeger, 2004.

Peristiany, J. G., ed. *Honor and Shame: The Values of the Mediterranean Society.* London: Weidenfeld and Nicolson, 1965

Pettifer, James, ed. *The New Macedonia Question.* Basingstoke: Macmillan, 1999.

Pettifer, James, and Miranda Vickers. *The Albanian Question: Reshaping the Balkans.* London: I. B. Tauris, 2009.

Pezzullo, Ralph. *Plunging into Haiti: Clinton, Aristide, and the Defeat of Diplomacy.* Jackson: University of Mississippi Press, 2006.

Philips, John. *Macedonia: Warlords and Rebels in the Balkans.* New Haven: Yale University Press, 2004.

Piaget, Jean. *The Child and Reality: Problems of Genetic Psychology.* New York: Grossman, 1973.

Pillar, Paul. "Intelligence, Policy, and the War in Iraq." *Foreign Affairs* 85 (March/April 2006): 15–27.

———. *Intelligence and US Foreign Policy: Iraq, 9/11, and Misguided Reform.* New York: Columbia University Press, 2011.

Pollack, Jonathan. *No Exit: North Korea, Nuclear Weapons and International Security.* New York: Routledge, 2011.

Pollack, Kenneth. *The Threatening Storm: The Case for Invading Iraq.* New York: Random House, 2002.

Pond, Elizabeth. *Friendly Fire: The Near-Death of the Transatlantic Alliance.* Pittsburgh: European Union Studies Association, 2004.

Posen, Barry. "After Bush: The Case for Restraint." *American Interest* 3 (November/December 2007): 6–32.

———. "Command of the Commons: The Military Foundation of U.S. Hegemony." *International Security* 28 (Summer 2003): 5–46.

Posen, Barry. "Pull Back: The Case for a Less Activist Foreign Policy." *Foreign Affairs* 92 (January/February 2013): 116–28.

———. "The War for Kosovo." *International Security* 24 (Spring 2000): 39–84.

Posen, Barry, and Andrew Ross. "Competing Visions for US Grand Strategy." *International Security* 21 (Winter 1996/1997): 5–53.

Powell, Colin. *My American Journey.* New York: Random House, 1995.

Posen, Barry, and Andrew Ross. "US Forces: The Challenges Ahead." *Foreign Affairs* 71 (Winter 1992): 32–45.

Power, Samantha. *A "Problem From Hell": America and the Age of Genocide.* New York: Basic Books, 2002.

Prados, John. *Hoodwinked: The Documents That Reveal How Bush Sold Us a War.* New York: New Press, 2004.

Prebble, Christopher. *The Power Problem: How American Military Dominance Makes Us Less Safe, Less Prosperous, and Less Free.* Ithaca: Cornell University Press, 2009.

Press, Darryl. *Calculating Credibility: How Leaders Assess Military Threats.* Ithaca: Cornell University Press, 2005.

Prestowitz, Clyde. *Rogue Nation: American Unilateralism and the Failure of Good Intentions.* New York: Perseus Books, 2003.

Prins, Gwyn, ed. *Understanding Unilateralism in American Foreign Relations.* London: Royal Institute of International Affairs, 2000.

Prunier, Gerard. *The Rwanda Crisis: History of a Genocide.* New York: Columbia University Press, 1997.

Rachman, Gideon. *Zero-Sum Future: America's Power in an Age of Anxiety.* New York: Simon & Schuster, 2011.

Rampton, Sheldon, and John Stauber. *Weapons of Mass Deception: The Uses of Propaganda in Bush's War on Iraq.* New York: Penguin Books, 2003.

Rashid, Ahmed. *Descent into Chaos: The US and the Disaster in Pakistan, Afghanistan, and Central Asia.* New York: Penguin Books, 2009.

———. *Pakistan on the Brink: The Future of America, Pakistan, and Afghanistan.* New York: Viking Books, 2012.

Renshon, Jonathan. *Why Leaders Choose War: The Psychology of Prevention.* Westport: Praeger, 2006.

Rice, Condoleezza. *No Higher Honor: A Memoir of My Years in Washington.* New York: Crown, 2011.

———. "Promoting the National Interest." *Foreign Affairs* 79 (January/February 2000): 45–62.

———. "Rethinking the National Interest." *Foreign Affairs* 87 (July/August 2008): 2–26.

Rich, Frank. *The Greatest Story Ever Sold: The Decline and Fall of Truth in Bush's America.* New York: Penguin Books, 2007.

Ricks, Thomas. *Fiasco: The American Military Adventure in Iraq.* New York: Penguin Books, 2006.

———. *The Gamble: General Petraeus and the American Military Adventure in Iraq.* New York: Penguin Books, 2009.

Riedel, Bruce. *Deadly Embrace: Pakistan, America, and the Future of Global Jihad.* Washington: Brookings Institution, 2011.

Rohde, David. *Endgame: The Betrayal and Fall of Srebrenica.* London: Farrar, Strauss and Giroux, 1997.

Rosecrance, Richard. "A New Concert of Powers." *Foreign Affairs* 71 (Spring 1992): 64–82.

———. *Rise of the Trading State: Commerce and Conquest in the Modern World*. New York: Basic Books, 1986.

Rosecrance, Richard, and Gu Guoliang, eds. *Power and Restraint: A Shared Vision for the US-China Relationship*. New York: Public Affairs, 2009.

Rosen, Stephen Peter. *War and Human Nature*. Princeton: Princeton University Press, 2005.

Ross, Robert, and Zhu Feng, eds. *China's Ascent: Power, Security, and the Future of International Politics*. Ithaca: Cornell University Press, 2008.

Ross Robert. "China's Naval Nationalism." *International Security* 34 (Fall 2009): 46–81.

Ruggie, John Gerard, ed. *Multilateralism Matters: The Theory and Praxis of an Institutional Form*. New York: Columbia University Press, 1993.

Rumsfeld, Donald. *Known and Unknown: A Memoir*. New York: Sentinel, 2011.

Sanger, David. *Confront and Conceal: Obama's Secret War and Surprising Use of American Power*. New York: Crown, 2012.

———. *The Inheritance: The World Obama Confronts and the Challenges to American Power*. New York: Harmony Books, 2009.

Saurette, Paul. "You Dissin Me? Humiliation and Post 9/11 Global Politics." *Review of International Studies* 32 (2006): 495–522.

Scheffer, David. "The United States and the International Criminal Court." *American Journal of International Law* 93 (January 1999): 12–22.

Schelling, Thomas. *Arms and Influence*. New Haven: Yale University Press, 1966.

Schiff, Benjamin. *Building the International Criminal Court*. New York: Cambridge University Press, 2008.

Schlessinger, Arthur. *Robert Kennedy and His Times*. Boston: Houghton Mifflin, 1978.

Schlessinger, James. "Quest for a Post–Cold War Foreign Policy." *Foreign Affairs* 72 (Winter 1993): 17–28.

Schroeder, Paul. "The New World Order: A Historical Perspective." *Washington Quarterly* 17 (Spring 1994): 25–44.

Schweller, Randall. "Realism and the Present Great Power System: Growth and Possible Conflict over Scarce Resources." In *Unipolar Politics: Realism and the State Strategy after the Cold War*, edited by Ethan Kapstein and Michael Mastanduno. New York: Columbia University Press, 1999.

———. *Unanswered Threats: Political Constraints on the Balance of Power*. Princeton: Princeton University Press, 2006.

Schweller, Randall, and Xiaoyu Pu. "After Unipolarity: China's Visions of International Order in an Era of U.S. Decline." *International Security* 36 (Summer 2011): 41–72.

Sell, Louis. *Slobodan Milosevic and the Destruction of Yugoslavia*. Durham: Duke University Press, 2002.

Sewall, Sarah, and Carl Kaysen, eds. *The United States and the International Criminal Court: National Security and International Law*. Lanham: Rowman & Littlefield, 2000.

Sifry, Michah, and Christopher Cerf, eds. *The Gulf War Reader: History, Documents, Opinions*. New York: Random House, 1991.

———, eds. *The Iraq War Reader: History, Documents, Opinions*. New York: Simon & Schuster, 2003.

Sigal, Leon. *Disarming Strangers: Nuclear Diplomacy with North Korea*. Princeton: Princeton University Press, 1998.

Simon, Herbert. "Motivational and Emotional Controls of Cognition." *Psychological Review* 74, no. 1 (1967): 29–39.

Smith, Anthony. *Chosen Peoples: Sacred Sources of National Identity*. Oxford: Oxford University Press, 2003.

Smith, Derek. *Deterring America: Rogue States and the Proliferation of Weapons of Mass Destruction*. New York: Cambridge University Press, 2006.

Smith, Tony. *America's Mission: The United States and the Worldwide Struggle for Democracy in the Twentieth Century*. Princeton: Princeton University Press, 1994.

Snyder, Glenn, and Paul Diesing. *Conflict among Nations: Bargaining, Decision-Making and System Structure in International Crises*. Princeton: Princeton University Press, 1977.

Snyder, Jack. "Imperial Temptations." *National Interest* 71 (Spring 2003): 29–40.

———. *Myths of Empire: Domestic Politics and International Ambitions*. Ithaca: Cornell University Press, 1991.

Spykman, Nicholas. *America's Strategy in World Politics: The United States and the Balance of Power*. New York: Harcourt, Brace, 1942.

Stern, Paul. "Why Do People Sacrifice for Their Nations?" *Political Psychology* 16 (June 1995): 217–35.

Stewart, Frank Henderson. *Honor*. Chicago: University of Chicago Press, 1994.

Steinberg, Blema. *Shame and Humiliation: Presidential Decision-Making on Vietnam: A Psychoanalytic Interpretation*. Pittsburgh: University of Pittsburgh Press, 1996.

Stelzer, Irwin, ed. *The Neocon Reader*. New York: Grove Press, 2004.

Stephanopoulos, George. *All Too Human: A Political Education*. Boston: Little, Brown, 1999.

Stiglitz, Joseph, and Linda Bilme. *The Three Trillion Dollar War: The True Cost of the Iraq War*. New York: Norton, 2008.

Suettinger, Robert. *Beyond Tiananmen: The Politics of US-China Relations, 1989–2000*. Washington: Brookings Institution, 2003.

Suskind, Ron. *The Price of Loyalty: George W. Bush, the White House, and the Education of Paul O'Neill*. New York: Simon & Schuster, 2004.

Swaine, Michael. *America's Challenge: Engage a Rising China in the Twenty First Century*. Washington: Carnegie Endowment for International Peace, 2011.

Talbott, Strobe. "Democracy and the National Interest." *Foreign Affairs* 75 (November/December 1996): 47–63.

———. "Post Victory Blues." *Foreign Affairs* 71 (Winter 1991): 54–69.

———. *The Russia Hand: A Memoir of Presidential Decision-Making*. New York: Random House, 2002.

Tajfel Henri, and John Turner. "An Integrative Theory of Intergroup Conflict." In *The Social Psychology of Intergroup Relations*, edited by William Austin and Stephen Worchel. Monterey: Brooks/Cole, 1979.

———. "The Social Identity Theory of Intergroup Behavior." In *Psychology of Intergroup Relations*, edited by William Austin and Stephen Worchel. Chicago: Nelson-Hall, 1986.

Tajfel, Henri, ed. *Differentiation between Social Groups*. London: Academic Press, 1978.

Taliaferro, Jeffrey. *Balancing Risks: Great Power Intervention in the Periphery*. Ithaca: Cornell University Press, 2004.

———. "Security Seeking under Anarchy: Defensive Realism Revisited." *International Security* 25 (Winter 2000): 128–61.

Tang, Shiping. "Reputation, Cult of Reputation, and International Scholarship." *Security Studies* 14 (January/March 2005): 34–62.

Taylor, A. J. P. *The Struggle for Mastery in Europe, 1848–1918*. Oxford: Oxford University Press, 1954.

Terraillon, Eugène. *L'Honneur: Sentiment et Principe Moral*. Paris: Librairie Félix Alcan, 1912.

Thucydides. *History of* the *Peloponnesian War*, translated by Rex Warner. London: Penguin Books, 1972.

Tunç, Hakan. "What Was It All About after All? The Causes of the Iraq War." *Contemporary Security* 26 (August 2005): 335–55.

Turner, Brian. *Status*. Minneapolis: University of Minnesota Press, 1988.

Unger, Craig. *House of Bush, House of Saud: The Secret Relationship between the World's Two Most Powerful Dynasties*. New York: Scribner, 2004.

US Department of Defense. *Soviet Military Power 1990*. Washington: Department of Defense, 1990.

US News & World Report. *Triumph without Victory: The Unreported History of the Persian Gulf War*. New York: Random House, 1992.

Van Selm, Joanne, ed. *Kosovo Refugees in the EU*. London: Pinter, 2000.

Védrine, Hubert, with Dominique Moisi. *France in an Age of Globalization*. Washington: Brookings Institution, 2001.

Voeten, Erik. "Outside Options and the Logic of Security Council Actions." *American Political Science Review* 95 (December 2001): 845–58.

Volgy, Thomas, Renato Corbetta, Keith Grant, and Ryan Baird, eds. *Major Powers and the Quest for Status in International Politics: Global and Regional Perspectives*. New York: MacMillan, 2011.

Wallace, Michael. *War and Rank among Nations*. Lexington: D. C. Heath and Company, 1970.

Walt, Stephen. "Alliances in a Unipolar World." *World Politics* 61 (January 2009): 86–120.

———. *Taming American Power: The Global Response to US Primacy*. New York: W. W. Norton & Company, 2005.

Waltz, Kenneth. "The Emerging Structure of International Politics." *International Security* 18 (Fall 1993): 45–73.

———. "Structural Realism after the Cold War." *International Security* 25 (Summer 2000): 5–41.

———. *Theory of International Politics*. Reading: Addison Wesley, 1979.

———. "Why Iran Should Get the Bomb." *Foreign Affairs* 91 (July 2012): 2–5.

Wedgewood, Ruth. "Fiddling in Rome." *Foreign Affairs* 77 (November 1998): 20–4.

Weller, Marc. "The Rambouillet Conference on Kosovo." *International Affairs* 75 (April 1999): 213–53.

———. "The US, Iraq, and the Use of Force in a Unipolar World." *Survival* 41 (Winter 1999): 81–100.

Wendt, Alexander. *Social Theory of International Politics*. New York: Cambridge University Press, 1999.

———. "The State as a Person in International Theory." *Review of International Studies* 30, no. 2 (2004): 289–316.

Williams, William Appleman. *The Tragedy of American Diplomacy*. New York: W. W. Norton & Company, 1984.

Wohlforth, William. "The Stability of a Unipolar World." *International Security* 24 (Summer 1999): 5–41.

———. "Unipolarity, Status Competition, and Great Power War." *World Politics* 61 (January 2009): 28–57.

Wolf, Reinhard. "Respect and Disrespect in International Politics: The Significance of Status Recognition." *International Theory* 3 (February 2011): 105–42.

Wolfers, Arnold. *Discord and Collaboration: Essays on International Politics*. Baltimore: Johns Hopkins University Press, 1962.

Wolfowitz, Paul. "The Clinton Administration's First Year." *Foreign Affairs* 73 (January/February 1994): 1–25.

———. "Remembering the Future." *National Interest* 59 (Spring 2000): 35–44.

Woodward, Bob. *Bush at War*. New York: Simon & Schuster, 2002.

———. *The Choice: How Clinton Won*. New York: Touchstone Books, 1996.

———. *Obama's Wars*. New York: Simon & Schuster, 2010.

———. *Plan of Attack*. New York: Simon & Schuster, 2004.

———. *Shadow: Five Presidents and the Legacy of Watergate*. New York: Simon & Schuster, 1999.

———. *State of Denial*. New York: Simon & Schuster, 2006.

Wright, Robert. *The Moral Animal: Evolutionary Psychology and Everyday Life*. New York: Vintage Books, 1995.

Zakaria, Fareed. *From Wealth to Power: The Unusual Origins of America's World Role*. Princeton: Princeton University Press, 1998.

———. *The Future of Freedom: Illiberal Democracies at Home and Abroad*. New York: W. W. Norton, 2004.

———. *The Post-American World*. New York: W. W. Norton, 2008.

INDEX

Printed and bound in the United States of America